ALSO BY SALLIE ANN GLASSMAN

The New Orleans Voodoo Tarot

Vodou Visions

An Encounter with
Divine Mystery

VILLARD ♛ NEW YORK

Vodou Visions

Sallie Ann Glassman

Copyright © 2000 by Sallie Ann Glassman

All rights reserved under International and Pan-American Copyright Conventions. Published in the United States by Villard Books, a division of Random House, Inc., New York, and simultaneously in Canada by Random House of Canada Limited, Toronto.

The illustrations in this work are by the author and were previously published in *The New Orleans Voodoo Tarot*, published in 1992 by Inner Traditions, Rochester, Vermont.

VILLARD BOOKS and colophon are registered trademarks of Random House, Inc.

Library of Congress Cataloging-in-Publication Data

Glassman, Sallie Ann, 1954–
Vodou visions : an encounter with divine mystery / Sallie Ann Glassman.—1st ed.
p.   cm.
Includes bibliographical references and index.
ISBN 0-375-75370-2 (alk. paper)
1. Voodooism.   I. Title.
BL2490 .G62   2000
299′.675—dc21   99-088214

Villard Books website address: www.villard.com

Printed in the United States of America on acid-free paper

2 4 6 8 9 7 5 3

FIRST EDITION

Book design by Carole Lowenstein

To those who came before:
Jane, James, and Sallie T.

To those who walk with me:
My partner, Shane.
My brothers, Andrew and Peter, and John Spadola.
My sisters, Nancy, Karen Lam, Claudia, and Polly.

To those who carry on:
Emily, Nicholas, and Ray-Ray.

Acknowledgments

I offer honor and respect for all those who have helped me, shared knowledge with me, and encouraged this work.

In Haiti:

I must thank my Papas especially, Edgar Jean-Louis and Silva Joseph, who initiated me into the Vodoun Mysteries, and sustain me before the Lwa. In addition, I thank my Godfather and patron, Dr. Jacques Bartoli, who offered me welcome in his country, and contact with like souls. I am indebted to him for his Kreyòl translations of my litanies and for his legendary, limitless generosity. Sylvain François graciously provided additional assistance with the Kreyòl translations. My Godmother in Vodou, Tina Girouard, opened Vodoun doors for me, and continues to hold the flame at the back flank of my neighborhood. In addition, I thank André Pierre for his vision and faith, and for sharing coffee, claret, words of wisdom, and visionary images of the Lwa. Florvil Michel Junior has helped also with Kreyòl translations, and Hélène Pinaud graciously and patiently corrected my faulty French litanies. I also thank Tiben Francillon for his largesse and guidance. I thank the Spirit of Cherel Ito for the dream, and pray that she is having a good swim with her beautiful Teiji.

In the United States:

Thanks to Bill Breeze for suggesting a Vodou tarot many years ago.

Praise to my Padrino, Antonio Gil, who has helped me to know the Orisha, and has helped empower and protect me in countless ways.

Praise to Courtney Willis, whose long-term and consistent support, guidance, friendship, and gifts of knowledge and out-of-print books have accompanied me on my journey.

In addition to having a name worthy of a Lwa, my friend Juan Maria Guadalupe McDonald-Valasquez was kind enough to translate the litanies for the Orisha into Spanish.

I thank the extended family of Simbi–Sen Jak Ounfò, and the members of the former Kali Lodge for their participation, insight, and extraordinary sincerity in support of the ceremonies that were performed for *Vodou Visions*. Most particularly I thank the Oungan, J. Shane Norris, who has shown magnificent tolerance and support. He has lent voice, heart, rhythm, and spirit, as well as tending to the practical, everyday needs of a working Ounfò, and he has watched all our backs. I thank these many others as well: Lorien Bales, Geoff Beardsley, Kerry Brown, Victor Cypert, Clara Earthly, Chris Feldman, Reverend Goat, Barry Hale, Jane Harvey, Michael and Loretta Hayman, Byron Hensley, John Herasymiuk, Eric Hussey, Darius James, Steve and Petra King, Brendan Malone, Gretchen McNee, Hart McNee, Michelle Moo, Anne Moore, Margrat Nee, William Neusom, Anthony Ryan, Seth Shearer, Christine Short, Kerri Simpson, Sharon Singleton, Gregg Wyldes, and Kenneth Wooten. Don Dufrane is surely still keeping the beat and complaining in the Waters.

Thanks, too, to Brooks and Diana Smith, as well as Debbie and Wilbur Reynaud for their support, patronage, and encouragement. Thanks to my Turkish Godfather, Suleyman Aydin, for employing me throughout the first years of this project.

Special thanks to Andy Antippas, who has been a real mentor to me, while never failing to live up to his many reputations!

I thank my editor, Christi Phillips, who recognized the worth of this project and believed in it from the beginning. Without her tireless efforts and midnight e-mails, *Vodou Visions* would not have been born. My agent, Kim Witherspoon, and Gideon Weil helped me navigate the most mysterious seas of publishing. Thanks to Bruce Tracy, Oona Schmid, and the editorial staff at Villard for selecting *Vodou Visions,* and for their patient, knowledgeable guidance and understanding.

Thanks to the eternally gracious Joan Rivers for making the dream real.

I thank the city of New Orleans for her tolerance and open mind. Her exotic soul dances to the rhythm of Spirit.

My family and my partner, Shane, were of immeasurable help to me, bringing their collective expertise, talent, and intelligence to bear, and bailing *Vodou Visions* out of deep waters in the final hour. I cannot imagine a moment without them in my heart.

My dear and lifelong friend Darius James always said I should write a book, so *Vodou Visions* is really his fault.

Finally, I offer all thanks and praise to my Mèt tèt, Lasirèn and Ogou Sen Jak, and to all the Lwa and Orishas who have allowed me to serve them through this work. They guide all things in the universe, under Bondye.

ASHÉ!

Contents

Note on Orthography ✳

The spelling of Vodou terminology presents many issues that may in the end be impossible to resolve to everyone's satisfaction. As Vodou defies orthodoxy, so too does the orthography of its Kreyòl terms. While Waldman's recent dictionary, published by the Creole Institute of Indiana University, provides an academic standard for terms, the Kreyòl of Vodou—born of the encounter between African dialects and the French spoken by colonists in Haiti—remains phonetic, and wildly divergent in both pronunciation and spelling. Relying upon Gallic spellings would provide a standard reference, but would be disrespectful to the power, history, and struggle of both the Kreyòl language and the Vodou religion. I have decided to work with the standardized Kreyòl spellings for the main body of the text, and have conformed to certain grammatical conventions of Kreyòl, such as the lack of pluralization of nouns, even though that is occasionally uncomfortable or confusing within an English text. I have attempted to use the article "the" whenever a name is plural, e.g. "the Gede are," or "the Manbo are." The litanies in the Visions, however, are written in the Kreyòl of common usage, bearing in mind that there are probably dozens of possible variants for the spelling of each word. The academic standardized version simply lacks the animated and lyric quality of the spoken language. French and English versions of each litany are provided as a more standard reference.

The word "Vodou" and its adjectival form "Vodoun" in particular have been selected to differentiate the religion from the lurid, celluloid image suggested by the common American term *Voodoo*.

In the same way, the spelling of "magick" in reference to Western Ceremonial practices distinguishes the occult science from sleight of hand.

About This Book

There is nothing that isn't Vodou. Vodou encompasses the principle and rhythm of life itself. Spirit is a present reality. It flows in and around every act and expression of the universe. It fills all things; informs all life; is the spark of the Divine within all people. Anyone can approach Spirit, whoever, however, and wherever they are. You start with what you know, where you came from, and then it grows.

The best way I can show all that is wondrous and blessed in Vodou is through my personal experience of the Vodoun religion. *Vodou Visions* is an attempt to guide you through Vodou in theory and practice. I am a visionary artist as well as a Manbo, a Vodou priestess initiated in Haiti. I am also a student of Santería, Vodou's sister religion as practiced in Cuba. During my Haitian initiation, I offered myself in service to the Lwa, the guiding Spirits of Vodou. I asked to be allowed to serve the community in any way that I could—through art, in word, in ritual action. My work is guided by the Lwa, and the Orishas, the Gods of Santería. This book is part of my offering of service to the Spirit. It is my work as a Manbo to help others awaken to a sense of awe before the Divine. As you read through the pages of the book, I hope you will begin to remember yourself as the child of Spirit.

There are those who would fault my work because I am initiated as a Manbo only, and not as a Santera as well. Or they might say that it is inauthentic to work with creative applications of old traditions. Some reject any creative or visionary developments in Vodou or Santería. There is always confusion and resistance when new forms and applications emerge. But it is that exact creative originality that I would like to encourage in my readers. It is not my intention to tell anyone that *Vodou Visions* is the authoritative Vodou canon. In fact, Vodou has no canon. *Vodou Visions* is a record of a direct encounter with Spirit, and offers guidelines on how anyone else can have a similar experience.

The principles of Vodou can be applied to creative ends in uncharted regions. In the new millennium, it is time for people to move into a new understanding of creative spirituality. Priests, church doctrine, dogmatic rules and canon only intimidate and alienate people from their own spiritual potential. You have the right and the ability to develop your own way of being, your own unique expression of spiritual evolution. There is meaning and redemption to be found in offering the allegory of your experience in service to the Spirit. Each practitioner works out original applications of Vodou trance. My friend Darius James, for instance, is a wildly creative, underground author who writes in a style that he calls "Vodoun gumbo literature." His writing blends bits and traces of his experience, which he seasons with outrageous and flavorful language that simmers together to form spellbinding literature. He does not write books, he writes spells. I am doing visionary art in which I use ritual and meditation to alter my normal, waking consciousness so that the Spirit can guide my hand and eye. Do not be afraid to do new work. Take drums and your dancing feet with you into the thick forest; leave cornmeal vèvè as markers. Call out to the Lwa, who will help you forge a path.

I have learned through my work as a Manbo that it is possible for people of any culture, race, religion, or upbringing to reawaken deeply spiritual experiences within the psyche. Some people are said to be "born with the Spirit." These people do not require initiation to awaken their dance with Spirit. Spirit is with them from birth. It is in each of their footsteps and perceptions, it is in each moment of their experience, and clearly visible to others as they look into this type of personality. It is much like the metaphor of the alchemical wind. Alchemists, the precursors of modern chemists and metallurgists, practiced the ancient art of transmutation of dross metal into gold while simultaneously inducing a mystical transformation of their consciousness. The alchemical wind symbolized the inevitable force that catches a person up into destiny. This wind thrusts a seeker into the very lap of the monster of identity that fears change or revelatory truth. If you are born with this wind at your back, there is nothing you can ever do to get out of it; it will eventually blow you to your destiny, and to the crisis of transformation.

I believe that it was my particular condition to have been "born with the Spirit," for the Spirit has been a relentless taskmaster, as well as a bestower of great boons and mysterious gifts all my life. I have also long been an initiate of an ancient international Order of magicians who claim their origins in the esoteric rites of the Knights Templar that accompanied pilgrims to the Holy Lands during the Crusades. The Order encourages individuals to recognize their True Will, or their purpose for incarnating, in accordance with Divine Will. My study of Western Hermetics and Ceremonial Magick through this Order has rounded out my lifelong devotion to the Yogic systems and the even greater portion of my life spent studying tarot, Qabalah, and crystal scrying. I have also for most of my life been driven to produce works of art, the bulk of them involving magical perception of the mysterious content of image, and all of them involving automata or trance technique. In addition, my own career has been profoundly influenced by friendships formed with people from around the world that have allowed me to grow beyond my own given circumstances, and by a family that both encouraged tolerance and acceptance of exotic points of view, and insisted on scholarly excellence.

In 1976, I was drawn to New Orleans to study Vodou, having heard in songs, movies, and books that New Orleans was the Vodou capital of the United States. It was Spirit calling. I have been studying and practicing Vodou ever since. Spirit called out again in 1989 that I begin work on a tarot deck based on the Vodou Lwa and the Santería Orishas, consistent with the traditional, Qabalistic framework of the mystical tarot. The work extended over three years and involved ritual invocations to the Lwa and Orishas who expressed themselves imagistically through my hand and eye. But the visions were more complete than just pictures. They were rounded perceptions that concentrated greater meaning in image. It has been my hope that the tarot images of the Lwa and Orishas would function as containers of Spirit that others could hold in their minds when they call the Spirits into their bodies and hearts. There was, however, much expressed to me beyond and within the images that I feel needs further expression. The Lwa and Orishas presented the essence of their nature with spellbinding clarity. I have included in this book the original visionary material that completes the power of the tarot images, so that the Lwa and Orishas can speak for themselves.

Upon publication of the tarot deck, I expected to be labeled "evil" or, conversely, to be inundated with requests for spells to bring back errant lovers and the like. Instead, the deck has been, with few exceptions, received warmly and with respect. Perhaps what I always thought was a personal burden of perception was actually a reflection of a greater current of influence from the Lwa. I have been fortunate in that I have given myself leave to "follow my bliss," as Joseph Campbell once taught. But there must be many others who hunger for relationship with Spirit and feel that alchemical wind at their backs. Perhaps Ayizan, the Mother and Manbo of our race, calls to the housewives who are sinking into boredom at home. Perhaps Ogou's heartbeat drums through the booming of the battlefield for soldiers far from home. Gede is the strange and cocky bedfellow who sits with legs crossed and arms folded, watching through dark shades as we walk through our lives—glimpses of him may be caught here and there, reflected in shards of glass and in the chance echoing of the sounds of his gluttony. And in thousands of villages all over the world, Ezili lends her glamour to women, and her dreams to us all. I have discovered that this is not some odd, wrong-planet perception of my own, but rather a kind of enduring truth and indwelling knowledge within our souls that have brought the Lwa to light within our culture. We look up from the trance of the everyday to see Spirit whom we already know intimately, like an old friend.

It is my hope that my own path and unfolding perception of the Lwa and Orishas will add to the knowledge of them. The same forces and soul needs that brought my path to the Lwa may be common to many, and may be applicable on a cultural level. People universally may have noticed that generation after generation perpetuates pathologies that endanger individual well-being, and distort and unbalance communities. The same dissatisfaction that forced me to look beyond the boundaries of my own upbringing may be working on a grand scale. Perhaps it is common to experience this same sense of dissatisfaction. The principles and techniques of Vodou can be applied to encourage a sense of meaning and fulfillment in communities. What has proven to be healing and genuine to me can be significant to others. The Gnostics speak of wisdom that is to be found discarded among the unwanted things of this world. We can reclaim this discarded wisdom. It may be that individuals who have reendowed their psyches with the ability to see, hear, and receive promptings of Spirit can affect the human condition. If some chords are struck within you, you might find yourself wanting to make the huge leap from theory to practice. To that end, practical rituals are included that can guide interested persons into direct experience of the Lwa and the Orishas who have guided me, enriched my life, and expanded my consciousness.

I have found, during the hundreds of readings I have done with the tarot and through crystal ball scrying, that all people—with a greater or lesser degree of awareness—are searching through time for the meaning of their immortal souls. It is my intention that this book be a further marker for those who are searching for their paths. Through it, I hope others will experience greater inspiration and a deepening presence of mystery. It is my intention that the healing, sensual, and living qualities of Vodou be actively experienced through this work; that the visions open within you as they opened within me. Here are patterns and methods of inviting the Lwa and Orishas into your life, as well as visionary expressions from them.

There are many paths that lead to the Vodoun. My own path is just one. Sometimes it is not so easy to recognize the graceful action of Spirit in your life as you live it. But listen and watch. Pay attention. Ritual action takes time out from the thick frenzy of life and fixes attention on the sacred. It is possible to retrace one's steps and find significant patterns unfolding. Messages are written within experience, as if in cipher. It is possible to learn the language of the Lwa. Call them. They have been with us since the beginning, sustained us, and continue to dance within our world and experience.

Vodou Visions

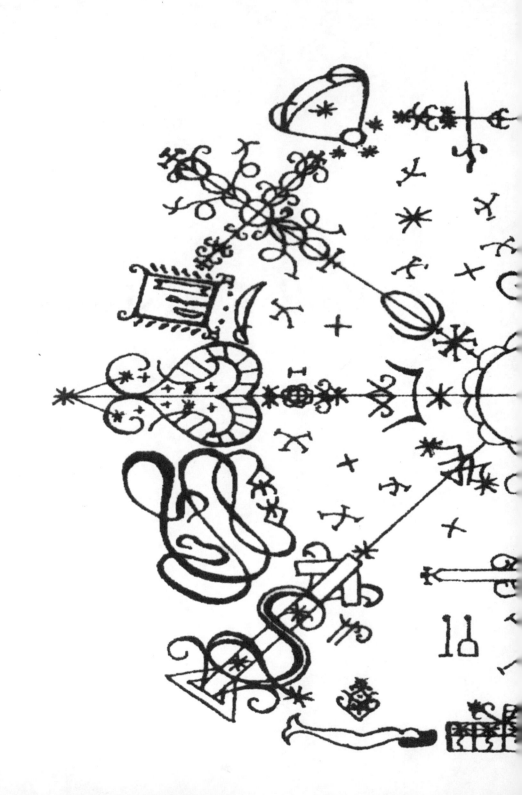

Why Do Vodou?

In November of 1995, I found myself wondering what a nice, middle-aged Jewish woman like me was doing in the midst of a bizarre and arduous Couché initiation in a squalid Haitian Ounfò. It seemed like a silly question at the time, since there I was, and I probably ought to have just done gladly what I had to do. Fate. Positive compulsion. Destiny. Since then, I've asked myself many times at many junctures—almost hourly, in fact—"Why are you doing Vodou?" Perhaps it's a test I give myself of my honesty, intensity, or truthfulness of Will. The simple answer, of course, is "Because it feels right. I like it." The long answer is a whole journey, a path through a thick and tricky forest. Maybe it's due to a persistent sense of what it means to be human. Or a need for Gods who are present in creation, and willing to walk through it with their creation. I like Gods that are accountable to their children, and whose approach is covered in blessings.

I imagine that many people all over the world have wondered why they were drawn to Vodou. I believe it's because the forms, rhythms, and mysteries of Vodou are universal and fundamental to the human experience. Vodou offers archetypal principles from which no one need be excluded. The truths that it offers are recognizable within the framework of human experience, no matter where one is from, or what the color of one's skin.

So the first reason I do Vodou is that I can.

Vodou is tolerant. It receives. It honors and respects us all as though we were gifts. It tells us that we are precious, whoever we are, Jew, Catholic, Hindu, Muslim, white, or black.

Vodou is based on ancestor worship. We come into the Vodoun with a whole heritage in our DNA. Our bloodline and heritage are important. Where do you come from? What powers and strengths were passed to you through the generations? It's also important to recognize whatever distorted baggage or crippling viewpoints were handed down. By accepting our heritage, it is realigned, balanced, and made whole, so that we can pass radiant power to subsequent generations. The seeds of future evolution are in us now. In the process of remembering, honoring, and reinstating our ancestors, we find our place in our own heritage. A fine web radiates from us, back into Mother, Grandmother, and Great-grandmother, and back beyond memory of time, while the seeds of the future extend forward. We approach the Vodoun as multidimensional beings with the legacy of the past in our bodies and with the seeds of the future in our intentions. As our place is found in history, the doors of time open and dissolve.

In Vodou, the definition of family also extends to include the community of the Ounfò or Sosyete. This family provides spiritual support and welcome encouragement from like-minded people. It is essential to remember that the Vodoun Gods are helpful and healing. Raising a community into the greater community of the Lwa provides spiritual focus and direction. The focus goes out from limited self-interest to more communal goals. Vodou teaches a unique combination of empowerment and humility in communal service to the Vodoun.

The community is guided by the Manbo, the priestesses, and the Oungan, the priests. They are the Mama and the Papa of the family. When you are in Silva Joseph's Ounfò, you are in your Papa's house. His circle of protection and concern goes with you everywhere you go. You are not under the ring and rule of the clergy. They are not "Holier than thou," spiritually superior, and therefore judgmental and repressive. There is no kissing of the holy ring. Just respect and honor. It sits comfortably with me, too, that the women Manbo play such a huge and equal role in Vodou, if only because the men were too exhausted from working the fields in the days of slavery to be much help in ceremony.

There is no orthodoxy, no central church in Vodou. It is refreshingly free of dogma, of all vestiges of dualistic judgment. Dogma is replaced with an ancient source of tradition that serves as inspiration and foundation for evolving forms of creative spiritual expression. The emphasis on creative application helps push past self-consciousness into the ecstatic realm where the Lwa thrive. The Lwa are often dramatic or outrageous or silly. They laugh and strut, and through them we laugh and strut ourselves. By laughing at ourselves, the human condition is transformed from one of limitation and suffering to that of joyful expression.

You can do Vodou in a group community, or you can do it alone. A crowd in the street, or just you and the Spirit. You can call the Lwa in an Ounfò, by a river, a lake, in your bedroom, in a bar. You can build an altar to call them, or dream them into your head in sleep. You can feed them, yell at them, take them into your body, lend them your flesh and blood. You can speak their words, dance their songs, draw their form. You can create new forms to give them. You can honor them, benefit from their protection and help. You can appeal to them, you can be their horse. You can explore the most inner, silent centers of your soul. You can explore the outer reaches of potential and inspiration. Whole areas of the psyche that lie dormant can be exercised in Vodou, can become powers. We have the power to transform our experience of the world.

I remember when I first went to art school to study painting. Suddenly I saw the same old universe with new eyes. There were colors I had never seen before—the world was brighter, more vibrant. Composition, form, movement, the dance of shadow and light. Texture, value, intensity, subtlety, and richness piled all on top of each other, building substance. The visual world was suddenly fascinating, as though I was observing it for the first time, unveiling its secret layers before my eyes. Vodou reawakens this fresh awareness of the sacred within the everyday. It reifies Nature. There are Lwa in the trees! Ashé! Intelligence in the rivers! Ashé! Wisdom in the rocks! Ashé! Everywhere Ashé!

In the midst of the deadening, hideous rush of urban distraction, there is a steady, ancient drumbeat. In our urge to become "comfort zombies," we give away our souls to the financial machine. We feel dead inside, so we think the whole world around us is dead. We kill off any evidence of soul in the world. Long ago we sold God to the highest bidder. Vodou turns our attention away from the competitive, corporate spell. It puts our souls, minds, and imaginations back in our bodies. Priorities and values change. How we treat ourselves, each other, and the world suddenly becomes more important than how far did we manage to claw our way up the corporate ladder today. We begin to relabel such things as "worth" and "meaning." A person becomes rich with "konesans" or Spiritual knowledge. The meaning of experience breaks through the resistance of literal reality, and we start to connect with ourselves, with each other, with the Lwa.

Listen to your heartbeat—it is a gift from an ancient bloodline. Remember your heritage. Remember the Gods who dance with us through the land of shadow. That's Ogou hefting the iron load of the industrial world. The world is full of potential, abundant. Every part of the world is sacred. The world is the Peristil of the Lwa. They dance with us. Ashé!

Vodou is a religion of survival and hope. It transforms dirt and squalor and minimal subsistence into brilliant and flashing, sequined displays. Each movement is fully attuned. Each person holds the birthright to potential.

And, finally, Vodou is sophisticated, rich, deep, graceful, and entrancing. However deep you dig, however intelligent, swift, demanding, disarming, adept, or creative you are, the Vodoun remains profoundly mysterious.

Why do Vodou?
Because you are precious. You are rich. You deserve to live from a sense of abundance.

Why do Vodou?
Because it is beautiful, and it bestows blessings.

Why do Vodou?
To get right with the Lwa.

Why do Vodou?
To bring the world back to life.

Why do Vodou?
To find our potential strength, our right to live and be.

Why do Vodou?
Because it meets the rhythms of our souls.

Why do Vodou?
Because it honors our destiny, our dignity, our ancestry, and our legacy.

Why do Vodou?
Because it is the Lwa calling.

They roll up out of the dark, secret earth.
They whisper in the currents of wind, the
    rhythms and roll of the drums,
in every heartbeat and the pulse of the
    world.

They come through the scent of our
    prayers,
the fire of our Will,
and the cool points of our dreams.

Why do Vodou?
Because when we call to the Lwa, they come.

What Is Vodou?

BLACK MAGIC, SORCERY, AND DEVIL WORSHIP: THE STUFF THAT MOVIES ARE MADE OF

The word "Vodou" sends chills down the spines of most people, and conjures up age-old terrors of sorcery, black magic, and bogeymen lurking under the bed. It's not surprising. Ever since 1884, when Spencer St. John wrote *Haiti or the Black Republic,* a fictional and lurid account of human sacrifice and cannibalism among Haitian natives, Vodou has been labeled an evil religion, and haunted by repression and misunderstanding. More recently, B movies with titles like *Voodoo Black Exorcist* and *Chopper Chicks in Zombietown* have provided Vodou with the worst image of any religion on earth. Hollywood has conjured up an intoxicating image of crazed natives running with ungodly powers through dangerously pounding dark nights of evil and primitive rites. Good, decent white women are seen in erotic frenzy, tormented by the relentless rhythms of libidinous natives till their lust for forbidden powers rips their soul to shreds. We are drawn to these lurid images in the same way that people pause in passing roadside accidents to see whatever horrors might be displayed for their fascination there. In *Heart of Darkness,* Joseph Conrad referred to this sort of disturbing titillation as the "Fascination of the Abomination." We take a posture of deep shock, and would never consider such behavior in ourselves, yet we hypocritically lap up sensational and defamatory images of Vodou in film and literature.

Western civilization thinks it knows Vodou through these offensively inaccurate movies and books. But through sensationalized versions of Vodou, Westerners give a face to their own darkest fears of the shadow. We fear what seems like a loss of control, which is embodied by Vodou's possession experience. Perhaps those raised in a rigid, corporate culture are alarmed by the implications of possession trance. Fear is inspired by the perilous crossing over the ecstatic bridge that spans the chasm between the solid and the invisible, the living and the dead, the mortal, individual self and the Divine. Western civilization feels itself to be more spiritually sophisticated, more composed morally. Although Vodou is labeled a primitive cult, it may be a more spiritually advanced one. While Western culture tends to honor and respect the scientific, the rational, and the technological, it simultaneously discredits and diminishes the value of the spiritual. The focus is entirely on the material, on the surface of reality. Perceptions concerning the nature of eternal truths or mythological reality cannot be proved by empirical science. We can build high-rises, subway systems, and bridges. We can prescribe pills for whatever ails us. We can break down the atom, isolate and tamper with genes. We can pass mind-boggling amounts of information in milliseconds. But the ability to see beneath the surface of the apparent to the invisible meaning within has atrophied to the point that there is no longer respect or recognition of systems that turn their attention directly to spiritual vision. Perhaps modern Judeo-Christian civilization has simply lost touch with those very values and perceptions that are central to the Vodoun experience. We fear what we don't understand but recognize however dimly—and possibly threateningly—as a repressed force within ourselves. That which is not understood, that which challenges restricted psyches, is called unsophisticated or primal or superstitious.

When I first saw some books about Vodou at a friend's house more than twenty years ago, my gut reaction was one of fear and mistrust. I felt the need to protect myself against what I imagined were uncontrollable, malicious forces. What if I were forever jeopardizing my immortal soul? Soon I understood that my fear sprang from ignorance, and it was foolish to be afraid of something that I knew nothing about. The more I learned, the more my fear subsided. Vodou as it is generally practiced has nothing to do with black magic, devil worship, or filmmakers' gory fantasies. What I discovered instead was a vibrant, beautiful, and ecstatic religion that was free from dogma, guilt, or coercion.

Vodou certainly is not an "evil" practice, but rather one that affirms relation with ongoing cycles of life and Spirit. Vodou engages in relationship with Spirit as the intelligence of energy that is immanent in humans, in all of nature, in thought. Spirit is the essential and ensouling force of being that is invisibly present, and guides the experience of life. Vodou is not a primitive practice that lacks order, insight, and cohesion. The living experience of the Divine that one encounters through actual Vodou practice requires a sophisticated philosophy, an elegance of participation in the mysterious, and an intimate knowledge of soul. Perhaps it is the honest sensuality of Vodou that is threatening at first, until one realizes that this sensuality allows us to take into our bodies the spirituality that feeds our souls.

It would be naïve to insist that Vodou doesn't have a shadow side. Perhaps all the fear that Vodou inspires is an indication of the powers inherent in its practice. The dictator "Papa Doc" Duvalier seized on the terrifying shadow aspect of Vodou to intimidate the Haitian people. In so doing, he further exaggerated Vodou's negative connotations.

Haitians acknowledge a distinction between Vodou, the religion, and magic. There is a distinction between Oungan and Manbo, the priests and priestesses of Vodou, and bòkò, or sorcerers, who are limited to working with magic, and are considered to operate on a lower spiritual level than a Manbo or Oungan. The Western paradigm that insists things are either good or evil is perhaps not applicable here. Bòkò "work with both hands"; their work can be malevolent or wholesome. Bòkò are dealing with time *now*, in very practical terms. They seem able to effect magical or supernatural transformations, but only for the time being. The magic is temporary. An Oungan or Manbo is working more in terms of the Eternal, effecting real healings that take time to develop, but which are less ephemeral, and which take into account the well-being of the whole community, and the revelation of Spirit. The bòkò may perform a spell to control a force in a person's fortune. The Manbo conducts a religious ceremony to align the life force within a person. While the bòkò might trap a Spirit into a "wanga" bottle in order to work a spell to bring riches or material success, the Oungan would do a ceremony, perhaps honoring Legba, who opens the door to opportunity, to find out how someone's life may be misaligned, and to discern the ways in which the problem may be rectified, adjusted, and healed. A bòkò's work is more restricted to individual desire, is more self-serving, and temporary. They are generally frowned upon, and even feared in Haiti, but that is not to say that they don't have a steady stream of customers who are willing to pay for their services and knowledge. Oungan or Manbo may work on a higher level of spirituality that is inclusive of, but not limited to, magic.

In spite of prejudice and fear, in spite of sensational disinformation, Vodou is a religion that has seen dramatic growth in recent years, growth that is crossing racial and cultural lines. People of all races, cultures, and religious upbringing are turning to it for an irreplaceable and undeniable experience of the Divine. Vodou is not a primitive cult; it is a healing practice and religion of ongoing creation. Vodou survived slavery and sustained a people who lost all but their rhythms and their Gods. The religion continues to grow, transform, and respond to the needs of practitioners, even as the servitors bring the Lwa, or Vodoun Gods, into the twenty-first century.

TI GINEN AND IFE: THE SCATTERED SONS AND DAUGHTERS OF THE LEGENDARY CITY

Let us stop for a moment and say praise for the nameless ancestors whose courage, backbone, and inspiration founded a religion of survival and hope.

Let us give honor to the human Spirit that imagines a heaven in even the most poisonous of environments.

Let us remember the history of Vodou, which in itself is a kind of initiation into the enduring power of Ashé. If we cannot remember, then let us imagine ourselves with them, the first slaves to land in Hispaniola. Finding ourselves thrown in with people of diverse African nanchon, diverse cultures and customs. Forced together to find a common way of survival, to find strength and meaning.

Let us offer respect to the treasures they carried in their memories, their imaginations, their rhythms and grace. They carried the Lwa with them. Ashé!

Vodou is based on the Yoruba and Fon traditions of the West Coast of Africa—Benin, Dahomey, and Togo, referred to as the Guinea Coast or the Slave Coast. During the sixteenth century, the slave trade began taking the people of the West Coast of Africa to work on plantations in the Caribbean, creating Vodou and its cousin religions, Santería, Candomblé, Macumba, Lacumi, Umbanda, and Quimbanda. Subsequent movements of the slave trade carried these religions to the port of New Orleans, and to the Carolina coast. Vodou is practiced primarily in Haiti and West Africa, although large Vodou societies exist in parts of the United States, particularly in New Orleans, New York, and Miami. Worldwide, Vodou is reported to have more than fifty million followers.

Slavery tore people from their families, from their cultures, and from their place and position in the community. They were left with only their Gods. But bits and traces of differing religious practices were culled from each of the African nations that combined in Haiti's slave population. Out of its diverse sources, a central core of knowledge developed that gave Vodou its strength and coherence. The word "Vodou" means "Spirit" or "Deity" in the Fon language of Dahomey, now a part of Nigeria. Vodou is monotheistic, recognizing one supreme God, "Bondye." This God is an unfathomable, abstract force. Beneath God are the Lwa, the ancestral and archetypal spirits that form the Vodou pantheon, and that interact with human beings. The Lwa are often referred to as angels, zanj, or even as Gods, but they are distinct from the Supreme God, Bondye. Vodounists believe that all things serve the Lwa under God, that everything in life is an expression of Divinity.

The first revelations of the Lwa were received in Ife, a city in Ginen, West Africa. Everything in creation and all spiritual strength comes from Ife; after death, the higher soul of the devotee returns to Ginen to reside with the Lwa and the ancestral Spirits. Because of this, all Vodoun practitioners refer to themselves as Ti Ginen, sons or daughters of Ginen. When people practice Vodou, they are entering the sacred gates of Ife to offer respect and honor to the legacy of those who came before. They replenish, in contemporary time and space, the inspired seeds of potential that the first children of Ginen planted in a harsh new world.

Vodou is syncretic, meaning that it takes on qualities of the cultures that it encounters. Vodou acquires. It draws into itself all that it recognizes, relates to, can use. The original Yoruba and Fon religions were Creolized through contact with French and the native Taino Indian cultures in Haiti, where it became what we think of today as Vodou. It transformed in Spanish-speaking cultures to become Santería, Candomblé, Macumba, and Lakumi. To the original complex cultural roots, stemming from the different African nations—Congo, Nago, Ibo, Rada, and Djouba—Vodou added traces of colonial French culture. The formal pirouette dances of the Oungan and Manbo at the beginning of Vodou ceremonies bear the mark of colonial dances. Religious gestures of the imperialist cultures present in Haiti can also be traced in the predominance of Catholic imagery and iconography associated with the Lwa—even the cross returns to its pre-Catholic roots as it has been pressed into service as Legba's crossroads, and Gede's home. The bush priest's, or Prèt Savann's, recitation of Catholic litanies and the names of the saints at the beginning of Vodou ceremonies are a remnant of Catholic dominance in Haiti. The Portuguese priests left significant traces of their Masonic brotherhoods in the Oriental and Qabalistic knowledge that filters through the Vodoun, as well as in Gede's standard-issue Masonic clothing and regalia. The predominance of Haitian sequined drapo, or Vodou flags, are certainly reflections both of Haiti's militaristic past and of Masonic standards. The few Native Indians that were alive when the African slaves arrived influenced the use of rattles and cornmeal in Vodoun ceremony. The slaves even transformed characters of the Italian cabaret or three-penny opera that was present on Saint Domingue into the attributes of some of the more charismatic Lwa, such as Ezili.

The history of the development of Vodou over several centuries in Haiti was not written down. The names are largely forgotten, with the exception of some leaders of the Haitian slave uprising who may have used Vodou Petwo rites to incite and sustain the long and bloody Haitian revolution. While it is difficult to speak of any sort of linear development of Vodou, traces of memory are coded into its assemblage of art forms, its dances, songs, altars, and ritual gestures, its Qabalah of meaning.

The Qabalah is the mystical tradition of Judaism that attempts to express God's essence. The Zohar is the most famous Qabalistic book. Written in the thirteenth century in Aramaic, the Zohar interprets the Torah (the first five books of the Hebrew Bible) as symbolic revelation of universal and Divine secret truths. For the most part, however, Qabalah is an orally transmitted tradition. By meditating on a series of ten Divine emanations, called "Sephiroth," that are pictured as aligning on a glyph called the "Tree of Life," a mystic can follow a symbolic map that leads to God, and can help bring grace into the world from its first issuance out of the three veils of the limitless. The limitless is beyond human comprehension, but the ten Spheres, and the twenty-two paths that connect the Spheres, form a kind of meditational filing cabinet in which all thought and experience can be organized and referred. Each Sphere expresses or contains a particular quality and force. All existence, potential or manifest, particular colors, smells, psychological states, angelic forces, and pantheons of God-forms from world religions can be attributed to each sphere and path, allowing the mystic to see meaningful patterns and secret wisdom revealed through relationships between the emanating Spheres. Qabalah was considered so powerful, and potentially so dangerous, that its study was traditionally restricted to married men who were over forty years old, and had already mastered study of the Torah and Talmud.

Qabalah's influence has spread beyond Orthodox Judaism. It is said to be the basis of the tarot system of divination, and forms the foundation of Western Ceremonial Magick, as well as the rites of Freemasonry.

Vodounists use Qabalah especially to catalogue the colors, corresponding Saints, offerings, food, drink, animals, ceremonial objects, symbolic tools, herbs, natural forces, symbolic animals, sacred trees, rhythms, and dances that are associated with each of the Lwa. Knowledge of the Qabalah of the Lwa allows an individual to approach the Divine and encourages the Divine to emanate grace into the world from the realm of Bondye.

AN ART, A DANCE, A DRUMBEAT: THE CREATION OF SOUL IN THE WORLD

Money, greed, competition, and aggression are the keys to success in the United States today. Spiritual and emotional needs, and the need for meaning, are regarded as idealistic at best. Our religion is the economy. We worship the dollar. As nothing has inherent soul value, everything and everyone is disposable. We are taught to detach and not care about ourselves or each other. We take our lead from corporations and deny responsibility for our interconnectedness with one another. Systematically, modern, corporate blind greed kills off the soul of the world.

Vodou, on the other hand, brings the world back to life, recognizes and creates soulful content. I believe humans only feel fulfilled when engaged in what John Keats called "Soul-making." Vodou relocates spiritual content within the discarded world. It listens to and extracts the underlying rhythms that connect life force to life force. It calls to us as we call to the Lwa. It tells us that each of us can dance within the archetypal waters. By recognizing, affirming, and honoring the spiritual content within the world, within all life, within ourselves, Vodou accomplishes the act of "Tikkun Olam"—the redemption, repair, and transformation of the world. ("Tikkun Olam" is the central purpose of Jewish life, and refers to the obligation "to perfect the world under the rule of God." The words "Tikkun Olam" are from the Aleinu prayer, which is repeated three times a day.)

In contrast to strict Judeo-Christian tradition, Vodou rites and rituals focus on bringing about enlightenment through direct contact with the Spirit. Vodou concerns itself with direct, living experience of Divine Mystery.

Anthropological, cultural, and historical studies of Vodou objectify and flatten the multidimensional experience of Vodou. Books are written about Vodou from an objective remove. It is difficult for the reader to translate from the two-dimensional study to the actual, living experience of Vodou. Vodou's sources are complex. Each individual that approaches Vodou is complex. Vodou requires a leap beyond the rational, logical restrictions of cool intellect to dive into the vibrant, molten core content of the Vodoun: "The Christian goes to church and talks about God, while the Vodounist dances in the Ounfò and becomes God."

In order to practice Vodou, we must approach from a completely different perspective: from within, rather than from a safer intellectual distance. Dive into the core of the Vodoun experience with your body, with all of who you are, where you came from, where you are going. For in Vodou all aspects of experience are present in multiple dimensions. Our rational mind is overwhelmed by the entrancing and marvelously abundant symbolic reference of Vodou.

Music, dance, and artistic expression are the heart and soul of Vodou. The religion itself is an art, a dance, a drumbeat, and is inseparable from the rhythms, forms, colors, and images that animate it. I've found this is true no matter where Vodou is practiced, whether in Haiti, or in New Orleans, where I live and work.

With its mix of French, Spanish, African, Native American, and Haitian cultures, New Orleans provided fertile soil for Vodou's syncretic nature, and gave birth to its own style of Vodou. Slaves were permitted to hold "dances" on Sundays in New Orleans's Congo Square. These dances were actually Vodou ceremonies, and allowed the slaves to maintain the forms of their religion. Southern Baptist and Spiritualist churches provided recognizable ground for Vodou to establish a foothold. Various waves of Vodounists reinforced Vodou's presence, both before the Haitian revolution and again after New Orleans was reopened to fleeing colonial plantation owners and their households. A few extraordinary and charismatic figures, such as Marie Laveau and Dr. John, kept Vodou's image alive, adapting it to the dominant Catholicism of the city. Vodou shifted, flowed, and undulated its way into the rich cultural heritage of the city, lending it its rhythms, its Afro-Caribbean flavor, and its slippery backbone. Traces of Vodoun influence can be found throughout New Orleans's many spellbinding cultural forms. The beaded costumes and second-line parades of the Mardi Gras Indians are a direct take on the mystical RaRa Parades of Haitian Carnival. The Cajun "traiteurs," or "root doctors," surely exchanged botanical treatments with Vodoun healers. The Hoodoo, or spell work, that is so dominant in New Orleans practice seems to be a watered-down version of the bòkò's trade.

There seem to have developed distinct strains of Vodou in New Orleans. The more noticeable strain is engaged in Hoodoo work—stereotypical spells and hexes—as opposed to Vodou, the religion. Hoodoo practice is predominantly directed to the tourist dollar, with sensational displays of ceremony and possession trance thrown in for effect. The tourist shops and performers strike me as more than a bit demeaning, capitalizing on the most corrupt and unsavory aspects of Vodou. Unfortunately, many Vodounists in New Orleans seem to have confused their spirituality with mercenary materialism. However, it may be the ironic truth that tourist fascination may have helped to keep Vodou alive and funded. In the meantime, there have also been Vodounists working quietly, with sincerity, in order to serve the Lwa through more authentic, and more demanding, ceremonial forms. It is rare for tourists to run across these groups, but they seem to be growing, and they appear to be earning recognition for the practice of Vodou in New Orleans. It may, in fact, be more possible to practice Vodou openly in New Orleans than in Haiti, where Vodou has consistently been persecuted or outlawed. It is certainly more possible to practice Vodou in New Orleans than in other parts of the United States, where it is still perceived as evil. In New Orleans, after all, Vodou is a marketed tourist commodity!

But I do recognize a growing movement in New Orleans to make the practice of Vodou more "real," to research and reproduce the Haitian, Cuban, and Brazilian roots of Vodou. While Vodou in New Orleans remains toned down compared to its practice in Haiti, I find that Manbo and Oungan in town are increasingly devoted to reproducing authentic Haitian rhythms, songs, and forms in their ceremonies. While there is some blurring in New Orleans of Haitian and Latin forms and rhythms—the Lwa and the Orisha worshiped together, there is also an unparalleled opportunity here for creative exploration beyond the confines of tradition. A real key for the development of Vodou in New Orleans will lie in a sincere and knowledgeable attempt to establish a link with authentic Haitian practice while still exploring the creative edge of inspiration. The real question is always whether the door has been opened at the crossroads so that the magic of transformation can take place. Have we passed from describable, reproducible words and forms to move into the other, ineffable dimension of Mystery?

The practice of Vodou is as individual as human lives and ancestry. The rituals I work in my Ounfò may differ from those worked in Haiti, just as rituals in Haiti differ from village to village, Ounfò to Ounfò. But my rituals are no less effective simply because they are different. They remain works in progress as we continue to develop technique and ability. There is no orthodoxy in Vodou, no central church, no holy father, and precious few "rules." There are techniques that are effective. Each ceremony can be a work of art. Effort, knowledge, sincerity, and practice make for more perfect offerings. Each Sèvitè is an instrument to be honed. It is not by coincidence that New Orleans is also the birthplace of jazz. It could be said that Vodou is to religion what jazz is to music: a form that grew from African roots and rhythms, absorbed influences from various sources, and enjoys its ultimate expression in the interpretation of improvisation of the practitioner.

LÈ MARASA, OR SACRED TWINS

The Marasa are the sacred Twins. They are the first children of God. They are the first Dead, and so the first Ancestors. They are always the first honored in Vodou ceremony.

In many cultures around the world, twins are seen as magical or taboo. In Vodou, the Twins represent two bodies that share one soul, and so span the abyss that separates the inner and outer worlds, the world of Spirit and the physical world. Vodou carries this idea throughout the symbolism of the crossroads—the cross in Christianity—whereby the horizontal arm of the crossroads represents the earth plane of time and space. The vertical arm represents the flow of Spirit throughout the world. At the top of the crossroads lives Papa Legba, the keeper of the gate, who walks on the power points of the sun. Legba is old, lame, and worn from walking with his children throughout the world. At the base of the crossroads walks Gede, the God of death and sexuality. He is the sun at midnight. Between the two flows the Spirit. At the center of the crossroads is the door that separates one world from the other. We call Legba to open the door to let Spirit flow into the physical world. In the symbolism of the Ounfò, the centerpole is the vertical axis, and the Peristil floor is the horizontal. The two worlds exist simultaneously. Each is revealed through relation with the other. The invisible is clothed with the visible, and the visible is ensouled by the invisible. At the axis of the crossroads, where the two worlds intersect, the magical energy of transformation is experienced. It is as the guardians or containers of this transformative mystery that we first honor the Marasa.

The Marasa's symbol is formed by two intersecting V's. The Twins are exactly opposite but exactly the same. Opposites in Vodou are not antagonistic. They reflect, reveal, and interpenetrate each other. The Marasa's twinning is honored with ceremonial bowls that have three partitions: two supernal elements create the child that is formed by their combined essence, but which transcends them.

From the union of the Marasa comes all things.

LÈ MÒ, OR THE DEAD

The Dead float in the Waters of the Abyss, which flow through everything, are everywhere, and inform all existence. The Abysmal Waters are the great wash of time, and the sweet—or perhaps salty—waters of creation. The Dead, our Ancestors, made us who we are. The earth we walk on is made of their very bones. We, in turn, create future generations. No rigid walls separate the past, present, and future, the living and the Dead. Through it all flow these eternal Waters.

Realities intersect. Life dances with Death. The Dead wait within the Waters to be called upon to influence, guide, and protect the living.

The Dead are composed of the Gwo Bon Anj of every human being who ever lived.

In Vodou, a person's soul is a metaphysical double with two aspects: the Gwo Bon Anj or Big Good Angel, and the Ti Bon Anj or Little Good Angel. Upon birth, the Magic Mirror that is the reflective surface of the Waters reveals this soul double, or Gwo Bon Anj, to the individual. The reflective soul lives with us throughout our lives. It is the spark of Bondye, which connects us to our Divine source. It's the life force within our consciousness and creativity, and is the dynamism that flows through the blood, breath, and energy in our bodies. The Gwo Bon Anj is not our breath or the beating blood itself, but is the life force that motivates these functions and informs the body with the cosmic will to live. The Gwo Bon Anj is contained within the body during life.

A living person's Gwo Bon Anj can be placed in an earthenware jar, where it is protected by the individual's Oungan or Manbo. But it can also be stolen and forced into slavery, or used in sorcery to great harm. A Zonbi's Gwo Bon Anj has been stolen, leaving only the Ti Bon Anj in residence. It is considered immoral for a person to entrap another person's Will, or Gwo Bon Anj. However, the Gwo Bon Anj can move aside in order for the Lwa to enter into or "borrow" a body during the possession experience.

The Ti Bon Anj is attached to the Gwo Bon Anj, and is a bit like the conscience that is incapable of lying. The Ti Bon Anj determines the moral choices made by a person, and is the conscience that distinguishes between good and bad, right and wrong. It is the individual personality, and particularly the ego. Through the Ti Bon Anj, people experience emotional response to their own moral behavior. The Ti Bon Anj mirrors the presence of the Gwo Bon Anj into visible manifestation, as reflected physically in the body as tears or laughter that express joy or regret. The two parts of the soul mirror each other and, ideally, resonate in harmony with one another.

Upon death, the aspects of the soul separate. The Ti Bon Anj is exhaled with the dying breath, and rises beyond the dead shell of the body. The body returns to the navel of the earth, where it dissolves back into clay and water. It awaits the Will of Bondye to be reformed and reanimated as a new body. The Ti Bon Anj stands before Bondye, but it loses its personal individuality. It has no further bearing upon the living, and can neither influence the Lwa, nor can it be used for sorcery or magic. The Gwo Bon Anj, however, lingers by the grave for nine days after the death of an individual. Death rites separate the body from the soul, and from the Mèt tèt, which has patronized people throughout their lifetime. The Gwo Bon Anj is returned to the Immortal Waters of Ginen, where it joins with the community of the Ancestral Dead. After a year and one day, reclamation rites call the Gwo Bon Anj back into the community of the living, where it offers guidance, advice, understanding, and perspective from its new body, formed of a specially prepared earthenware jar, called a govi jar. If properly performed, the Gwo Bon Anj can become a Lwa eventually, or can be reincarnated in the form of succeeding family generations.

Vodou accepts the cycles of life and the processes of death. The categories are simply not rigid. Death is a process that leads to further rhythms. We reach through the doors to touch and communicate with the Dead in honor of the Mystery of their initiation. We don't understand the level on which we are operating until we have achieved the next level of initiation. The Dead have achieved the next level of initiation, and we can benefit from their perspective. Likewise, they benefit from our memory and the honor we pay them. Through our love and memory, their lives attain ongoing meaning. If the doors between the living and the Dead are closed, whatever is lurking on the other side becomes monstrous and frightening. If they are open, the atmosphere and qualities of both sides are free to exchange.

LÈ MISTÈ, OR THE LWA

The Mysteries are unseen but eternally present Spirits or Gods known as the Lwa. The Lwa were once living people who passed through the initiation of death. As Vodou evolved, people with particularly charismatic personality traits were remembered and honored over generations. As living memory of the person died out, some stories were forgotten, others were embellished. Sometimes different people's stories were combined. Over time, an archetypal Lwa developed.

The Lwa are intermediaries between an abstract and distant God, Bondye, who is too far removed for humans to contemplate. Nor does Bondye seem to engage himself in his human creation. As the Lwa have experienced mortal life, they understand the human condition and are willing to concern themselves with the struggles and needs of the human community. Like most people, they have qualities that can be at times charming, powerful, difficult, or demanding. While they can manifest in some outrageous forms, the Lwa are helpful and healing Spirits.

THE ARCHETYPAL LWA

The Lwa, the living Gods or Spirits, are universal, ongoing archetypes. They are not stagnant, but develop through their relationship with their Sèvitè, and their continuing concern for the living. New aspects of old Gods develop, such as when Ogou, the old African warrior-god, became the patron of the United States because of our fascination with things militaristic. He also became the Lwa invoked for protection on car trips in connection with his role as master of the iron forge. Simbi, the serpent Lwa who transports the energy of communication, has become the patron Lwa of computers. Some Lwa have become more important as the world changes, while others have fallen into neglect and obscurity.

There is ongoing controversy over whether these Gods are exterior, independently existing beings, or whether they are creations that emerge from the deep psyche. I'm not sure that it matters. Perhaps they do emerge as archetypal images from the collective unconscious, are exteriorized, and, like a psychological complex, take on an independent life of their own. What is important is that they are recognizable, familiar, and empowering. We know them, for they characterize universal truths.

The archetypal Lwa maintain natural forms as well as characteristic powers in the universe. The Lwa live in Nature, in the trees, water, and stones. But they also reside in one's psyche as a sort of psychological symbol or trait. Legba, the guardian of the spiritual gateway, is also the radiance of the sun. Agwe is the God of the ocean and the sense of abundance in the world. The archetypal Lwa walk through life with us, and help us to form, as Joseph Campbell said, "myths to live by."

LWA NANCHON

The archetypal Lwa are divided into different nanchon, or nations, originally based on the ritual styles and cultural qualities of the different African tribes that influenced Vodou. There are said to be seventeen nanchon, but only a few are still commonly known in Haiti. The best known would include Rada, Petwo, Kongo, Nago, Ibo, and Djouba, with the Gedes forming the family of death and regeneration

Mysteries. The Rada nanchon comes from the Arada kingdom in Dahomey. The Petwo nanchon takes its name from Don Pedro, who was supposed to have been a leader of the maronage movement, a rebellion of runaway slaves. Some scholars contend that the Petwo nanchon's origins can be traced to the Kongo people of Africa. Others insist that it is a purely new world development, while Maya Deren suggested the possibility that the Petwo nanchon rites were born from the exchange between escaped slaves and the Native Indian population who had themselves escaped slavery to the remote mountains within Haiti. At any rate, the Petwo rites reflect the violence, danger, and rage that grew out of slavery, as well as a real need to effect transformation of experience. While the Rada rites are airy, formal, and ceremonial, the Petwo rites are fiery, revolutionary, and magical. The Rada and Petwo rites are usually, but not always, kept separate, in separate Peristils, even. The temperaments of the two main Vodou nanchon are certainly easily distinguished from one another. The Petwo rituals, drums, and dances are distinct, as are several Petwo ritual touches, for instance the use of flashing powders or gun powder, the use of a plain gourd rattle instead of an asson, and the cracking of a whip to announce the ceremony, or the arrival of a Petwo Lwa, and often rum replaces water for the libations. While the Rada Ezili Freda Daomé is a coquette who revels in luxury, lace, and finery, the Petwo Ezili Dantò is full of rage and vengeance, but is not above rolling up her sleeves to do hard work for her Sèvitè. The Petwo nanchon has often erroneously been labeled "evil," while the Rada has been characterized as purely beneficent. But Vodou defies such convenient dualism. The Lwa of each nation can provide protection and empowerment, and each can manifest anger or even malice when neglected or disrespected. The nanchon rather reflect each other, perhaps refracted by different angles of disposition and temperament.

The other main nanchon, though sometimes categorized in either the Rada or Petwo nanchon, are distinct. The Kongo nation Lwa, coming from the Kongo region of West Africa, have been the most absorbed by the Petwo nanchon. The Nago nation is imbued with pure power. The Ibos are full of pride, can be arrogant even, and maintain a kind of national identity. The Djoubas are agricultural and earthy, and are characterized by the stylings of peasants. The Gedes, with their Banda dance, are erotic and provocative.

The Vodou nanchon no longer refer to places of origin, but to the general categories of attributes and disposition characterized by all the different families of Lwa. All the pantheons of all the nanchon, with their individual forces and intelligences and aspects, are present and sustained within Bondye's universe.

FAMILY LWA

The family Lwa are your Ancestors, who continue to be remembered, consulted, and fed by their surviving family members. Your lineage and legacy are important. There are messages in your bloodline. Maybe your Great-grandmother was a source of power, wisdom, insight for you. It's best to be on good terms with the family Lwa, to know who you are and where you came from, what gifts and difficulties you have inherited. As Ishmael Reed said in *Mumbo Jumbo*, "Don't forget to feed the family Lwas."

The current head of a family conducts ancestral ceremonies for the family Lwa. These Lwa are fed, honored, and remembered; in return, they give guidance, divination, and help. They can be a real source of strength, of hope, coherence, and meaning.

WORK LWA

There are also work Lwa that are particular to one Manbo or Oungan or one Ounfò. The work Lwa give useful information on how ceremony should be conducted, and the work that is needed for the Ounfò. They are also useful in bringing about the necessary conditions that will help the Ounfò meet its needs. The work Lwa can be of tremendous practical importance to a Sosyete, though they are not held in the same regard as either the archetypal Lwa or the family Lwa.

There are hundreds of archetypal Lwa and innumerable family Lwa and work Lwa, further colored by nanchon, as well as by the temperament and understanding of the Sèvitè. Each of the Lwa presents a particular attitude or perspective that fuses with the Sèvitè's psyche in possession.

The Lwa and the Sèvitè share a symbiotic relationship. The Lwa are created by human honor, and maintained by human memory. They are not so absolutely above us as, say, Yahweh. The Lwa register neglect. They can be resentful and are saddened by forgetfulness. They can be hurt or angry or pleased, even comical. The Lwa act through their possessed Sèvitè in ceremony. In return, the Sèvitè are nourished through contact with Spirit. The Sèvitè honor and propitiate the Lwa, but the Lwa bow to the Oungan's or Manbo's direction.

VÈVÈ

Every Lwa has its own vèvè, or ritual drawing, which a Vodou practitioner uses to summon the Lwa. The vèvè, which is usually drawn on the ground with cornmeal, represents a path between the Lwa and the practitioner. The Lwa can follow this path to the physical space occupied by the ritual.

The vèvè generally is drawn by the Oungan or Manbo, who has a large repertoire of these graphic designs memorized. Each vèvè portrays a kind of magical alphabet where different repeating symbols hold coded meanings. For instance, is said to represent horns, or animal force. A star shape represents the crossroads extended into the fourth dimension of time and space. In the same way, a vèvè is not restricted to purely linear expression, but extends multidimensionally.

Each Oungan or Manbo puts infinite care into the drawing of the vèvè. The vèvè reflects their artistic ability as well as their aesthetic and visual interpretation of the basic qualities of the Lwa.

Try drawing a vèvè. It isn't easy! A plate with the cornmeal is held in one hand. A small portion of cornmeal is allowed to trickle out between the thumb and first finger of the other hand, as the lines of the vèvè are drawn. The act of drawing the vèvè is magical. It holds the quintessential force, and is the essential signature of the Lwa. Drawn with power and focus, the vèvè itself can be enough to call the Lwa. The iconography of the vèvè establishes the link between the Lwa and the community.

The vèvè can be drawn either before the ceremony begins, or during the ceremony, accompanied by singing. The vèvè can also serve as a mouth, or two-way door, for feeding the Lwa. Offerings are often placed on the vèvè, to entice the Lwa forward to communicate. Once the vèvè is completed, however, the magical act itself is complete. Libations are poured, a lighted candle is offered by a barefoot Ounsi, and the vèvè is activated. The dancers dance directly on the vèvè, scattering the cornmeal to disperse its energy and charge the space.

MAKING SACRED: OFFERINGS TO THE SPIRIT

In Vodoun work, sacrifice is the means to transcend the purely physical and get movement going both ways between the imagined and the real. Physical material must be made sacred, and, conversely, a physical medium must be provided through which the invisible can manifest. Vodou sacrifice is a kind of reverse Eucharist, whereby precious pieces of the everyday are set aside, honored, baptized, or consecrated. In return, the Lwa consume these sacred objects to become more manifest in the physical world.

As a vegetarian, I don't practice or condone animal sacrifice. I can't imagine any desire of mine that could warrant causing an animal to suffer in my stead. I'd like to see the practice of Vodou in the United States give up the use of live animals, but I do understand that animal sacrifice is viewed differently in a Haitian cultural context. Haitian initiates contend that the Spirit requires the vital life force in order to manifest. The sacrificial animals are kept, cared for, and slaughtered with compassion and respect. The majority of sacrificed animals are cooked and eaten by the community in a feast that follows the ceremony. The one noted exception is when an animal has been sacrificed as part of a healing ceremony. Then the animal is thought to have taken on the contaminants and toxins from the human, and so is not eaten. It's argued that Americans eat millions of animals annually that are slaughtered in the most inhumane and unconscionable ways. Americans politely camouflage their slaughter in neatly wrapped cellophane packages. The fact that Americans do not relate to it as such does not mean that some poor animal didn't give up its life in that process.

Finally, it's suggested that Vodoun animal sacrifice is not any different from the Catholic Eucharist in which the flesh and blood of Christ is consumed, "transmuting meat and drink into spiritual substance." In Vodou, food and drink are fed to the Gods so that they can become more material. "The Word made Flesh." The unseen incorporated. Spirit manifest.

My long training in Yogic techniques has taught me that an individual may achieve ecstatic states without the use of drugs, and that the life force can be directed from one's own electromagnetic circuitry without the sacrifice of any animals. Time and effort are the only sacrifice required. In my Ounfò, we have been working with manipulating prana, the life force or life energy. Local practitioners are concerned that individuals with Western values usurp traditions and alter them to suit their tastes and needs. In the process, they diminish the tradition. I believe that work with pure prana—the Ashé of Vodou—does not in any way water down the rituals, but in fact requires an even more raw vulnerability and intensity at the most immediate and central core of our being. In my ceremonies, I offer this prana to the Lwa, along with a whole lot of fruits and vegetables. There are those who say that you are not doing Vodou if you are not making blood offerings to the Lwa. But I have found that the Lwa accept my Ounfò's offerings, and continue to come to our ceremonies even without a literal blood sacrifice.

Fortunately, there are many traditional offerings for each Lwa, including salt or river water, various herbs, rum, cigars, perfume, jewelry, seashells, tobacco, candy, flowers, and trinkets, that don't require the taking of animal life. Each Lwa has his or her own particular tastes. The more tumultuous or difficult Gods are propitiated with offerings that will satisfy them. A list of the favorite and characteristic offerings is provided for each Lwa in the visions chapter of this book.

Sacrifice may seem to be a superstitious practice, but all things resonate at their own vibratory level. Each color holds a particular vibration and will affect the human psyche at a certain level. In ritual, all color, sound, scent, image, and movement combine to overwhelm the psyche with a particular, emphasized force. All people, all things, are ensouled with intelligent energy vibrations of Ashé, the creative life force. We can go into the archetypal realm to sublimate, direct, transform, or harmonize physical reality. Vodounists see Spirit as universally present within all natural forces, so it does not strike them as supernatural when the force of a Lwa intercedes for them or alters their perception of reality.

Everything that we are is food for the Lwa. Our attention to them is food. The consumption of food that turns into the energy of life is a miracle.

Even the rhythm of the drums and the bodies of the dancers are given to the Lwa. The drum rhythms carry our prayers, dreams, and hopes to the place where the Dead wait to answer. The Lwa walk from the realm of the invisible, over the drumbeats, as if they were stepping stones through the Waters, into the bodies of the dancers, who offer themselves as horses for the Gods to ride when possession occurs. It's the drummers' job to offer up a relentless wave of rhythm that overwhelms the dancers' conscious resistance to possession. While the rhythms and dances maintain corresponding appropriateness for each Lwa and nanchon, the drums further emphasize the crisis of consciousness that occurs in possession by slapping beats back against the dominant rhythm. All effort is given in offering to the Lwa, who reciprocate by entering into the community.

It is possible to see the whole of life as an offering to the Lwa. If we make the effort to fulfill the potential of our lives, keep our vision clear and constant, then all that we are and all that we do become an offering. With foreknowledge of the great leveling of death, we can make our lives and our work a beautiful offering to Spirit.

THE VODOU COMMUNITY

A Vodou community, or Sosyete, is composed of an extended family of Sèvitè—individuals who serve the Spirit. A child in Haiti grows up within a particular Sosyete, learning the style and techniques of that Sosyete. In the United States, it's a bit more difficult to gain admittance into a Peristil. It is also more difficult to find appropriate members who can all work together powerfully and peacefully. All members of a Sosyete must be able to apply their individual talents and personality to the well-being and coherence of the whole group. For the space of the Peristil to transform into sacred space, and for the Lwa to appear, all the people present must be able to put aside their own egos at the door. "Respect" and "honor" are the first words spoken upon entering the temple.

The Sèvitè must maintain sincerity of intent, openness to their most central self, and a focus on aiding their community in service to the Spirit. Each Sèvitè gives trust from the center, and each receives support and protection from the group, which provides a safe space in which to explore the unknown.

Since it is unlikely for the Lwa to appear without a core group of knowledgeable and competent ritualists, drummers, dancers, and singers, a balance of both talent and tendency is important, as is a symmetry of experience and spontaneity. The individuals in a Sosyete must trust themselves and each other sufficiently to reach into the molten core of experience. The Sèvitè are the natural resource of the Sosyete, and the ultimate offering to the Lwa.

There are levels of initiation reflected within the hierarchy of the Sosyete. The konesans are general participants. The Ounsi are initiates devoted in service to the Vodoun. The Kanzo are more profoundly devoted, and more completely initiated through trial by fire. From their ranks, the Laplas, or master of ceremonies, is selected. The two Drapo—the initiates who carry the sacred, sequined Vodou flags of the Sosyete—are also usually Kanzo. There is a choir, and so a choir leader, or Ounjenikon, who has mastered the sacred songs of the Sosyete, is selected on the basis of his or her knowledge of repertoire, as well as singing ability. Finally, there are the priests, the Oungan, and the priestesses, the Manbo, who provide leadership for the community.

Each Sèvitè's nature resonates with one particular Lwa, known as his Mèt tèt, or Master of the Head. Here, too, a mélange of personalities in the Sosyete works best, so that there is an Ezili, the beautiful, luxurious coquette of dreams, balancing an Ogou, the iron man, warrior spirit; a Lasirèn, the enticing mermaid sorceress of song, balancing a Simbi, the magician-serpent of communications. A matrix or web extends between the Sèvitè's psyches and energies, against which power points converge, and upon which the Lwa will walk. The Lwa who come most often or in the greatest power to the Sosyete are graciously honored with sequined Vodou flags, pictures, special celebrations, and richly embellished altar chambers dedicated to them.

Of course, since many readers will be practicing Vodoun rituals alone, a variety of solitary ceremonies are included in the ritual chapter of this book that should help to make the most of a solitary experience. Group work holds many dangers: the danger of falling into performance or posturing before others, and the danger of compromising one's personal integrity when pressured by a group's Will. Solitary work can lack perspective and focus on service, giving way to delusion or ego bloating. I feel that the most effective Vodoun practice involves both group and private ritual, but if you are restricted to working alone, develop as many of these talents and attitudes as you are able.

The core focus of a Vodou Sosyete is on service. Be true to yourself and make your life the most beautiful offering that you can give. Service to the Lwa is service to the community. Service to the community is service to the Lwa. It is amazingly difficult to work with a group. It is amazingly difficult to be real with yourself.

OUNGAN AND MANBO, OR VODOU PRIESTS AND PRIESTESSES

In Vodou, the Sèvitè enters into direct experience with Spirit. There are no set rules for this experience; people respond in accord with their own spontaneous intuition. There's no need for a priestcraft in the traditional, Catholic sense of the word.

What is the role of an Oungan or Manbo? The primary difference between them is one of gender. The Manbo are female and the Oungan are male. Otherwise, the Manbo and Oungan are equal in power and action. Being a Manbo myself, I'll make reference to Manbo only, with Oungan always implied as well.

When I was initiated in Haiti, I was told that I had been given the full powers of a Manbo, but I was not told what those powers might be. I was not given any specific instruction about the powers I would have to seize in order to come through the Manbo initiation. It was part of the undisclosed Mystery to discover what powers would be drawn from me by the Spirit. While I imagine that those powers are different for each person, it's probably a common truth that a Manbo doesn't know what, exactly, she is able to do until a member of her extended family—or the family of the Lwa—asks it of her.

There are perhaps duties that are common to almost all Manbo. She is a spiritual guide and teacher who accompanies and commemorates the major life passages of her extended family: birth, marriage, death of loved ones. She is a root doctor and healer with knowledge of both the medicinal and the magical qualities of numerous herbs, and has skill in applying them. The healing work extends into any area where there may be an imbalance in life energy, and often includes psychoanalytic and social work. But just as important are her roles as trusted confidante and Mother to many. I find myself being drawn out of my assumed limitations by the needs and requests of others. For myself, this process has drawn out psychic and divinatory abilities, healing abilities, the ability to communicate with the Dead, and the ability to neutralize and banish various forms of "hauntings." While I personally don't feel that I understand these abilities or even necessarily recognize them, I try to remain open to the possibility of them. Unless their requests directly compromise my personal integrity, I always try to help people who are in need. Just as the belief and memory of the community make Lwa of the Dead, so the community's belief draws ability from the Manbo. The Manbo must be able to put aside self-doubt in order to respond to these needs, even when charting unknown territory.

Each solution is different, each need, each remedy and response must be effective. Vodou is a religion of resilience and survival. People have very little in Haiti; there are so few resources to spare that the religion must be effective and practical. People need here and now, flesh and bone results for their extreme needs. The Gods must be accountable for their actions, and for the extremities of the human condition. The Manbo choreograph the dance between the Lwa and the community. They approach the Lwa on behalf of their community by going to the crossroads where human prayer knocks on spiritual conscience. In turn, they receive and express the needs of the Dead and the Lwa to the community. What offerings are needed? Are people neglecting their Mèt tèt? Are people forgetting their responsibility to their family Lwa? Ritual technique is mastered to this end. The Manbo explores crucial pathways between worlds in order to bring prayer and response back and forth across the crossroads.

Once the Lwa are contacted, the Manbo intercedes so that they don't hurt people. The Gods play hardball. Possession is not an easy experience. I've seen a pregnant woman possessed by Gede. In spite of her large belly, Gede gyrated her pelvis, ground her hips, even had her doing somersaults. While people usually don't have such extraordinary possessions, a person can be blasted by the Lwa. Initiation implies a degree of adeptness in the technique of possession. A noninitiate may struggle more intensely at the moment of crisis when the God comes and the individual identity moves out. A Manbo or Oungan can handle the Gods with more finesse. Their individual Will can recognize the moment of crisis. They are more able to agree or disagree to its onset. A Manbo can discourage or soothe the possession in a person who can't handle it. If the Lwa requires too much of his Sèvitè, the Manbo must explain the human limitation to the Lwa. A man is dedicated to Ezili. She requires lace, champagne, pearls, pastries. He cannot afford all that she requires, and has not enough money left over even to feed himself. The Manbo works out an understanding between the two parties.

In psychological terms, a Manbo integrates the many powerful archetypes of the Lwa within herself, within the individual, the individual within the community, and the human community within the greater community of the Lwa. Integration is a kind of psychic alchemy through which the disparate aspects of a person's psyche are recombined, balanced, and made whole or holy. In Haiti, I was deeply impressed by my Oungan's ability to handle and direct the delicate and often frightening psychic and psychological states that passed through my head during my Couché. Though he had probably never read Jung, he knew the subtle tricks and challenges of the mind, and probably was able to work with greater psychic resources than most psychologists. He had an understanding of common human psychological pathways, and was able to apply that recognition of the universal to each individual's psychology. Having walked the paths himself, he was an able guide through the thick forest. Walking these labyrinths myself did not rid me of psychological confusion, but did help me recognize dangerous crossroads and the guardians of inner sanctums. Now I am in a position to understand them when others are walking those same paths, and I know some of the favorite foods and offerings that placate the monsters that stand guard.

Most important is the Manbo's ability to see through the dark, external mirror of individual identity to the potential within each person. The Manbo perceives the Spirit that is ensouled by the material and coaxes it out to unveil itself. It is exactly in their most sacred, central self that people are most vulnerable and most easily damaged. The Manbo draws potential out of people by providing an environment of respect and honor in which their best selves can emerge. Ceremonies are created in which a person's spiritual vibration or Ashé is aligned with archetypal forces. Readings and divinations also help people see their true Will, accept it, and seize their power.

As a Manbo, I'm called upon to do psychic readings. During these readings, I'm exposed to what is most beautiful and most wretched in the human condition. I see the possibilities and the desolation of everyday reality. Some-

how there is an unspeakably huge gulf between the potential of the human spirit and the corruption of the mundane world. Why do people suffer so? I believe that the majority of people who seek readings are actually quite sensitive to spiritual urgings, but they struggle daily with themselves, with a crass and competitive culture, with a crazy and broken world. To survive in it, they must develop two faces. The one, a circumspect public mask that deflects the inner face of the spiritual seeker, displayed only in the perfect silence of revelation. The wasteland that separates the two suggests the treacherous journey of the shaman, the prophet, the crazed artist, between the points of power, between the safety zones. Not here. Not there. The uneasy distance of the in-between.

An old friend complains that he spends all his time, energy, passion, organizing a people's movement to overcome oppression, to attain freedom and equality for all. Only he's not sure anyone actually wants freedom and equality. No one seems to care. They'd rather watch TV. He's alone and tired. I tell him that, traditionally, prophets have not been very happy people. He doesn't know that he's an Oungan. He must accept himself. Accept his work. Seize his power.

I think of my conversation with a Haitian metal artist who sees how the world is and how it could be. He makes art from the abyss that lies in between. He says to me, "I am not a happy person. Why should I make happy art?" I think, *An Oungan is an artist who makes beauty out of hope.*

A driven, hard-core, to-the-bone, front-trench Charity Hospital emergency room trauma nurse needs a reading. She's difficult and confrontational, with a molten heart of pure human love. It's her heart that's bleeding all over that cold steel exterior. She's covered in the blood of a violent society. She says we have got to do better. She's looking for a way to tolerate the shamanic burden of the intermediary. Nobody said it would be fun. Joseph Conrad said we must endure "the unendurable."

"Papa Legba is at the door. Open the door for your children, Papa. Your children wait for you."

My friend, the nurse, is angry at the rules. Angry at the Gods who she says must be held accountable. Then she goes to stick her hands back in someone's chest. Trial by fire. She is Kanzo. As advocate, she pledges before Divine law and human law. She calls for respect and for integrity. She is groping in the in-between. She is a Manbo.

We can stay locked inside our climate-controlled, burglar-proofed, Internetted isolation booths. Or we can face and integrate the descent into grief and loss that allows us to look fully at how destroyed our world is—plunge our hands into the exploded chest of the world and reconnect the tubes to its damaged heart. Better to be lost and wandering in the desert of the in-between than stuck in the inertia and hopeless acceptance of unacceptable terms. The Manbo can't help people escape from life's conflicts, but she can help them figure out on what terms and at what level to engage those conflicts.

Children are born gifted, with a graceful state of innocence and wonder. Most people go through a progressive shutting-down process in which their natural being is negated, diminished, disallowed. Culture and society teach that only certain socially accepted and regulated behaviors will be tolerated within very limited and limiting boundaries. School enhances this crippling of natural Spirit by rewarding standard perception and punishing children for the odd point of view. What is most vulnerable and precious in each gets locked into a rigid external mask. Teachers teach what to think instead of how to think. The job market seals our fate, and the media lures us into willingly

giving up our power in order to fill an image of success and beauty. The Manbo teaches individuals how to reach the most vulnerable part of themselves to find the source of self and power, and shows them how to do their own creative work, based upon a command of traditional knowledge and universal ancient inspiration.

Her work requires the Manbo to remain out on the edge of taboo—respected and trusted, but somewhat intimidating in her requirement for brutal honesty. There can be no compromise for the sake of comfort or social acceptance. Always there is responsibility before the unwavering gaze of the Lwa, responsibility to the community, and finally responsibility for her own personal integrity. To be of help to others, she must first know herself, and be able to trust in herself and her relationship with the Lwa. Her powers come always through the bonds of service. Her ritual dance with the Laplas and the Drapo at the beginning of each Vodou ceremony represents the battle between the Spirit and the whole Sosyete with the Manbo. They vie for supremacy of power. In the course of this conflict, the Manbo forces the Laplas and the Drapo to kiss the Peristil floor. The Spirit is willing to be commanded by the Manbo's initiated direction. But then the Manbo kisses the hilt of the Laplas's machete and the Drapo's poles to acknowledge that the source of power is always in the Spirit. No one would ever confuse her for the power that comes through her.

The Oungan and Manbo must ultimately be artists in the Spirit. They give themselves over to the ecstatic creation of soul in the world. Like my Haitian artist friend, they see the world as it could be. They also see the world as it is. They create from the uncharted region in between. Their acts of creation are the result of the positive compulsion to serve, just as the Vodoun "horse" is overwhelmed by the Lwa. The next step—the initiated step—is to agree to this process; to create from the throes of chaos. To agree to service.

A Manbo is an artist who makes beauty out of hope.

POSSESSION

Although centuries of Christian context have made the word "possession" synonymous with demonic attack, the reality is completely different. Vodoun possession is not descent into darkness, but an expansion of self, a melding of self with the Spirit. It is entrance into the mystery of the Divine that is the Vodoun's most precious gift. All the spells and powers that are often mistaken for Vodou pale in comparison with the experience of Divinity's presence within our bodies and blood.

Possession is the paramount means of giving transport to the Spirit. In full possession trance, a person's Ti Bon Anj is put aside for a time so that the Divine intelligence of one of the Lwa can enter into a human body in order to act and communicate through that body. The human becomes the chwal, or horse, that is mounted by the God.

There are many stages and degrees of possession trance, which can include anything from a light trance or visionary condition to the state of full possession in which a person's whole conscious self vacates the body for the duration of the trance. Even partial possession can serve as an avenue through which the Lwa can communicate their wishes and wisdom; full possession is something I would not recommend without the assistance of an experienced practitioner.

In group rituals, possession usually occurs within the bodies of the dancers, but can happen to anyone in the Ounfò. It is generally quite clear when a possession is happening. The dancer stumbles or staggers, or may sway and lean on someone else as the God mounts the horse and takes up the reins of their body.

A dramatic shivering of limbs or torso that has the appearance of a seizure sometimes occurs. Often one foot will get "rooted" to the spot and the other foot will pivot around it as the Lwa moves up out of the earth and into the horse. Or, if the Lwa descends from above, the horse may seem groggy or drunk. Other times, there's a sudden, spontaneous explosion of extraordinary dancing or singing. In all cases, there's a crisis of identity that occurs in the psyche of the possessed individual as her consciousness resists fusion with the Lwa. It's natural for the Sèvitè's sense of identity to oppose this opening beyond herself.

Westerners are terrified of losing "control." We think that our sense of identity will somehow maintain a cage around Spirit. But Spirit flows freely beyond and through us. The crisis of possession is attended initially with confusion, or fear. As people let go of identity, they enter into an uncharted, amorphous territory that eventually opens into the presence of the Gods. It is Simbi that acts as the guide through the nowhere realm that is traversed after the identity has melted, and before the Lwa enters. Simbi delivers the psyche to the energy intelligence of the Lwa.

The horse has no memory of all that the Lwa does and says while using her body. The complete amnesia of the horse indicates that there really is a vast difference between our everyday waking state of consciousness and awareness of the spiritual realm. Possession is a social act, an offering for the greater benefit of the community. It is brought on through the ritual efforts of the community. On the other hand, demonic possession or psychosis is maintained within the individual, generally hidden from the community; it is an antisocial act. The possession experience directly benefits everyone in the community except the horse. Individuals integrate the experience later when told what has happened, but they are transformed by the residual effect of having incorporated a God. All of us, no matter how damaged or ruined or unglamorous, are ensouled by the Gods.

The different Lwa display characteristic attitudes, gestures, and personality traits that are universally recognizable when they possess a horse. Ezili displays her arms in graceful movements of elegance. She holds up her little finger in the gesture of the coquette and disdains the other women in the room. She requires that she be draped in lace and jewelry. But her possessions end with the horse sobbing inconsolably, as Ezili is the Mother of Sorrows whose disappointment in the real world cannot be consoled. Danbala, on the other hand, slithers and undulates on the ground as a serpent. Because he is a serpent, he makes guttural sounds in lieu of discernible speech. Other Lwa may be more or less dramatic, but they are always recognizable and true to form.

Possession appears to be somewhat similar to extraordinary performance art. A fine actor's whole way of being is cast aside in order to move fully into a role. For the time that he is onstage, he is Hamlet. The human horse expands upward as the God refines itself to fit the human container. Each horse develops a slightly different aspect of the Lwa. Edgar Jean-Louis's Gede is different from Silva Joseph's Gede, which is different from Brendon Malone's Gede, but they are all Gede, cocky and outrageous, graphic yet grand. In the same way, Sir John Gielgud's Hamlet is different from Mel Gibson's Hamlet, even though they are both certainly Hamlet.

The great danger of possession is that of getting "blasted," of not being able to handle the crisis of fusion with a God. Sometimes the Manbo or Oungan has to intercede so that the Lwa does not hurt the horse or demand too much. It is suggested that you work gradually with the techniques for attaining trance states that are described in the vision and ritual chapters. Pay attention to fear. Don't be afraid to move back from a precipice and take small, careful steps. Be relentlessly honest with yourself, for there is a terrible danger of posturing or pretending with possession that thoroughly robs a person of the actual presence of the Spirit.

Why do something that sounds so frightening? Because possession builds a bridge to Spirit so that the Lwa can reach out to us as we reach out to them. Opening the floodgates to the source allows the individual and the community to receive advice and guidance, or inspiration and encouragement, from the Spirit.

Just as important, the person possessed experiences the world from another point of view, and learns that his or her way of seeing is not the only way. One time the world is Ezili's, washed in love and expectant of the dream of perfection. The next time it is Ogou's realm, where the world is a battlefield. By engaging in archetypal Spirits, it becomes possible to get beyond carried baggage and think in a new manner. It's not unlike experiencing personal transformation through years of psychotherapy. I call it "getting right with the Lwa," or balancing Ashé.

Sacred Space, Sacred Time: Altars and Rituals

It's the time that you have wasted for your rose that makes the rose so important.
—Antoine de Saint-Exupéry, *The Little Prince*

Rituals are moments of grace that expand outward into eternity. Ritual lifts your consciousness out of the everyday mode, heightens and expands it. In the process, you create or recognize something sacred. It doesn't matter how hard it is to do, or how long it takes. People who hold nothing sacred are lost. The value of ritual work is immeasurable, for there is no gauge against which to measure it. In the mundane world, things like money and time are measurable, and hold value. In the interior world of ritual, it is symbol and myth and modes of consciousness that hold meaning. Ritual opens the doorway into the internal reality of universal imagination where life is unlimited and Spirit reigns. Ongoing ritual practice creates a pool of the sacred into which the practitioner can dive.

A valuable ritual effects change and growth, encouraging strength and self-knowledge. Rituals have opened me to interior riches, where life pours itself from a limitless source, and articulates its meaning through art and vision. When we put our attention into the realm of soul, we participate in soul making, increasing the presence of soul in the world.

ALTARS

It's important to establish an altar for spiritual work. If you can create a pleasing environment, you can entice the Lwa and draw your own psyche into the dance. Your altar is your starting point for Vodoun ritual. It is sacred, focused ground, and absolutely personal. As with all Vodou work, begin with what you know and let it grow from there. Trust your instincts. If you see some discarded trinket in the road and it reminds you of a particular Lwa, pick it up and offer it in front of that Lwa's image. Vodou is a religion that honors abundance, and your altar should be embellished from this sense of abundance. An altar is not a static creation. It grows as your relationship with a Lwa grows. You want to leave your altars to a trusted, honored friend when you die, for your altar will not just be imbued with the Lwa's presence. It will become the created child of your intimate exchange with the Spirit.

There are many theories on how an altar may be constructed. Some people will tell you that the Orishas and the Lwa may not be honored on the same altar. Or they will tell you that Petwo deities and Rada deities will not tolerate being on the same altar, or even in the same Peristil, with one another. Others will tell you that you must balance the representation and presence of all the nations, and all the archetypal or elemental forces of all the Lwa, on one main altar. It seems to me that there are different rules in different parts of Haiti, or in different Ounfò. Sometimes lack of finances or simply lack of room dictates the need for one central altar, on which the major deities served in that Ounfò are represented, while several side alcoves are dedicated to particular Lwa, such as Ezili or Ogou. Most commonly, there are two distinct altars, one for Petwo, and one for Rada deities. But that is certainly not always the case. There is room for all manner of styles and interpretations of the cosmic order of things. In New Orleans, where the worship of Santería Orishas and Vodoun Lwa is merging, it makes sense that altars here would reflect relationship between the two worldviews. On the other hand, don't be surprised if a Santero or an Oungan shrieks at you for placing Ezili on the same altar as Oshún! Be creative and artistic in your approach to assembling an altar, but make sure that your work makes sense to you. Altars establish a kind of imagistic, or Qabalistic, language. Vodou altars were originally created by people who were largely illiterate. The pictures, bottles, statues, packets—all the objects on the altars—were words that came together to express meaning. What I think is important is that the language of your altar be internally coherent. The various images and symbols should not contradict or antagonize one another. Even more important, your altar should communicate your feelings to the Spirit. You can always change, adapt, and adjust your altar as your understanding increases, or as you receive inspiration and instruction from the Lwa. You may, inevitably, run into some Vodou or Santería "expert" who screams in outrage at the sight of your altar, but if you and the Lwa are well pleased, if the altar is alive and meaningful to you, then that expert's opinion is really of no consequence.

My home contains numerous altars. One is for my Ancestors, and includes family photos as well as personal items belonging to loved ones. I feed this altar with food and drink that I associate with my family as well as with my heritage. I offer green grapes and Glenlivet scotch for my father, caramels and martinis for my mother. To all the Ancestors reaching back to our native home in the Ukraine, I offer borscht and potatoes, blintzes and vodka. Glasses of water and white candles are maintained on the altar for each named Dead. Because I wish to honor my Jewish cultural heritage, I keep a Star of David on the altar. The altar itself is draped with a prayer shawl for an altar cloth.

Another altar is dedicated to Spirit. The objects on this altar change frequently, but there are always candles, incense, glasses of water, and images of the sacred feminine force. Because Oshún and Ezili are important to me, I have painted glass novenas for them on the altar, and my *Vodou Visions* images. But Ezili Dantò is also an important aspect of the divine feminine. Though she is fiery and hot, and some say she shouldn't share an altar room with Freda, I have novenas for her on a facing altar, and for Mator Salvatoris and Our Lady of Prompt Succor, who are her corresponding Catholic images. My feminine trinity is completed with Manman Brijit, the crone of the cemetery, and with gifts for Oyá, the Santería Orisha who guards the gates of the cemetery. From the Hindu pantheon, I have collected statues of Kali, my favorite Goddess of destruction, and ashes from the many rituals I have performed for her. These mirroring altars may challenge long-standing perceptions of feuding aspects of the feminine, but they reflect my own efforts to integrate all aspects of the feminine into a powerful whole.

Another altar is consecrated to Gede, a trickster Spirit associated with sexuality and the Ancestral Dead. Gede's altar is a wood cabinet topped by a wooden cross, the same symbol used in Gede's vèvè. Inside the cabinet is another cross that sits at the top of three steps. A statue of Saint Gerard—Gede's Catholic counterpart—stands on the top step. Strings of peppers, and the found bones of small animals, collected pebbles, and shards of brick and stones from outside the entrances to cemeteries are strewn on the bottom stairs of the altar, for the benediction of the Dead.

Other altars grow in my house as I focus attention on other archetypal Lwa. The small altar for Oshún and Ezili is covered with an amber altar cloth, and white lace, and painted novenas and images from *Vodou Visions*. There are traditional religious pictures and statues of Caridad del Cobra, Our Lady of Lourdes and Guadalupe, and Mater Dolorosa, heart milagros from Mexico, and stones from freshwater rivers and streams. I collect vials of water from all Oshún's rivers that I visit. I use these waters as both offering and anointment, and as substance into which I release currents of Will. Oshún's house is made from a calabash that is adorned with a peacock-colored scarf, and filled with jewelry and her sacred power symbols. Gold bells are draped over the calabash, and a fan of peacock feathers crowns the whole. There are jars of honey and cinnamon, and pumpkins for Oshún, atomizers of Anaïs-Anaïs perfume, pastries, and champagne for Ezili. At this altar, I approach Spirit in power and request blessings. I ask for guidance in how to be anointed into powerfulness. I call on Oshún and Ezili, and offer them my gifts, in return asking for the ability to see, hear, know, receive, and accept Spirit.

Shangó's altar is dressed in red satin cloth. A large statue of Santa Barbara, Shangó's Catholic counterpart, is surrounded by painted novena candles with images of Shangó from *Vodou Visions*. There is a horse, small drums, and stones and herbs that are sacred to Shangó, along with a plate of red apples and red berries. I approach Shangó from a place of personal power and demand his protection! I spend time at this altar every day, and slowly a surety of power comes to me, through water and flame, in Spirit.

As Lasirèn is one of my Mèt tèt, I put particular attention into my altar for her and Yemayá/Olokun—her closest corresponding

Santería Orisha—which I keep in my bathroom. On this altar are mermaid images and statues of Saint Martha and Regla, seashells, mother-of-pearl, sand dollars and rocks that I've collected from various beaches, decorated mirrors, and scarves and sequined cloth in all shades of blues and sea greens. I also collect vials of beach sand and ocean water from all of my travels. Whenever I bathe, I sprinkle water on this altar. Whenever I swim in the ocean, I am anointed from my ocean mother's great altar.

Ogou is my other Mèt tèt. His altar is covered in his favorite red. There I keep a sword that I inherited from my father, along with a sequined Haitian Vodou flag of Ogou Sen Jak and various military regalia. Pieces of iron—spikes from the railroad tracks and bullets off the street—are kept in an iron cauldron. I keep this altar hidden in a closet, as a secret strength and a forge of inner mettle.

In addition to all these individual altars, I keep a main altar for all the Lwa in my Ounfò. This is a large, many-tiered altar that is divided into different sections for the different nations. Black and violet cloths cover the Banda section for the Gede. A red cloth marks the Nago nanchon for the Ogou. A white lace cloth covers the Rada nation. A vibrant, scarlet satin of the Petwo nation's fire points balances a soothing blue for the cool water points. The entire pantheon of Lwa is represented and balanced on the altar with painted bottles, religious pictures, associated symbols, and assembled images for each Lwa. The main altar also houses and protects the Ashé of the Sosyete. There are Po tèt ("head pots," or earthenware jars that hold the souls of Sèvitè for safekeeping) of the members of the Ounfò, as well as Pakèt Kongo (wrapped and tied packets that are prepared with herbs and substances sacred to a Lwa, which impart the essential force of that Lwa), and power points (items or icons that concentrate magical powers) belonging to individuals in our group. Ceremonial beaded necklaces are kept on the altar, as are the Laplas's machete and swords. There are people in the U.S. Vodoun community who criticize me for serving all the nations on one altar. They say that the Petwo and Rada Lwa will fight, or will punish me. But my experience has taught me differently, and this balance of all the Ashé and sacred forces in the universe makes sense to me. I wonder how the Gods can expect humans to get along if they cannot even live on the same altar together!

Whatever anyone may think of it, the main Spirit altar grows and transforms continually, having taken on a life, intelligence, and aesthetic of its own. Prayers and offerings are placed on this altar during all our ceremonies for the Lwa. The altar is enlivened through daily ceremonial attention. The Ashé of the Lwa and the Ashé of the Sèvitè create an awesome and sacred beauty that does not sit still in one dimension. The Ashé sparks its own living language in symbol and image that extends from the everyday into deep realms of meaning.

RITUALS

It is perhaps the most daunting step in Vodoun practice to move from theory to actual ritual work. There's a bit of a catch-22 involved here: you can't experience the Vodoun without doing ritual, but you can't do rituals until you've experienced the Vodoun. You may feel silly or awkward or afraid at first, but you can gentle your way into dialogue with the Spirit. Allow yourself to learn as you grow until awkwardness and fear give way to confidence and grace. Make a start, then let Spirit guide and refine your work.

A good way to begin ritual work is by cleansing and purifying your house, and taking a ritual cleansing bath.

Ritual to Cleanse and Purify House or Ounfò

There are several formulas for making a house-cleansing solution.

A traditional recipe begins with a large bucket of water, into which you add:

A bottle of rum.
A bottle of rubbing alcohol.
Perfume.
Three egg whites.
A bottle of Florida Water (a skin bracer or cologne, extracted from oranges, cinnamon, and florals, in an alcohol base).
Cascarilla (ground-up eggshell).

Or you can simply use some of your favorite perfume.

First, make a broom from camphor branches, or any very leafy branches that are available in your area. Dip the broom in perfume, or in the cleansing solution. Starting at the back of the house and moving forward, shake the broom all over the furniture and into the corners of each room. Hit the broom hard on all the doorjambs and don't be afraid to yell at the negativity to get out of your house. When you reach the front of the house, shake all the collected negative energy out the front door. Finally, burn scented candles in every room until the air is filled with perfumed smoke, then open all the windows and let the smoke out. After the smoke has cleared, put small mirrors on all the doors to your house, facing out. Use cascarilla or chalk to make *X*'s on the outsides of all the doors to encourage protection.

Go to a river. Turn your back to it, and throw the leftover branches over your head into the water. Don't look back as you go home by a different route. If possible, stop at a friend's house and take a spiritual bath before you go back into your house.

My all-time favorite house-cleansing ritual was taught to me by a Santera named Mother Mercedes. Place a coconut behind

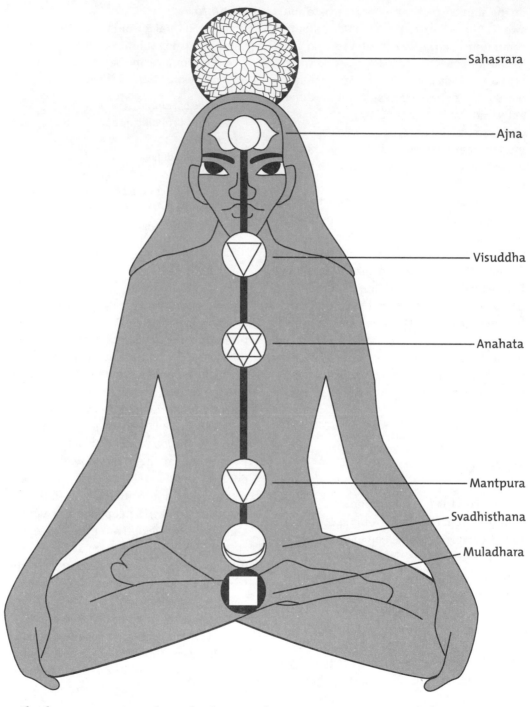

Sahasrara

Ajna

Visuddha

Anahata

Mantpura

Svadhisthana

Muladhara

Chakras: spiritual and physical energy points in the body

your closed front door. Squat over it and pee on it. Then open the front door and kick the coconut out onto the street while you shout, "Get the hell out of my house!!!"

Ritual Cleansing Bath

Ritual baths are vital for the cleansing of the self before other work can be done. It's best to have an assistant help with this so that you can remain entirely passive throughout the ritual, like a newborn baby. The assistant prepares the space, and cleans up afterward. The bathroom is lit with candles and scented with incense, and the bath itself is prepared with bath salts or crystals and an infusion of basil and rosemary.

Allow yourself to be placed in the bathwater. The assistant stirs the water and consecrates your chakras, saying prayers for each nexus of energy. For instance, at the crown chakra, your assistant could pray for the purity of your inspiration; at the Ajna, or forehead, for clarity and focus of thought; at the throat, truth in word and open communication; at the Anahata, for your heart to be open to love; and so forth. Your assistant should speak spontaneously, according to the inspiration at the moment. Soak in the bath while consciously releasing the restrictions of your old self into the water. When you feel that you have finished, your assistant lifts you out of the water, towels you dry, and dresses you in new, white robes or in clothes that you will use only for ritual work. Later, take the collected herbs from the bath and leave them at a far-off crossroads, or in a great body of water. Throw the herbs over your shoulder and never look back at them.

Ritual for Presenting Yourself to the Spirits of Your Ritual Space

Face each of the four directions and speak to the elements: air in the east; fire in the south; water in the west; earth in the north. Light incense in the east and a candle in the south.

Pour libations of water in the west and sprinkle salt or earth in the north. Again, don't prepare what you say to the elements. Let your speech be spontaneous and from the heart.

Face your altar and dedicate yourself to mastery and to service. Burn papers on which you have written all your self-doubts. Offer food, drink, and flowers to Spirit. Crush flower petals and press them onto each of your chakras. Dance for the Lwa and/or drum until you feel yourself move into a sense of ecstatic presence with Spirit. After the ritual, collect the flower petals and offerings and take them to a crossroads or a place that is appropriate to the Lwa with whom you feel most empathetic, and leave them there with prayers of thanks.

Ritual for Shedding the Negative Self

By the dark moon, go into your ritual space in old clothes. Dance on the floor like a snake and shed your clothes in the way that a snake sheds its old skin. See your skin there, gone.

Burn the old clothes, the old skin. Put on a new, feathered snakeskin, or at least picture this new skin as you put on clean new robes. Stand tall and erect, in charge. Have an assistant who sees you as a king or queen put a crown on your head and hand you a silver bowl of water in which grapes float.

Take a grape into your mouth. Bite into it and feel the juice in your mouth. Feel the seeds of the grape going into you, and know that they will grow into a magical being. Tell the Lwa that you are here and that you want to know their presence within you.

Ritual for Empowering the Positive Self

In order to empower the new self, work a self-portrait ritual. Take a bowl of water and two glass mirrors. Paint the back of one piece of glass with black enamel paint so that it creates a black mirror, and leave the other glass clear. Look deeply into the bowl and release emotion into the water. Particularly allow pain and sorrow to ripple away. Pour the rest of the water over the two mirrors. As you gaze into the mirrors, an image will come to you of yourself as you wish to be, or as you are capable of being. Draw this image in pastel chalks on paper. Keep your gaze fixed on the mirrors rather than on the paper on which you draw.

I do these rituals periodically, when I feel drawn to them. At first, I saw images of ways in which I felt trapped in pathologies or endangered, but they gradually came to suggest release into surety and beauty. Gradually, I am painting the power and beauty and strength into my own image as I move behind the mirrored surface, into the waters of imagination.

There are also rituals to help get "with" the various Lwa and Orishas, as they are present in the world around us.

Ritual for Oshún, Santería Goddess of Rivers

Pour flower petals, honey, cinnamon, and perfume over your head before taking a spiritual bath. Collect the flower petals from the tub, along with honey and cinnamon sticks, and go to a river. Call on Oshún, Goddess of rivers, of beauty, luxury, and love. Put some honey on a stick of cinnamon and pour it into the river, being sure to taste it first because Oshún was once poisoned with honey. Toss the flower petals into the river, asking for release from all that binds and holds you down. Place your fingers in the water. Send prayers out to Oshún, and receive her blessings as the rippling water comes back over your fingers. Anoint yourself with her water. Feel the benediction of her touch.

After many of these rituals, the Spirit of the river has become animated for me. The river flows through the Crescent City like honey, like the blood of Oshún.

Vèvè Ritual

A vèvè ritual allows people to work alone with some of the main principles of Haitian ritual and to call the Lwa into their life. It is possible to build upon this basic vèvè ritual in order to further dedicate yourself to a particular force.

First, clean a space on the ground, preferably outside on clear dirt. Take a pinch of cornmeal in your hand and make a crossroads in the air above the area you will be working on. Toss the cornmeal through the center of the crossroads to move it into the spiritual realm. With full concentration on devotion to the Lwa that you are calling, start drawing the vèvè on the ground. Take your time. Be aware of who you are, of all that you bring into the act. Feel the cornmeal passing through your fingers as you trace out the signature of the Lwa. Feel the force of the Lwa moving into the grainy meal as you lay it down.

When finished, place offerings for that Lwa on the vèvè, then hold a candle and a pitcher of water. Stand and make three pirouette turns with the water and candle, turning first clockwise, then counterclockwise, then clockwise again. Place the candle in the center of the vèvè to light the way for the Spirit. Pour three libations of water before the vèvè to acknowledge that you come from the water, are made of water, and will return to water. Kiss the vèvè three times, then kneel before it with your arms open and your palms facing up. Say prayers or litanies in praise of the Lwa. Kiss the vèvè three more times, then scatter the cornmeal drawing to activate it. Anoint yourself with some of the cornmeal and go about your day.

"Head washing" Ritual for Purification

Head washings are done before or during initiations. They are also done to clear a person's head when he or she is too easily possessed.

Conversely, they are done in order to anoint a person's head in service to the Lwa. By "washing" your head, you make your head a sanctified temple for the Lwa. You further harmonize or ally yourself with the forces embodied by a Lwa. For instance, if you feel a need to enhance love and beneficence in your life, you could do a head washing for Ezili and Danbala.

Prepare all of Ezili's and Danbala's favorite foods. Drape an altar space in white lace and white satin. Place flowers and images of Danbala and Ezili on the altar. Wearing white clothes, draw Ezili's heart vèvè with Danbala snakes on either side in cornmeal. Place offerings on the vèvè: milk, champagne, white wine, white grapes, bananas, an egg, white cake, perfume, popcorn, and Florida Water. Place a bowl on the vèvè. Make three pirouettes with water and a candle. Place the candle on the vèvè, then pour three libations of water into the bowl. Add all the other offerings into the bowl of water. As you say prayers to Ezili and Danbala, mash all the ingredients together with your fingers. You are releasing the life energies of your offerings into the water in which the Lwa flow. When you have finished making the head-washing mix, kiss the vèvè three times and place yourself in a receptive, open state. Dip your hands into the water and say heartfelt prayers to Danbala and Ezili for guidance, assistance, and benediction. Then anoint your arms, your neck, throat, and heart, your knees, feet, and face, with the wash. Finally, scoop up the mix into your hands and cover your whole head. This can be an intensely moving experience, often inexplicably cathartic for such a simple act. Cover your head with a clean, white scarf that you have tied snugly. You can wash off your face and the rest of your body, but leave the head wash on, wearing the scarf to bed. Take the wash and the Lwa with you into your dreams. Be sure to record any dreams you re-member, then you can wash your hair in the morning. Dispose of any extra head wash at a crossroads, or pour it into a river.

It is vital to work personal rituals in addition to group rituals. The personal rituals establish intimacy and knowledge of Spirit. Each practitioner should maintain a personal connection to power. Carry this intimate knowledge of Spirit, and the inroads into spiritual realms, with you when working a group ritual. This group ritual is adapted from books that I have read on Haitian and Cuban tradition, studies, and conversations with many Vodou practitioners, including Kathleen Marie Tway, Louis Martinie, and the Oungan/artist André Pierre, as well as personal ritual experience with my Padrino, the Santero who acts as my Godfather, Antonio Gil, and the Oungan who initiated me, Silva Joseph and Edgar Jean-Louis. In addition, I have incorporated some elements of Western Ceremonial Magick as well as elements of my own Jewish heritage, and direct inspiration from Spirit. It is the ritual I use to contact the individual Lwa and Orisha that inspired the images of Vodou Visions. It is only a basic outline for ongoing group work. We insert some stylistic or formal ritual differences when we are calling an Orisha, such as the various prostrations that are performed before the altar, as is appropriate for the different Orishas. We adapt the ritual each time to our specific needs, sometimes doing a ritual to call one Lwa, sometimes calling all the Lwa of all nations in their traditional order, sometimes incorporating head washings or healings or divinations into the main body of the ceremony. All of the litanies that are included in this book are my own writing and are not traditional. You may insert them at the appropriate point in the ceremony, or you may write your own. The ceremony may be adapted to individual use, or you may embellish it however you or your group chooses.

If you are doing a Petwo ceremony, salute Bawon Kalfou, the Petwo Legba, first. Replace the response "Ayibobo!" with "Bilolo!" You may want to add flashing powders or gunpowder, whistles, sparklers, or the cracking of whips to announce the arrival of a Petwo Lwa. Of course, if a Lwa comes, that Lwa will take over and conduct the remainder of the ceremony however it sees fit!

We have been learning the sacred Kreyòl songs for each of the Lwa. When we are doing Rada ceremony, we begin with several songs for Legba while offerings are being made. We usually draw vèvè for the Marasa, Legba, Loko, and Ayizan before the ceremony begins. During the ceremony we sing songs, perform pirouettes with a candle and water, and pour libations before each of the vèvè of the Lwa who accompany Legba, and for the Lwa whose vèvè is being drawn in the body of the ceremony. We are also learning the appropriate drumbeats and dances for the different Lwa and Orishas. This is difficult, long-term work, requiring a committed and devoted group. Clearly, there is a lifetime of exploration and development available within the outline of this one ritual. Take it as a possible guide, and make it your own.

Ritual for Contacting the Lwa or Orishas
You will need:

> A candle.
> A cup or bottle of water.
> Incense.
> Cornmeal.
> Offerings for the Lwa (see "Visions" chapter for lists of appropriate offerings).
> An asson (ritual rattle strung with beads and an attached bell) is required if there is a Manbo or Oungan present; if not, you can use any rattle.
> A machete.
> Drapo (sequined Vodou flags) are optional.

You can place on an altar the appropriate image from *Vodou Visions* or card from *The New Orleans Voodoo Tarot* or any image of the Lwa that you like or may have that has been covered with a cloth of the color sacred to that Lwa.

1. A conch is blown, with a drumroll.

> Sing: "Annoncé, annoncé, annoncé!"
> Ounfò responds: "Annoncé, annoncé, annoncé!"
> Kreyòl: "Anonsé, anonsé, anonsé!"

Libations are poured from the doors, to the centerpole, in the form of a crossroads.

2. Laplas dances backward in a circle with two drapo carriers, cutting the air with his machete.

3. Laplas and Manbo engage in a mock battle, which culminates with the Laplas kneeling and placing the tip of his machete on the ground while the Manbo kisses the hilt. The two drapo carriers kneel and place the top of the flags to the ground, while the Manbo kisses the bottom of the flagpoles.

4. Any Manbo and Oungan present salute each other by making three pirouettes, one counterclockwise, one clockwise, and another counterclockwise, in order to reorient perception to the way in which the Lwa see on the other side of the mirror. Double handshakes are exchanged to symbolize the crossroads.

Ounsi pirouettes three times with Oungan and Manbo. Oungan and Manbo stand in place, holding the hand of the Ounsi above their head, while the Ounsi pirouettes, clockwise, counterclockwise, and clockwise. Double handshakes are exchanged.

5. Manbo and Oungan orient their offerings and the ceremonial objects to the four quarters by making three pirouettes in each quarter of the circle. They then kiss the altar three times and the ground three times. They make

a crossroads (+) with their offering in the air, passing the offering through the center of the crossroads while letting it slip out of the hands for a second so that it can move from the outer world to interior reality.

Each participant then makes an offering, saying personal prayers at the altar. While they are making their offerings, the choir sings a song of praise and invitation to Papa Legba.

6. Pour libations to Legba at the doors or entrance to the ritual space, draw libations in crossroads pattern from each door to the centerpole, and to the altar, saying:

> "A Legba, qui garde la porte."
> Kreyòl: "Pou Legba, kap véyé pot'la."
> "To Legba, who guards the door."

Make crossroads with the libation bottle in front of all the drummers, saying:

> "Aux tambours."
> Kreyòl: "Tambou."
> "To the drummers."

Pour three libations in front of the drummers and/or salute with the asson on the ground three times. Songs may be sung to the drums. Pour libations into the cupped hands of all the participants.

7. Opening prayer: Kneel on the ground with the container of cornmeal in front of you. Make a crossroads (+) in the air with the container and say:

> "En faisant ceci, nous touchons Guinée."
> Kreyòl: "Lè nou fè sa, nap man sid."
> "In doing this, we touch Ginen."

Take a pinch of cornmeal in each hand and make crossroads (+) in the air, saying:

> "La famille de ma mère, la famille de mon père, touchent Guinée."
> Kreyòl: "Fanmi Manman'm, Fanmi Papam' ap manyin Ginen-yo."

> "My Mother's family, my Father's family, touch Ginen."

Dip your fingers into the cornmeal and take some up, saying:

> "Nous dansons ici, et en Guinée on danse."
> Kreyòl: "Isit´nap dansé, nan Ginen yap dansé."
> "We are dancing here, and in Ginen they dance."

(The opening prayer establishes the practitioner's work within the continuum of heritage, with ongoing tradition, and within spiritual, interior reality.)

8. Draw vèvè for Legba while Legba's songs are being sung. Manbo and Ounsi pirouette with a candle and water. Kneel, pour three libations before Legba's vèvè, and kiss the vèvè three times. These actions may be repeated with vèvè for the Marasa, Loko, and Ayizan. Draw the appropriate vèvè for the Lwa in cornmeal on the ground.

The choir sings songs for the drawing of the vèvè and initial songs for the Lwa being invoked. (Sometimes the vèvè is drawn before the ritual begins. In that case, the congregation must take great pains to avoid disturbing or stepping on the vèvè. With two barefooted Ounsi, the Manbo performs three pirouettes in the Four Quarters with a candle, a libation bottle, and an asson. One Ounsi places a candle on the vèvè and all three pour three libations before the vèvè. They kiss the vèvè three times, then the Manbo says the litanies as follows. If the vèvè is drawn during the ceremony, the Ounsi and the Manbo sometimes wait till after the vèvè has been sprayed to do their pirouettes and to kiss the vèvè.)

9. Orientation of the vèvè to the Four Quarters:

Fire: Make a crossroads in the air with the candle over the vèvè, saying:

> "Aux Loa de feu au Sud."

Kreyòl: "Pou Lwa difé nan sid."
"To the Lwa of Fire in the South."

Pass your hands through the flame to heat them, then hold your hands over the vèvè to impart warmth to it, saying:

"Ko Ba Ni Jo!"
"Come dance with us!"
Congregation: "Ago! Ago-é!" ("Attention!")

Water: Make a crossroads in the air with the libation bottle over the vèvè, saying:

"Aux Loa de l'eau à l'Ouest."
Kreyòl: "Pou Lwa nan dlo nan lwès."
"To the Lwa of Water in the West."

Pour four libations around the vèvè to symbolize the four cardinal points of the universe, saying:

"Ko Ba Ni Jo!"
"Come dance with us!"
Congregation: "Ago! Ago-é!"

Air: Make a crossroads in the air with the incense, saying:

"Aux Loa de l'air à l'Est."
Kreyòl: "Pou Lwa nan lè nan lès."
"To the Lwa of Air in the East."

Hold the incense between your hands and blow the smoke over the vèvè, saying:

"Ko Ba Ni Jo!"
"Come dance with us!"
Congregation: "Ago! Ago-é!"

Earth: Make a crossroads in the air over the vèvè with some cornmeal, saying:

"Aux Loa de la terre au Nord."
Kreyòl: "Pou Lwanan la tè nan nò."
"To the Lwa of Earth in the North."

Sprinkle an outward spiral of cornmeal over the vèvè, saying:

"Ko Ba Ni Jo!"
"Come dance with us!"
Congregation: "Ago! Ago-é!"

Spirit: Take the asson and make a gesture as if to open a veil over the vèvè, first with the

hands out at arm's length before you, then moving the arms outward till they are straight to your sides, shaking the asson throughout, saying:

"A l'Esprit surtout, royaume de Bon Dieu."
Kreyòl: "Pou Gran Mèt-la, nan wayom´Bondye."
"To the Spirit above all, realm of the Good God."
Congregation: "Ago! Ago! Ago-é!"

(Orienting to the Four Quarters aligns the working with the natural, elemental forces, and allows Spirit to descend.)

10. Open the door: Drumming begins slowly and softly at this point, as does any song that the choir may know for the particular Lwa.

Make crossroads in the air over the vèvè with the libation bottle, then pour libations on the vèvè, saying:

"Pour les Marassa, Jumeaux sacrés qui se reflè-tent de chaque côté du miroir."
Kreyòl: "Pou Marasa ki sou dé fas glas-la."
"For the Marasa, sacred twins who reflect each side of the mirror."

"Ago, Les Marassa!"
"Ago, Lè Marasa!"
"Ago, The Marasa!"

Congregation responds:

"Ayibobo!"
"Amen!"

Pour three libations over the vèvè, saying:

Respecte, honneur aux Morts. Famille Guedeh au Guinée.
Les Ancêtres qui vivent toujours dans nos mé-moires.
Des Eaux Abysmes jusqu'aux générations sans cesses."

Kreyòl: "Respè, honè pou Mò-yo. Fanmi Gede nan Ginen.
Zansèt nou you kap viv nan tèt nou.
Ki nan fon dlo, fon lamè."

"Respect, honor to the Dead. The family Gede in Guinen.

The Ancestors who always live in our memories.
From the Abysmal Waters, throughout endless
  generations."

Take water on your fingers, touch your wet
fingers to your lips, sprinkle the water behind
your head, saying:

"Respecte à ceux qui sont passés."
Kreyòl: "Respè pou sak mouri-yo."
"Respect to those who have passed."

Take water on your fingers, touch them to
your heart, and sprinkle the water before you,
saying:

"Honneur à ceux qui vont arriver."
Kreyòl: "Honè pou sak ap vini-yo."
"Honor to those who are yet to come."

"Ago! Les Morts! Ago!"
"Ago! Lè Mò! Ago!"
Congregation responds: "Ayibobo!"

Sprinkle water in a vertical crossroads above
the vèvè, saying:

"Pour les Mystères. Les Invisibles qui guident
  toutes choses au monde, sous Bon Dieu."
Kreyòl: "Pou Mistè-yo. Invisib kap guidé tou sa
  kap fèt sou Bondye."
"For the Mysteries. The Invisibles who guide all
  things in the world, under God."

Sprinkle water in a horizontal crossroads
above the vèvè, saying:

"Papa Legba est à la porte. Ouvrez la porte pour
  vos enfants, Papa. Vos enfants vous atten-
  dent."
Kreyòl: "Papa Legba nan pot'la. Ouvè pòt-la pou
  pitit´ ou-yo, Papa. Petit´ ou-yo ap tan´ ou."
"Papa Legba is at the door. Open the door for
  your children, Papa. Your children wait for
  you."

"Ago! Legba! Ago-é!"
Congregation responds: "Ayibobo!"

Shake the asson over the vèvè while reciting
the appropriate litany for the Lwa. End with
three repetitions of:

"Ago! ——— [insert name of Lwa]!"

Congregation responds each time: "Ayibobo!"

After last repetition, take water or appropriate liquor into your mouth and spray it onto
the vèvè to activate it.

11. Make passes over the dancers and drummers with the asson to charge their energies
and to raise the life force. Dancers begin
dancing backward in a counterclockwise, cir-
cular direction. In the process, they dance on
the vèvè to disperse the cornmeal. The drumming intensifies.

12. Consecrate all participants with cornmeal
(on the temples for inspiration or on the back
of the neck for possession).

13. Dancers and drummers continue until a
possession occurs or until exhaustion, at
which point all sit, meditating for a vision or
insight.

14. Closing prayer: Kneeling on floor, with
palms together, say:

"Merci à Legba, qui garde la porte, les Marassa,
  les Morts, les Mystères.
Merci à ——— [insert the name of the Lwa]. Re-
  tournez en paix chez vous. Laissez tranquille
  et la terre, et le temps. Cette fois ici dans
  l'Hounfor; la prochaine fois en Guinée."
Kreyòl: "Mèsi Legba, kap véyé pot´-la. Mèsi
  Marasa, Mèsi Lè Mò, Mèsi Mistè-yo.
Mèsi ——— [insert the name of the Lwa].
Rétounen la kay-ou nan la pè. Kité latè-a ak
  letan dèyè. Fwa-sa nan Ounfò-a. Apré-sa nan
  Ginen."
"Thanks to Legba, who guards the door. The
  Marasa, the Dead, the Mysteries. Thanks to
  ——— [insert the name of the Lwa]. Return
  in peace to your home. Leave the earth and
  time alone. This time here in the Ounfò; next
  time in Ginen."
Congregation responds: "ASHÉ!"

We have worked this ritual hundreds of

times in my Ounfò. Each time, we come away with a sense of benediction and personal blessing.

In the course of working rituals like these to the Lwa, the practitioner can unlock the meaning of symbols that have been distorted in outward expression. Within the inspired reality of ritual, the symbols present themselves as themselves in a kind of epiphany. Great horses can carry the meaning of these symbols back down the path to the outer world, where they empower and heal.

*

Vodou Visions

William Blake suggested that there is an inner, eternal realm that reflects outward onto the dark mirror of the world. Prophets, artists, and poets attune themselves to that inner realm to retrieve symbols that they bring forward into external reality as visions from the core of the psyche. Trance work also draws a person into this core, where the imaginative, creative, and expansive waters of the soul are encountered.

What I experience in vision trance is not just a pushing aside of my personality, but an expansion of self and a dissolution of the boundary between self and other. The universe of self becomes vast and timeless. My ability to create and express myself expands well beyond my ordinary limitations, and particularly beyond any limitations of culture and race. There is magic in the fluid core that is restorative and transformative and has the power to change and heal us.

Time and effort are required to consciously pursue visionary techniques, and technique is required to be able to express the full impact of the visions received. Diamanda Galas is a classically trained, operatic singer, and an acclaimed performance artist. In preparation for her performances, which she describes as "singing for the Gods," Galas must make a psychic descent into Vodoun-type trance. She draws material from the deep core, which she expresses through voice and vibration. In an interview in *ReSearch* magazine, she says, "When you are singing for the Gods, you must have a superlative technique to extrovert the ride." The conscious mind has its work to do, in cooperation with internal inspiration. It requires discipline to maintain conversation between the conscious mind and the subconscious mind, between the Gwo Bon Anj and Ti Bon Anj, to stand before the steady gaze of Spirit, to maintain your own conscious gaze in return, and to bring eye and hand with you into communion. With a mastered technique, able to balance outward expression with internal inspiration, you are able to remain on the creative and magical edge.

In Haiti, there is a cultural context that trains a person gradually to attain Vodoun trance states. Even Haitian Vodounists, however, must learn magic, drumming, and effective movements over years of apprenticeship. A tremendous discipline is required to focus the mind. This discipline does not come easily, but it can be developed. An integral awareness and competence can be reinforced through the daily practice of mental, physical, spiritual, and magical practices that focus attention, concentration, perception, Will, and directed imagination. Years of effort went into the trance states that now come rather readily to me. I studied and practiced and learned all that I could about Qabalah, metaphysics, Yoga, world religions, mythology, shamanism, and Western Ceremonial Magick. Without a doubt, however, I simply started from a place of personal interest, applied my own heritage and psychological makeup, developed discipline where I thought it was lacking, and learned little by little to trust my own innovations as they developed. The greatest obstacles to the work are inertia, boredom, and self-doubt. There are periods of descent, of the dark night of the soul, when self-doubt and frustration creep in, creating a wash of disgust and despair. Remember always, and especially at such times, that your actions and your efforts stand for more than yourself. If you want to sing for the Gods, you must master your instrument and offer all that you have in service.

YOGA MUDRA: ASANA, PRANAYAMA, MANTRAYAMA

Of greatest help to my own development has been the daily practice of several forms of Yoga that address the practice of asana, or postures; pranayama, the science of breathing; and mantrayama, the science of sound vibration. In particular, I have found that Yoga mudras—gestures or postures combined with meditation and breathing or chanting techniques—are conducive to altered states. Yoga unifies body, mind, and soul, and teaches the practitioner how to affect any one of these three aspects of self through the medium of any of the others. Subtle nerve endings are affected, energy flows are directed or harmonized; mind and being are transformed. I recommend study with an intuitive and gifted teacher as the only way truly to learn Yoga. For the purposes of this book, however, I will present a deceptively simple mudra practice that can help bring on trance states.

Sit in a cross-legged or lotus position, in which the heel of your right foot is firmly planted on your left thigh, and the heel of your left foot is planted on your right thigh. Rest your wrists on the tops of the knees, with the index and middle fingers curled under your thumbs. Your back should be straight, your shoulders relaxed, your head centered. Raise your right hand if right-handed, your left hand if left-handed, to your nose. With the two free fingers, cover your left nostril. Inhale slowly and with control for a count of four. Continue to cover the left nostril and, with your thumb, cover the right nostril. Hold your breath for a count of sixteen. Release your left nostril and exhale for a count of eight. Cover your left nostril again and hold your breath for a count of sixteen. Then reverse the breath. Uncover the left nostril, then inhale for four counts. Cover the nostril and hold for sixteen. Uncover the right nostril and exhale for eight. Cover and hold for sixteen. Continue this rhythm and pattern for at least eleven minutes, increasing to longer sessions as you are able. At first, it will be extremely difficult to maintain rhythmic consistency, and a comfortable volume of breath, but it's essential to keep your breathing even, gentle, and slow. As you develop capacity, increase the timing to eight counts, sixteen counts, and thirty-two counts. Your breath is like a kite string that holds your mind. As you control your breathing, you focus your mind and teach it to soar beyond the turbulence of thought and ego.

CONCENTRATION
It is well known that we use only a small portion of our brains. Fortunately, your mind is a muscle that can be exercised. Concentration exercises can help develop some of that area that has become vestigial in Westerners.

CANDLE CONCENTRATION EXERCISE
Sit comfortably at the table in a straight-backed chair, or sit cross-legged on the floor at a low table. Light a single candle on the

table at eye level. Place paper and a pen in front of the candle within easy reach. Set a timer for ten minutes. Hold the pen in your hand, poised on the paper. Relax, breathe deeply, and concentrate on the candle flame. Do not think of anything but the candle flame. Each time your mind wavers, make a scratch mark on the paper. You will notice several categories of distractions, including:

1. Physical. Your body will itch or twitch or feel cramped, or an appendage may "fall asleep."
2. Flights of fancy and trains of thought.
3. Boredom.
4. You will suddenly notice that you are successful, which will distract you immediately.
5. Diversions from the environment, for instance the ticking of the timer or a dog barking.

Each day as you practice this exercise, try gradually to reduce the number of scratch marks. I must confess that I always had an alarming number of marks, although I did this particular exercise every day for at least two years. It is exceptionally difficult for me to sit still. Yet, perhaps through the sheer discipline of daily effort, my concentration has increased along with my attention span. I am now able to sit for hours in trance in order to do readings, and, as a kind of magical mental weapon, when the subject is vital, I can maintain a sharply focused concentration.

MEDITATION
Concentration on the breath will take you deeply into a meditational state. Correct meditation does not produce myriad mental images or visions; it is a state of expectant receptivity in which there is no conscious mentation. Sit in the cross-legged asana, with your wrists resting on your knees and with your index fingers curled under your thumb.

Conversely, place one hand cupped gently in the other and hold it in your lap. Your breath should be rhythmical, slow, deep, and full. Allow your mind to follow the breath and focus on it. You may present a question to Spirit, offer prayer, or simply offer thanks. You may not receive any clear response during your meditation; it may come subtly into your awareness later, marked by a simple and complete clarity. Meditation should be practiced daily, even if only for ten minutes. Over time, the practice will build a cathedral of the soul, removed from the endless rush of time and space.

You may want to add mantra—a chant that combines breath and sound vibration—to your practice. Yoga books offer numerous "seed" mantras that effect specific awarenesses in the mind. The sacred songs of Vodou are comparable in effect, and I would suggest trying chanting the name of a Lwa in combination with Yoga asana and breathing, vibrating the Lwa's name on the outward breath vocally and inhaling it silently into the waters of the soul. The repetition of mantras stuns or overrides the intellect's resistance, allowing the mind to slide into an altered state.

By combining breathing, meditation, and asana, it is possible to direct or arouse life force. This life force can be offered to the Lwa for their manifestation in lieu of sacrificial animals.

VISUALIZATION
In order to obtain and maintain deep trance states, it is necessary also to develop visualization techniques. If your mind can hold an image for a period of time, it can follow it into the realm of its own expanded meaning.

VISUALIZATION EXERCISE
This exercise tends to come easily to visually oriented people; to others, it may prove quite frustrating.

It is helpful to begin with an aesthetically pleasing but unchanging visual, such as a silk flower. Choose something simple and colorful, like a tiger lily. For about ten minutes a day, stare at the flower until you have absorbed its image. Then close your eyes, and try to hold the entire image of the flower in your mind. Each time the flower fades in your mind—you find yourself seeing only one portion of the flower or you are distracted from the practice—make a scratch mark on a piece of paper. The goal is to extend the length of time that you can hold the complete flower steadily in the mind's eye.

Experiment with different sorts of images. Try using tattwa symbols, simple graphic Hindu symbols that represent the elements. A yellow cube represents earth, a silver crescent is air, a red triangle is fire, a blue sphere is water, and an indigo egg is ether. As you are able to hold these single images in your mind, begin combining the tattwas—a blue sphere within a yellow cube, for instance.

When you're able to hold visual images in your mind, you can go on to work with guided visualization. Sit cross-legged or lie on the floor on your back. Breathe deeply and rhythmically. Have someone recite a visualization for you, or play a previously recorded tape of a visualization that you have prepared. The visualization should include the description of a gradual descent into a tunnel and the eventual emergence into an extremely relaxing and soothing environment. A state of light self-hypnosis is attained, during which it is possible to perceive submerged intuitions and to receive spiritual guidance.

Guided visualization is particularly useful for learning how to work on astral levels. The astral plane is a more rarefied or subtle level of reality. The astral forms a kind of matrix or foundation of light energy upon which the physical world is formed. Magical theory holds that by manipulating the astral light image within one's mind, it is possible to affect the material manifestation on physical levels. This is the magicoscientific basis for sympathetic magic as applied to Vodou.

It might be appropriate to prepare for a Vodou ceremony by embarking on a guided astral journey to Ginen. Relax deeply, releasing all experiences and pressures of the day. Visualize traveling through a tree, deep into its roots, down through the centerpole of the earth into the waters below, on into Ginen. Give yourself time to explore Ginen, to inhale its atmosphere. Allow yourself to visit with Ancestors or with the Lwa, who may speak with you or show you signs. Return to your physical space and body, refreshed and enriched from your journey.

CEREMONIAL MAGICK, TAROT, AND QABALAH

Although I often forget the process of my own training, I realize that Western Ceremonial Magick techniques inform my Vodou practice. I spent years—literally all of my adult life—studying and reading tarot and Qabalah, the mystical Jewish tradition upon which tarot is based. In Ceremonial Magick, every color, word, image, gesture, and sound is intended to induce a particular mental state. When the conscious mental boundaries are overloaded, the mind gives way to an altered state. The drumbeats, dance steps, songs, altars, and offerings have the same effect in Vodou ceremonies.

It is far beyond the scope of this book to attempt even the most simplistic study of Ceremonial Magick, its theory, rituals, and formulas. A bibliography of some important books on the subject is included for any readers who wish to incorporate magical techniques in their Vodou ceremonies. I suggest that a beginner work with the Lesser Pentagram Banishing Ritual in particular. Though that concentrated ritual is not included in a traditional Vodou ceremony, the magical techniques necessary for the mastery of it are all applicable. If you make a mistake in your ceremonial work, it is also a good idea to have a good banishing ritual under your belt for housecleaning.

Many forms of Angelic and Elemental Magick can also be combined with Vodoun techniques. For instance, I suggest drums to accompany Angelic invocations together with call and response chanting. Or try drawing astral vèvè to invoke a Lwa during astral visions.

Western Ceremonial Magick claims roots in the Knights Templar, who supposedly resurfaced as the Freemasons after a period of persecution in the Middle Ages. One of Vodou's influential sources includes Freemasonry. Although each culture may scoff at the style and methods of the other, denying any resemblance, there are recognizable magical formulas in both rites.

QABALAH AND DIVINATION

QABALAH
It is a time-consuming discipline to study Qabalah. It is generally suggested that a person already have mastered Talmud and Torah before considering the study of Qabalah. There are several aspects of Qabalah. Some deal with the cosmos of numbers and letters. As you learn about the significance or revelatory nature of numbers, you could begin to think about which numbers are sacred to which Lwa and how many aspects or paths each Orisha has. Ask yourself what meaning might be hidden in the numbers and what they might reveal about the nature of the Lwa or Orisha.

Other aspects of Qabalah are said to teach the mind to think in the way that God dreams. This dream of God is visualized as extending upon a glyph, called the Tree of Life, that contains ten Spheres and twenty-two connecting paths. Each Sphere and each path represents an evolution from the unlimited into manifestation. The Vodoun, the community of the Lwa, manifest these same aspects or vibrations in the expression of Bondye into the diversity of creation.

It can be quite beneficial to organize one's knowledge of the Lwa according to the different Spheres and paths, noting how one bit of knowledge reveals hidden knowledge about something else that may have seemed inscrutable in isolation. Vodou seeks to discern the underlying cosmic meaning within experiences that can often seem disconnected or senseless. Because each of the Visions corresponds to a Sphere or path, it helps to lay out the images as they would appear on the Tree of Life. Experiences or information that seemed random or chaotic can reveal meaningful patterns as encompassed within the expression of Bondye, the Ain Soph Aur, in the parlance of Qabalah. Essentially, all correspondences and all pantheons from all religions, philosophies, and systems of thought can be traced along the glyph. Ezili relates to Venus, who relates to Aphrodite, all of whom have something to do with love. A limited list of Qabalistic texts in the bibliography provides a beginner with some approach to Qabalistic thought, particularly as it applies to occult theory.

READING THE CRYSTAL BALL
In Haiti, divination is conducted either through dreams or signs, or by reading regular decks of cards. While I have worked extensively with tarot, I also learned to read the crystal ball in order to find some way to turn psychic abilities on and off at will. André Pierre, a formidable Oungan and artist, re-

The Qabalistic Tree of Life

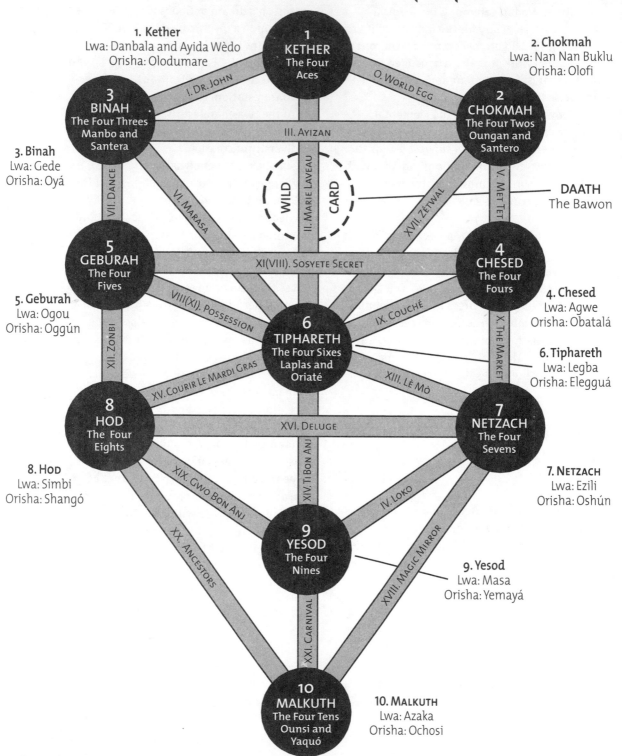

1. Kether
Lwa: Danbala and Ayida Wèdo
Orisha: Olodumare

2. Chokmah
Lwa: Nan Nan Buklu
Orisha: Olofi

3. Binah
Lwa: Gede
Orisha: Oyá

DAATH
The Bawon

5. Geburah
Lwa: Ogou
Orisha: Oggún

4. Chesed
Lwa: Agwe
Orisha: Obatalá

6. Tiphareth
Lwa: Legba
Orisha: Elegguá

8. Hod
Lwa: Simbi
Orisha: Shangó

7. Netzach
Lwa: Ezili
Orisha: Oshún

9. Yesod
Lwa: Masa
Orisha: Yemayá

10. Malkuth
Lwa: Azaka
Orisha: Ochosi

1
KETHER
The Four
Aces

2
CHOKMAH
The Four Twos
Oungan and
Santero

3
BINAH
The Four Threes
Manbo and
Santera

4
CHESED
The Four
Fours

5
GEBURAH
The Four
Fives

6
TIPHARETH
The Four Sixes
Laplas and
Oriaté

7
NETZACH
The Four
Sevens

8
HOD
The Four
Eights

9
YESOD
The Four
Nines

10
MALKUTH
The Four Tens
Ounsi and
Yaquó

WILD
CARD

O. World Egg
I. Dr. John
III. Ayizan
II. Marie Laveau
V. Met Tet
XVII. Zétwal
VI. Marasa
VII. Dance
XI(VIII). Sosyete Secret
VIII(XI). Possession
IX. Couché
X. The Market
XII. Zonbi
XV. Courir Le Mardi Gras
XIII. Lè Mò
XVI. Deluge
XIV. Ti Bon Anj
XIX. Gwo Bon Anj
IV. Loko
XVIII. Magic Mirror
XX. Ancestors
XXI. Carnival

cently told me that an Oungan must be a prophet; he must be able to divine for others. Increasingly, as I practice my technique in crystal ball reading, I experience the same amnesia that occurs during possession. Working with the crystal involves entering into a Vodoun trance. I can see two realities for each person: the archetypal level of the Gwo Bon Anj and the way that person's inner intention translates outward on the dark mirror of the world.

To read the crystal ball, sit comfortably before the crystal. Relax deeply, and breathe rhythmically. Let the crystal provide a kind of tractor beam that focuses the mind into receptive clarity. When an image emerges into the mind's eye, swoop down after it with avid attention like a bird descending out of the sky for its prey, until it opens into a full perception. Retrieving the perceptions that the symbols suggest brings them back to surface expression.

Crystal visioning involves a process of changing focus, changing channels. It feels much like being conscious in a dream, totally relaxed, but totally focused in the dream image. There is no reference to other realities. The visionary landscape is characteristically "crystal clear." To work with the crystal ball, I suggest that you just sit down and try it. Use your meditation and deep-breathing techniques to relax into concentrated focus. When an image appears in your mind's eye, follow it. It is only through repeated practice that you begin to learn the terrain and trust what you perceive. You can test out your visions by doing crystal ball readings for friends.

My experience in creating the images for *Vodou Visions* was extraordinarily similar to that of reading the crystal ball. I gave my hand and eyes to the Lwa that they might mark their own signatures. I often had no idea how a particular image would come out until, as the last stroke of the pastel was laid in, the Lwa's force would leap out of the image. The images became containers of Primal Spirit.

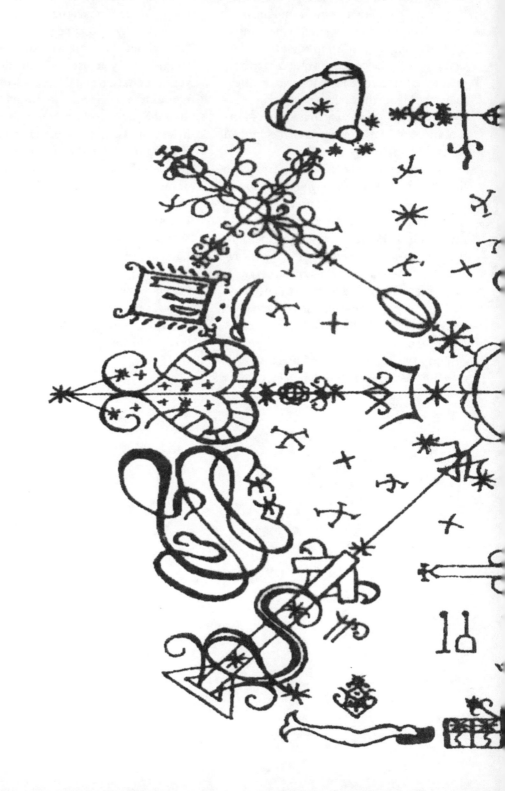

The Visions

VISIONARY ART

Visionary art requires more than simply pushing aside the intellect and allowing a greater presence to work for you. The conscious mind must be kept available as you expand outward to meet greater forces. As the door opens, allowing an exchange between the conscious and subconscious minds, the superconscious can flood through. Opening into vision, we move beyond the circumstances of time and place, into the inviolate archetypal that endures. The art that is produced reflects the crisis that fuses the abiding self with the mundane, temporal self.

When I am going into a vision, I find myself diving after a particular image or flow of images. There is no thought of what I hope to find; no preconceived idea of what I am going after. The visionary artist becomes the act of creation itself, just as the Vodounist dances in the Ounfò and becomes God. The visions are guardians of internal content. Though one moves down inwardly after the image, the image itself emerges outward. It turns itself out into the mind's eye, through the hand of the artist, into the world.

Attached to the images of the Lwa and their corresponding vèvè in this book is a written text of the visions I experienced for each of the Lwa. These visions were attempts to ask the Gods who they are. They may not fully agree with existing literature on the Lwa, but they were experienced in the fluid way in which a relationship is formed. There are always surprises, secrets to be revealed, subtleties to be explored. Finally, the Vodoun Mysteries, the Lwa, remain mysterious. They reach deep into the Waters of the Abyss. They are richly textured and vibrantly seasoned. One Lwa dances with another through the web of life.

Don't be content just to read the visions or flip through the images. Sit with them. Feed them. Construct and work your own rituals. The more you learn, the more you can apply. The greater your technique, the wider and deeper your field of reception becomes for these expressions of the Lwa. When creating visionary art, apply all the techniques you have mastered. Clear your mind of all distraction and focus into the core. You can chant the name of a Lwa or sing a sacred song for them. But give them your hand and eye for creative expression. The Lwa are not dead. The Waters are not stagnant, and the archetypes are not finished. Add yourself to them. Invite the invisible presence within the image to come dance with you. You can choose to swim on the surface or you can dive deep. The Waters of the Abyss are forever unfathomable and eternally replenishing.

Danbala and Ayida Wèdo's World Egg

88

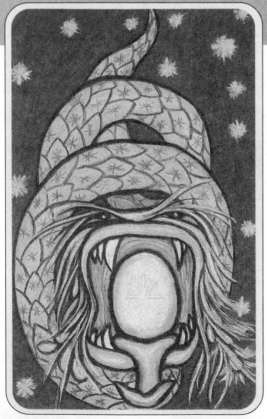

Call on Danbala and Ayida Wèdo's World Egg to bless any new undertaking or beginning. Call on it for a perception of the cosmic principle underlying a particular matter.

OFFERINGS

An egg, painted with a double crossroads, and placed on a mound of white flour. An egg, wrapped in a shed snakeskin, egg candies, *Vodou Visions* image of Danbala and Ayida Wèdo's World Egg.

LITANY

"Pour l'œuf mondial de Damballah et Ayida Wèdo. Montrez-nous les mystères de la gestation; les secrets que le monde détient. Qu'est-ce qu'il y a là-dedans? Chuchotez ce qu'il aura. Acceptez nos offrandes. Entrez dans nos cœurs, dans nos bras, dans nos jambes. Entrez ici, dansez avec nous."

KREYÒL

"Pou Danbala avek Ayida Wèdo. Montré nou mistè ak sékrè yo. Ki sa ki la dan'n? Aksepté ofran'n nou. Antré nan kè nou, nan bra nou, nan jam'm nou. Antré vin'n dansé avek nou."

TRANSLATION

"For Danbala and Ayida Wèdo's World Egg. Show us the mysteries of gestation; the secrets of the world in potential. What is in there? Whisper what there will be. Accept our offerings. Enter into our hearts, our arms, our legs. Enter and dance with us."

TRADITIONAL

Danbala, the creative principle, is pictured as a snake that arches across the sky. The arching snake meets his wife, Ayida Wèdo, the rainbow, who arches as his reflective complement back into the waters. Their sexual union is represented as a serpent coiled around the world, symbolized as a cosmic egg. The egg contains within its ovular symbolism all potential, all possible development. The egg is Danbala's favorite offering. He pierces the eggshell with his fangs, and sucks the egg out.

VISION

The power of the serpent and the egg meeting at the center of the crossroads is primal, beyond words and coherent sense. The quality of that power is both vulnerable and wild. The delicate egg of potential is carried around in the sharp teeth of the serpent. The double crossroads on the egg is luminous. Out of chaos, the egg of creative potential is posited, forming one crossroad of exchange. The serpent carries the closed, germinating world of the egg out through space and time, forming the second, fourth-dimensional crossroad. This is how we experience Danbala and Ayida Wèdo's World Egg—we move through space and time in the course of our lives, searching for the essential creative Will that is symbolized by the egg. When we discover the perfect circle of Oroboros, the snake that consumes its own tail, wrapped around the egg, we shatter through the eggshell, into the cosmos of self.

Dr. John

CALL ON DR. JOHN for inspiration for drumming. Call on him for assistance with healing. Call on him for power, for disciplined energy, and for charisma.

OFFERINGS

Drumheads, blue and red snake images, drumbeats, magical and medicinal herbs, snake vertebrae, Dr. John's image.

LITANY

"Pour Docteur John, John le Bayou, John Montanet, qui devient Loa. Maître de tambour, guérisseur racine, mystérieux et puissant, Docteur John, prettez-moi un peu de votre magie. Acceptez nos offrandes. Entrez dans nos cœurs, dans nos bras, dans nos jambes. Entrez ici. Dansez avec nous!"

KREYÒL

"Pou Doktè John, John Bayou, John Montanet ki tounin Lwa. Tanbouyè, doktè féy Doktè John prété'm pouvwa maji ou. Aksepté ofran'n nou. Antré nan kè nou, nan jam'm nou. Antré vin'n dansé avek nou!"

TRANSLATION

"For Doctor John, John Bayou, John Montanet, who is becoming a Lwa. Master drummer, root healer, mysterious and powerful, Doctor John, lend me some of your magic. Accept our offerings. Enter into our hearts, our arms, our legs. Enter and dance with us!"

TRADITIONAL

Dr. John was a free man of color who lived and practiced Vodou in New Orleans. He had distinctive blue and red snakelike tattoos on his face. He was an exceptional drummer, and a powerful root doctor, whose name evokes African mysteries and Vodoun magic. He was supposed to have been a sacred drummer at Marie Laveau's ceremonies. Historical fact is, no doubt, somewhat blurred with the legend of his powers. Dr. John was certainly dramatic and charismatic in life; in death, his legend is rising to the status of a Lwa.

VISION

The vision of Dr. John brings a sense of the demands of energy placed upon the man, and the Mysteries of the energies that he channels. His ordeal is to be able to handle the energy coming through him so that he can transform and distribute it. He has to be able to produce the needed energy whenever called upon. He breaks the energy into different rhythms with the drums. It is a tremendous requirement of his dignity and ego to be able to stand back personally and let this energy come through him.

In Dr. John is intense, burning energy passing through an intensely sweet and gentle man of extraordinary truth and service. His body has to hold up throughout all this channeling, leaving him exhausted in life, and creating a rather intimidating projection of him into legend.

He sits on the drum to channel the earth energies and to contain them in the conduit of the drum. His snake tattoos also channel this primal, Kundalini energy through and under the flesh, and into his head, the seat of Spirit.

Marie Laveau

CALL ON MARIE LAVEAU for empowerment in the Vodou arts, and for
help in healing. Marie Laveau provides
assistance in all workings.

OFFERINGS

Salt water, white and blue flowers, white and
blue candles, Voodoo doll, "Voodoo oil," gris-
gris bags, jambalaya and other traditional
Creole foods, hairdressing tools (Marie was a
hairdresser), Marie's *Vodou Visions* image.

LITANY

"Pour Marie Laveau, Loa historique de la Nouvelle Orléans. Reine du Vodou. Femme forte, intelligente, sage, et puissante. Pendant la vie vous dansiez avec les Invisibles, et dans la mort vous dansez encore avec nous. Acceptez nos offrandes. Entrez dans nos cœurs, dans nos bras, dans nos jambes. Entrez ici. Dansez avec nous!"

KREYÒL

"Pou Marie Laveau, Rèn'n Nouvèl Olèan. Fan'm vanyan, fan'm intélijan, fan'm fò. Lè ou té vivan ou té kon dansé avek Invisib-yo. Koun'n yé-a sé avek nou wap dansé. Aksepté ofran'n nou. Antré nan kè nou, nan bra nou, nan jam'm nou. Antré vin'n dansé avek nou!"

TRANSLATION

"For Marie Laveau, historical Lwa of New Orleans. Vodou Queen. Strong, intelligent, wise, and powerful woman. During your life you danced with the Invisibles, and in death you dance with us. Accept our offerings. Enter into our hearts, our arms, our legs. Enter and dance with us!"

TRADITIONAL

Marie Laveau was an historic Vodou Queen of New Orleans. She was the most famous, and possibly the most powerful and influential, of New Orleans's Vodou Queens. She was instrumental in combining Catholicism with Vodou in the United States. She presided over famous ceremonies, especially on Saint John's Eve on Bayou Saint John. Marie Laveau lived from 1794 to 1881, but there is some confusion concerning her life, and that of one of her daughters, also named Marie. There is similar confusion surrounding her final resting place. She remains mysterious. Her official tomb, in Saint Louis cemetery #1, is still visited by believers, who mark X's on the tomb and leave offerings. Marie Laveau remains a powerful and generous spiritual presence in the city. During her life, she was known to be exceptionally kind and caring to the poor, to prisoners, and to victims of the yellow fever epidemics.

VISION

Marie Laveau appears to be a very solid woman. She stands in front of a beaded curtain, which she opens to show that she's still initiating. Through the vehicle of her painted vision, she's still looking for followers. The vision's image is her link, and with it, she'll be pulling people through. Marie is doing a primal seductive dance with history and race.

As priestess, her experience is of intensely sacred personal isolation. She walks through crowds of people, but is not one of them. She is terribly lonely in this isolation, even though surrounded by followers and accompanied by Spirit. She only feels connection with her own life through her children, who make her life actual and real to her. Still, though, she lives in the shadow of her own myth.

Marie Laveau operates on many levels, most of which are misinterpreted, and all of which cause her much pain. She used these misinterpretations on the secular level during her life to promote awareness of the Lwa.

She is seemingly open, but actually she is intensely private internally. She is open to the core of the psyche, that dark, magical territory where she works creatively with the Lwa. She participates in the ongoing creation of the archetypes, and influences them. That is why she was so powerful in life, and why she was so influential, with the Lwa, and with humans, and in the history of Vodou. And that is why no one has ever quite filled her shoes since. They are not open to the indwelling Spirit on that profound core level. She opens the cowrie shell veil to that visionary core where initiation waits. Her eyes gaze directly into your core.

Hear her drum rhythms pulsing like blood. It is the ongoing passage of the bloodline in the eternal feminine.

Ayizan

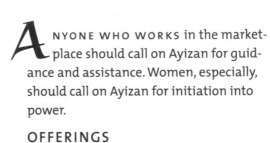

ANYONE WHO WORKS in the marketplace should call on Ayizan for guidance and assistance. Women, especially, should call on Ayizan for initiation into power.

OFFERINGS

Frayed palm branches, initiation materials, market wares, dirt from the crossroads of a market, plantains, cane syrup, mirlitons, flowers, yams, sweet liqueurs, Ayizan's *Vodou Visions* image.

LITANY

"Pour Ayizan, Loa racine d'ancêtre. Mère des Mambos qui initie par la palme effrangée. Nous vous recherchons dans les carrefours des marchés. Vous êtes cachées dans les denrhees du marche. Ayizan, au cœur pur. Acceptez nos offrandes. Entrez dans nos cœurs, dans nos bras, dans nos jambes. Entrez ici. Dansez avec nous!"

KREYÒL

"Pou Ayizan, Lwa rasin'n. Manman tout Manbo. Nap chèché ou nan tout kalfou maché koté ou kaché Ayizan. Aksepté ofran'n nou. Antré nan kè nou, nan bra nou, nan jam'm nou. Antré vin'n dansé avek nou!"

TRANSLATION

"For Ayizan, ancestral root Lwa. Mother of Manbos who initiates by the frayed palm branch. We seek you in the crossroads of markets. You are hidden in the wares of the market. Ayizan of pure heart, accept our offerings. Enter into our hearts, our arms, our legs. Enter and dance with us!"

TRADITIONAL

Ayizan is a root Lwa, the wife and feminine counterpart of Loko, and patron of the marketplace and public spaces. Yoruba tradition refers to the earth plane as "the Market." Ayizan brings the Mysteries to the human domain. She rules the fringed palm frond that traditionally covers the new initiates' faces as they emerge from the Couché into the Lever ceremony. She is the Lwa that purifies the initiate. Loko and Ayizan are related to Legba, and escort him, but they are much closer to the human race than Legba is, and often act as intermediaries on behalf of human interests. Ayizan imparts konesans to her human children. She is the patron of Manbos, and usually comes to Manbos in possession. Ayizan's full name is Ayizan Velequete. Her vèvè represents an intersecting *A* and *V*. Some say her vèvè reflects the Masonic symbol of the letter *G* within the tools of sacred geometry. Chromolithographs of Christ—usually Christ being baptized by John the Baptist—are used in association with Ayizan.

First Legba is called, then Loko and Ayizan, who control and direct the arrival of all the other Mysteries to the earth plane.

VISION

Ayizan enters under the frayed leaves of the palm that cover the initiate's eyes. We purify ourselves to receive internal fertility. Ayizan is empowering to women. She enables women to attain the mastery of the Manbo. Women who have separated from a lover perform a ritual in which they look into a mirror and thank generations of women before them—their Mother, their Grandmother, their Great-grandmother—for the attributes that they have received from them. They are empowered rather than destroyed by the failure of the romance. This mirror ritual is appropriate to Ayizan.

Ayizan is an ancient root Lwa. She is Sophia, exiled in the things of the world, in the wares of the marketplace.

Suddenly all the bustling figures in the market turn into sinister, sneering skeletons. Our culture has marketed everything, and has made even spirituality commercial, but Sophia can be found beneath the mask of the material. The faces of the market turn to frightening skeletons, but within the bone there is that which endures. Although the marketplace has become something that kills our values, it is also an enduring manifestation of the activity of the Spirit of life.

Mother of the race, Ayizan has been with us from the beginning, and is bought and sold and thrown away. But when we cover our eyes to the outside display, there she is, waiting with her gifts of purity and initiation in the things of the world itself. In this time of both great need and neglect of her gifts, Ayizan is calling strongly to people.

C ALL ON LOKO for healing and for mastery of the asson. Men especially can call on Loko for spiritual strength and empowerment. Loko can be called upon to give guidance for the running of the Ounfò.

Loko

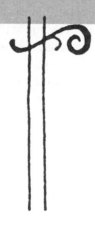

OFFERINGS

Images of fighting roosters, keys, leafy tree branches, healing herbs, butterflies, Loko's *Vodou Visions* image.

LITANY

"Pour Loco, Loa racine qui marche avec Legba sur les points des carrefours. Loco, le mari d'Ayizan, gardien de l'Hounfor et du Poteau-Mitan, patron des Houngans, et maître de l'asson. Roi Loco, guérisseur qui habite dans les arbres. Acceptez nos offrandes. Entrez dans nos cœurs, dans nos bras, dans nos jambes. Entrez ici. Dansez avec nous!"

KREYÒL

"Pou Loko, Lwa raisin'n kap maché ak Legba nan kalfou-a. Loko mari Ayizan, gadien ounfò ak Poto Mitan, patron oungan, mèt ason. Papa Loko, doktè fèy kap viv nan pyé bwa. Aksepté ofran'n nou. Antré nan kè nou, nan bra nou, nan jam'm nou. Antré vin'n dansé avek nou!"

TRANSLATION

"For Loko, root Lwa who walks with Legba on the points of the crossroads. Loko, husband of Ayizan, guardian of the Ounfò and the Poto Mitan, patron of the Oungan, and master of the asson. King Loko, healer who lives in the trees. Accept our offering. Enter into our hearts, our arms, our legs. Enter and dance with us!"

TRADITIONAL

Loko is an ancient root Lwa. He is the first Oungan, the master of the asson, the magic rattle that designates an Oungan's authority. Loko lives in the trees, and controls the Poto Mitan, which is the symbolic tree in the center of the Ounfò. He is the escort of Legba, and the husband of Ayizan. He is a great healer who uses leaves and herbs in his medicines. Loko's possessions can be wild and sometimes even destructive, especially if he is angry at the lax behavior of an Oungan. Once an Oungan himself, he must be stronger than the forces that he directs. He is a solar deity, and is often referred to as "King."

His symbols are the butterfly and the rooster, which came to symbolize Aristide's democratic struggle in Haiti.

Loco corresponds to Saint Joseph.

VISION

Loko is crouched way up high at the top of the Poto Mitan of the Ounfò. He is seen through the hole at the top of the roof, sitting in the treetops that are his home. He pulls aside the branches and peers down. He seems to say that Spirit requires something material to need Spirit before Spirit can be drawn into the Ounfò. Loko heals his worshipers, but it's the memory and respect of the worshipers that keep Loko alive.

Loko, at the top of the Poto Mitan, is the receiver and transmitter of Ashé. He travels down the Poto Mitan as a snake who leaves traces of himself in seeds that he implants along the length of the pole. The little butterfly who flits back up to Loko is the "soul bird" of people's hopes, aspirations, dreams, and prayers. The butterfly flits over Loko's sacred healing vegetation to pollinate it, and finally flutters back up to Loko. He receives this gentle, delicate prayer energy and transforms it into serpent energy, which spirals back down the phallic pole to the Sèvitè. All this process balances Ashé, which, when it is in imbalance, causes disease. The Ashé as symbolized by the butterfly and by the serpent are both Ashé—just different frequencies of Ashé.

We do not recognize the seeds that develop as Loko's answers to our prayers. We don't know how to translate this type of Ashé into a form that we can use without burning ourselves up. This is why we need to align our wants and desires with our True Will.

Master of the Head

CALL ON THE MASTER OF THE HEAD to help you discern which Lwa is your Mèt tèt. Call on the Master of the Head to develop self-mastery.

OFFERINGS

Candle, braided hair cuttings, head scarf, horse crop, appropriate offerings for the Lwa that rules your head, *Vodou Visions* image for the Master of the Head.

LITANY

"Pour le Maître-tête, Loa gardian, patron, Loa qui domine l'âme. Parent divin du Gros Bon Ange, agent psychique au monde des mystères. Acceptez nos offrandes. Entrez dans nos cœurs, dans nos bras, dans nos jambes. Entrez ici. Dansez avec nous."

KREYÒL

"Pou Mèt tèt la, Lwa kap kontrolé nan'm. Fanmi Gwo Bon Anj. Aksepté ofran'n nou. Antré nan kè nou, nan bra nou, nan jam'm nou. Antré vin'n dansé avek nou."

TRANSLATION

"For the Master of the Head, patron, Lwa that dominates the soul. Divine parent of the Gwo Bon Anj. Psychic agent in the world of the Mysteries. Accept our offerings. Enter into our hearts, our arms, our legs. Enter and dance with us."

TRADITIONAL

The Master of the Head is the Lwa who most closely resonates with the character and tendencies of a Sèvitè. The Sèvitè can handle that Lwa's possessions with the greatest grace. The Master of the Head may be the Lwa who first possessed a person, or possesses them most frequently, or may be discerned through divination.

VISION

One must master one's own head before the Master of the Head presents itself. It is only when one is mature, and master of the psychic self, that the Master of the Head becomes known.

There is an interesting relationship between the master drummer seen here, who beats on the head of the drum, and the Master of the Head, who beats on the Sèvitè's head. The drum must be finely tuned and properly fed before it can be an apt instrument for ritual drumming. The master drummer beats on its head and fills it with power and rhythm. They work together. The Master of the Head beats on our heads, fills us with its power, but we must be apt containers to be able to handle the force moving through us. The Sèvitè's soul doesn't just get wiped out during possession. The Sèvitè is not just some flailing pawn of the Lwa, but must simultaneously maintain mastery of his/her own self and, at the same time, service to the Lwa. The Lwa reciprocates by both mastering and serving the head of the Sèvitè. The Lwa and Sèvitè work together. There is a relationship of mutual respect and service.

Marasa

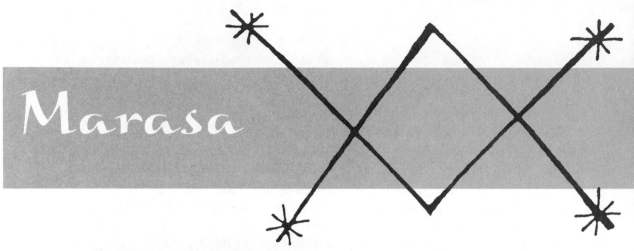

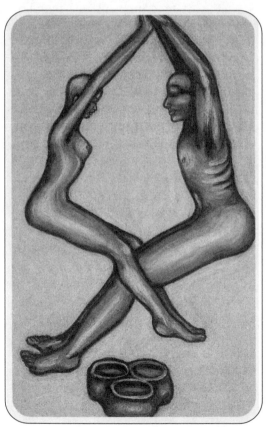

CALL ON THE MARASA for procreation, and to enhance the well-being of all children.

OFFERINGS

Candies, sweets, roasted corn, black beans and white rice, black and white candles, salt and pepper, molasses, honey, pudding, two dolls, three-chambered bowl, *Vodou Visions* image of the Marasa.

LITANY

"Pour les Marassa, Jumeaux sacrés qui se reflètent de chaque côté du miroir. Les Jumeaux qui partagent une âme, à la fois opposés, et égaux. Des deux, toutes choses. Acceptez nos offrandes. Entrez dans nos cœurs, dans nos bras, dans nos jambes. Entrez ici. Dansez avec nous."

KREYÒL

"Pou Marasa ki parèt sou dé fas youn glas. Marasa ki gen youn sèl nan'm pou yo dé. Opozé ak égal. Aksepté ofran'n nou. Antré nan kè nou, nan bra nou, nan jam'm nou. Antré vin'n dansé avek nou."

TRANSLATION

"For the Marasa, sacred duality that reflects on each side of the mirror. Twins who share one soul, at once opposite and equal. From the two, all things. Accept our offerings. Enter into our hearts, our arms, our legs. Enter and dance with us."

TRADITIONAL

The Marasa are the Divine Twins, and are associated with children. They are the first children of God, and the first Dead, and so they are the first honored at a Vodou ceremony. They are feasted on All-Souls' Night, November 1. The Marasa represent the duality of the human and the Divine in our nature. They also suggest procreation: it is through the union of two polarities that multiplicity is manifest. For this reason, the Marasa are often fed with a three-partitioned bowl. From duality, a third principle arises. The Marasa Twa represent love, truth, and justice.

The Marasa can be demanding, capricious children. They often exhibit jealousy toward one another if not treated fairly and with absolute equality. A ceremony for the Marasa is often followed by an abundant feast for children, as the Marasa have abundant appetites. The Marasa are syncretized with the Three Graces, or with Saints Damian and Comas.

VISION

The three-chambered bowl becomes the male and female polarities, issuing from unity. They come together again to retain a state of union. The third bowl is also the child that manifests from the union of opposites. This bowl is either Marasa Doca, the first girl child born after twins, or Marasa Docu, the first boy child born after twins.

Over this bowl, a male and female figure, naked, in a state of innocence and in the shape of the Marasa vèvè, pass back and forth, exchanging, like a double helix. Into the space between them, all things are manifested. From a distance, the space between the Marasa is seen to be made up of all colors from a distance, but is clear when you get close. In the same way, Sri Ramakrishna says that Kali seems black until you get close to her, as water is deep blue until you look closely and see that it is clear. This space between them is all magic. Beyond all manifestation, the Marasa remain the Marasa, innocent of their own creation.

The act of bowing to the infinite within is the action of the Twins; one half bowing to the other; the outer to the inner. The vèvè of the Marasa is the gateway to their graceful dance.

Dance

CALL ON DANCE to inspire your dancing, and to enhance appreciation for the body. Call on Dance to harmonize body, mind, and spirit.

OFFERINGS

Leotards, dancing shoes, photos or paintings of dancers, ribbons worn while dancing, do a dance for the Lwa. Dance image.

LITANY

"Pour l'Esprit de la Danse qui nous transporte hors du monde temporel jusqu'à l'avenir. En-voyez-nous les rhythmes des Dieux. En-seignez-nous comment servir l'Esprit avec les corps. Acceptez nos offrandes. Entrez dans nos cœurs, dans nos bras, dans nos jambes. Entrez ici. Dansez avec nous!"

KREYÒL

"Pou Lwa Dans´ yo kap transpôtè nou nan youn mond étènèl. Apran-nou sèvi espri yo avek kô nou. Aksepté ofran'n nou. Antré nan kè nou, nan bra nou, nan jam'm nou. Antré vin'n dansé avek nou!"

TRANSLATION

"For the Spirit of the Dance that transports us out of the temporal world into the Eternal. Send us the rhythms of the Gods. Teach us to serve Spirit with our bodies. Accept our offer-ings. Enter into our hearts, our arms, our legs. Enter and dance with us!"

TRADITIONAL

Dance is essential to Vodou. As the drum rhythms affect time, so do the dancers move through space. Dance and rhythm open an aperture in space and time. Ritual dance al-lows us to take our physical bodies with us into ecstatic trance, beyond space and time.

The traditional card that corresponds with the dance card is "the Chariot," the vehicle of Spirit. The ritualized movement of the physi-cal body sublimates and directs spiritual en-ergy and carries it beyond its own space-bound limitations.

VISION

The dancers suspend in the alchemical state of solutio: the ego melts, and is engulfed in a medium that is far more vast than itself. The ego is in danger of drowning in the Divine Ocean of Movement. The dancer here is pos-sessed by Spirit. She—or he—faces us aggres-sively, and dares us to plunge into power. The danger is of drowning, the promise is of mak-ing connection between the limited ego and the Eternal self.

The dancers move harmoniously, in their own orbit. They are stars in the great body of the heavens. As stars they hold the rhythm of destiny. The dancers step into their proper footsteps. The vèvè of the dance reflects this harmonious dance between the individual and the Spirit, the ego, and the Eternal. The vèvè spirals like DNA; like the energies of the Ida and Pingala (the upward and downward flows of energy, according to the Yogic sci-ences), exchanging, harmonizing. We dance our destiny through the great sea of life.

The Spirit spins a dancer like a will-o'-the-wisp. You can be spun out, flung out, drowned. Or you can hold on and combine your essence with the Divine.

M EDITATE ON POSSESSION when you want to bring on trance states (although it is suggested to refrain from attempting to experience full possession unless in the presence of a competent Oungan or Manbo), or when you want to feel your connection with Spirit.

Possession

OFFERINGS

Items that represent your sense of personal identity: especially those aspects of your personality that seem to have a hold over you (such as cigarettes), or that represent aspects of your personality that you wish to enhance (such as a paintbrush for an artist), *Vodou Visions* image of Possession.

LITANY

"Nous demandons l'expérience et la connaissance de la possession. Ennivrée de l'obscurité blanche, la peau est innondée de divin. Je suis plus que je suis. Acceptez nos offrandes. Entrez dans nos cœurs, dans nos bras, dans nos jambes. Entrez ici. Dansez avec nous."

KREYÒL

"Nap mandé ekspéryans ak konésans. Nan fè nwa blan sa-a Lwa-yo antré anba tout po nou. Aksepté ofran'n nou. Antré nan kè nou, nan bra nou, nan jam'm nou. Antré vin'n dansé avek nou."

TRANSLATION

"We request the experience and the knowledge of possession. Inebriated with the white darkness, the flesh is inundated with the Divine. I am more than I am. Accept our offerings. Enter into our hearts, our arms, our legs. Enter and dance with us."

TRADITIONAL

Possession is a trance state through which a profound connection is established with Spirit. During possession, a person's identity slips aside and allows the greater presence of a Lwa or Orisha to come through the vehicle of his body. The Spirit "mounts" or "rides" the person, who is referred to as "the horse." Some authorities feel that the possessing Spirit is an external force that overwhelms the personal. Others feel that the possession experience allows an internal, archetypal presence to emerge from within the person. Through possession, the Lwa and Orisha enter into the community. The crisis of possession is brought on by a combination of the focused discipline of a spiritual community, cultural expectation based on tradition, and the ecstatic release of "the horse."

VISION

There is a certain violence implied in the act of possession, in the fight to mount the horse, and in the struggle of the horse to contain the God—to bring on the possession, agree to it, and survive it. This all is not unlike the power plays and penetration of a sexual relationship. The vision is steeped in sexual tension. Here the horse takes the receptive female role, allowing penetration by the Lwa. The God takes the active, masculine role by mounting the Sèvitè and depositing the seed of its Divinity within the flesh.

The Lwa is huge, white, insistent, overwhelming. The small black horse could take all that power into her body. They are united by a serpentine rein that issues from within the Sèvitè's mouth and is held by the Lwa. The Lwa's clawlike hand rips through the image, spilling blood-red passion throughout the vision.

Though the Lwa's presence is huge, the Sèvitè will not remember the Other within herself. The tendency is to tear oneself away from the God to remain locked inside one's insistent personal identity. But in the eyes of our beloved, we recognize the indwelling presence of Divinity. In erotic love, we recognize the struggle and subsequent release into union. We extend beyond ourselves, into the Divine.

Couché

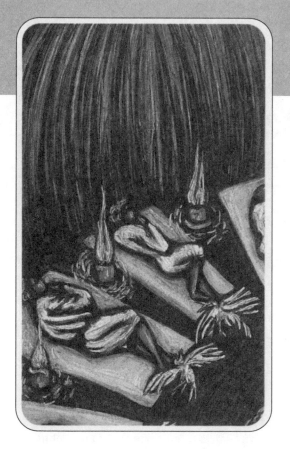

CALL ON COUCHÉ when you want to re-treat from the external world in order to reconnect with your spiritual center.

OFFERINGS
Carrots, potatoes (grown in the earth), organic initiation paste, grapes in water (seeds are swallowed during ritual so that they can grow into a new being), seeds, Couché image.

LITANY
"Nous demandons l'expérience et la connaissance de la rêverie initiatoire du Couché. Chaqu'un se retrouve en soi. La grâce qui germe dans les ténèbres silencieuses de la matrice. Acceptez nos offrandes. Entrez dans nos cœurs, dans nos bras, dans nos jambes. Entrez ici. Dansez avec nous."

KREYÒL

"Nou mandé ekspérians ak konésans ké Couché poté pou nou. Gras-la kap jèmin nan ténèb matris-la. Aksepté ofran'n nou. Antré nan kè nou, nan bra nou, nan jam'm nou. Antré vin'n dansé avek nou."

TRANSLATION

"We request the experience and knowledge of the initiatory dreaming of Couché. Each secluded within. The seed which germinates in the silent darkness of the womb. Accept our offerings. Enter into our hearts, our arms, our legs. Enter and dance with us."

TRADITIONAL

"Couché" means "put to bed." Couché is an initiation ritual that usually lasts from seven to nine days. The initiate is shut in a small initiation chamber and instructed to lie on the left side to "dream." Occasionally, the Couché is punctuated by intense rituals of one sort or another. During the Couché, chickens are sacrificed, and their feathers are attached to the initiate with blood. It is not established at the outset of the initiation whether one will "take up the asson" to become an Oungan or Manbo. This is determined by the Lwa. You may also Couché again, after taking up the asson, in order to get back in touch with the Spirit. The Couché may be seen as a spiritual retreat that symbolically concentrates many of the themes of the Vodoun experience: the concept of slavery, the descent into the raw depths of identity, and the whole life/death/rebirth cycle. The Couché represents the death of the old self, and rebirth in the Spirit.

VISION

Look into the scene of this vision through the eyes of an initiate. In the fetal position in the initiatory chamber, feel the cool, smelly dampness of organic paste on your forehead, and hear in the distance the drums of the community without the hut. In the womb, the baby's constant lullaby is the rhythmic beating of its mother's heart.

Gaze at the other initiates through candlelight and shadow. The glowing candles illuminate other forms here and there—a chicken, a grass mat, something half present in the shadows. All the reclining bodies in the fetal position next to each other look like bodies in a Pharaoh's tomb. There is the same silence and same mysterious quality that must be present in a Pharaoh's tomb. There's nothing you can really say about either end of it—the death of a king or the birth of an initiate. The vision is all feeling and image. It is not at all verbal, except for the word "bindu," which is Hindu for "seed," and the word "bijou," which is French for "jewel."

Planted in silence, the living seed becomes a gem.

The Couché is a period of seclusion that gives the initiate entrance into the great work of revelation. The point within the circle. The initiated member of the community emerges, newborn, from the silence of the hut. Sometimes we have to be put to sleep in order to put our doubts aside and receive Spirit. We must give blood—the sacrificed chicken here—to break through into konesans. The old self must die. Life eats life.

"Couché" in French can have several meanings. It can refer to death, or sleep, or to making love. In the initiation hut, feel the erotic desire of the initiate to attain union with Spirit, the willingness of the initiate to let his or her old self die, and the fertile, rich silence in which the world can reveal its true self.

See this through the initiate's eyes, even though those eyes are packed with a cool, fermenting compress that is organic and faintly foul. There are blood and chicken feathers sticking to your feet, and sweat sticking to your body. In Vodou, the Spirit comes into the body, into the earth within the womb of matter. Spirit made flesh.

The Market

WORK WITH THE MARKET when you are engaging in commerce, or when you seek to understand the underlying principles of economic realities.

OFFERINGS

Discarded food or items from the market, dust from the crossroads of a market, Market image.

LITANY

"Pour le Marché, centre matériel de la communité humaine. La Roue de la Fortune, où sont cachés les enigmes, les mystères. Tout est en vente; rien n'est gratuit au monde, et le Marché tourne toujours. Acceptez nos offrandes. Entrez dans nos cœurs, dans nos bras, dans nos jambes. Entrez ici. Dansez avec nous!"

KREYÒL

"Pou Maché sant matérièl kominate-a. Koté ki chajé ak mistè. Tout't bagay pou van'n. Anyin pa pou anyim nan lé mond. Maché-a ap fonktioné. Aksepté ofran'n nou. Antré nan kè nou, nan bra nou, nan jam'm nou. Antré vin'n dansé avek nou!"

TRANSLATION

"For the Market, material center of the human community. Wheel of Fortune, where riddles and Mysteries are hidden. Everything is for sale; nothing is free in the world, and always the Market turns. Accept our offerings. Enter into our hearts, our arms, our legs. Enter and dance with us!"

TRADITIONAL

The marketplace is a metaphor for human civilization. It stands on the crossroads between energy and value, the crossroads where the world meets. The oldest operating market in the United States is the New Orleans French Market, pictured here. An endless parade of visitors from every part of the world pass through its tumultuous array of produce, as well as crafts and trash, available for sale every day.

When people make saint in the Santería tradition, they are supposed to steal something from the Market to signify that everything in the world is owned by the Orishas, so they can take anything back from the material world whenever they desire. The Santero or Santera must accompany the initiate in order to pay the vendor surreptitiously for the "theft."

VISION

A great cacophony of action and motion unfolds in New Orleans's French Market. Hidden in plain sight, at the center of all the commotion, are the powerful beings associated with the tarot path of the "Wheel of Fortune": Hermanubis, the Serpent, and the Sphinx. Great Mysteries are embodied within the action of the Market, but they are hard to see for all the surface materialism. The world is completely driven by the economy of the Market. The competition drives people to be in control of the Market, like the Sphinx, at the center of the wheel. But it is a mistake to think that having the answers to the Sphinx's riddles will transform you into the Sphinx. Bear in mind that the Sphinx asks the riddles. She does not answer them. It is essential to ask who is being served, as it is essential to look into the sources of power. The Serpent represents the downward flow of power into nature; Hermanubis represents the evolution of power back to its Divine source. Both movements must be mastered and balanced before one can attain the powers of the Sphinx; to know, to will, to dare, to keep silent. Then one sits, poised at the eternal center, while the wheel turns and turns.

Put on the mask of Hermanubis, the Sphinx, or the Serpent, and walk through the chaos of the marketplace while embodying the invisible power of each of these beings. Are your perspective and experience of the Market altered by each ancient archetype?

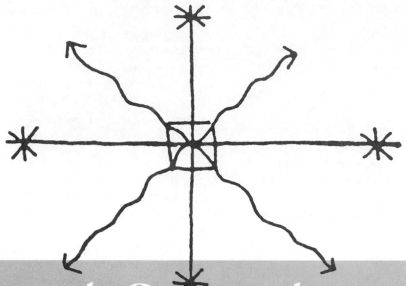

Secret Societies

CALL ON SECRET SOCIETIES for facing and integrating the shadow.

OFFERINGS

Fetishes, sigils of secret societies, ropes, chains, image of Secret Societies.

LITANY

"Pour les Sociétés Secrètes qui travaillent dans la nuit, dans les places secrètes, inconnues, souterraines. Enseignez-nous. Montrez-nous l'essence subtile et psychique sous le monde terreste. Acceptez nos offrandes. Entrez dans nos cœurs, dans nos bras, dans nos jambes. Entrez ici. Dansez avec nous."

KREYÒL

"Pou Sosyété Sékrèt kap travay nan nuit´, nan koté sèkrè. Apran'nou. Montré nou esans subtil ak psichie ki an la tè. Aksepté ofran'n nou. Antré nan kè nou, nan bra nou, nan jam'm nou. Antré vin'n dansé avek nou."

TRANSLATION

"For Secret Societies who work in the night, in secret places unknown, underground. Teach us. Show us the subtle and psychic essence beneath the topside world. Accept our offerings. Enter into our hearts, our arms, our legs. Enter and dance with us."

TRADITIONAL

Bòkò or sorcerers join together to form brotherhoods, or secret societies. These occult societies originated in sorcerer societies in West Africa. The supernatural practices attributed to secret societies may or may not be imaginary. They are supposed to meet at night—especially in the crossroads of cemeteries. They're reputed to commit all manner of terrible acts, including turning their victims into animals that are sacrificed in ritual or butchered at the meat market. They are said to confer Vodou passports that allow safe passage into secret ceremonies all over Haiti, where they hold special courts in which judgments are passed and penalties incurred upon those who have transgressed against their code. Some are said to be able to transform themselves into animals and birds at will.

It's more likely that most secret societies are made up of bòkò who share occult knowledge and acceptance of one another. They are certainly bound by their oaths and traditions of membership. The secret societies effect liaisons that are both dangerous and powerful. The secret societies may be seen as preservers of the magical techniques of transformation.

VISION

The image is expressed on two levels. In one, the person being judged is in the form of Justice, wearing a blindfold. This form of Justice is blind—no amount of arguing your case will alter its absolute rule. This form of Justice has everything to do with cause and effect. Nature affords just results according to its own inexorable rule. The community that sits in judgment are the animal faces. If you are not in sync with the community, it will judge you. These people with animal faces are also the shadow self. If you try to repress the shadow, it becomes monstrous and devours you. You can give it too much power. But if you lift up the blindfold and look at it fearlessly, it will communicate the secrets of your self to you. It will animate the darkness of the psyche, just as these animal eyes betray secret life in the shadows of the forest.

On another level, it is each of us that stands there before the dark forest. In searching for secret societies, we each search for our self. In standing before the judgment of greater powers, we judge ourselves. It is our own vigilant eyes that look into our secret selves. We keep secrets from ourselves. The secrets that we keep from ourselves keep our hands bound in fear. The vital animals loose in the forest offer empowerment. All we have to do is walk through fear and let go of that which restricts us.

To present yourself to secret societies, you have to be both humble and brave.

ALL ON ZONBI when you wish to temper an overly assertive nature, or if you wish to develop the perilous abilities of the shaman.

OFFERINGS
Snakeskin, govi jars, tea lights floating in water, Zonbi image.

LITANY
"Pour le Grand Zombi, à la fois mort et vivant, qui marche sur les points shamaniques entre les mondes. Entourez-vous autour de moi, serpent de la sagesse, chuchotez-moi vos divinations. Acceptez nos offrandes. Entrez dans nos cœurs, dans nos bras, dans nos jambes. Entrez ici. Dansez avec nous!"

KREYÒL
"Pou Zonbi, mò-vivan kap maché nan pwen shamanie ant dé mond. Antouré moin. Palé

Zonbi

nan zorey moin. Aksepté ofran'n nou. Antré nan kè nou, nan bra nou, nan jam'm nou. Antré vin'n dansé avek nou!"

TRANSLATION

"For le Grand Zonbi, at once dead and alive, who walks the shamanic points between worlds. Wrap yourself around me. Whisper your divinations to me. Accept our offerings. Enter into our hearts, our arms, our legs. Enter and dance with us!"

TRADITIONAL

The Zonbi in Haiti is a person whose Will or Gwo Bon Anj has been stolen, leaving a soulless body. The Zonbi has lost his soul, but continues to live as an empty, physical shell. These living dead are slaves to the bòkò or Zonbi master who has stolen their soul through a combination of magic, herbal paralysis, and psychologically traumatizing ritual.

When Vodou traveled to New Orleans, a snake was often used in ceremonies as a transmitter of the Spirit to the horses. The snake became referred to as "Le Grand Zombi."

VISION

The concept of the Zonbi in New Orleans is as the oracular Spirit that speaks through the snake, not the soulless shell of the Haitian Zonbi.

The Haitian Zonbi has her mouth sewn shut, but she is dancing with the snake of the New Orleans Zonbi. The Ti Bon Anj dances above the head of the woman Zonbi. Her hands are up as she reaches for Spirit. As the Ti Bon Anj comes to her, it entwines around her body as a serpent. What is the connection between the Zonbi and the traditional card of "the Hanged Man" that corresponds to this path? And what is the connection between the Zonbi concept in Haiti and its seeming opposite in New Orleans?

The Hanged Man corresponds to water, the Waters of the Abyss. In death, we become intimately involved with the Waters of the Abyss.

The body is gone, allowing the personality to become diffused and dissolved in the Waters as a person becomes a Spirit. Haitians live in terror of becoming a Zonbi for whom the body lives, but the Spirit is gone—the absolute perversion of the usual process.

The Hanged Man is suspended at the crossroads. He is in between, hanging in this suspended manner from the Tree of Life. He gives up his lesser self in sacrifice, and gives himself over to the greater power and greater support of the Divine, from which he is suspended. It is not his Will, but the Will of God, that is moving through his body and personality, thus reflecting the typical mode of shamanism.

As Haitian Vodou traveled into the United States, where shamanism was a powerful force among Native Americans, the concept of the Zonbi became a Lwa. The Zonbi became something that could be worshiped, an empowering force. There had to be a way to survive the experience of slavery—of becoming a Zonbi—and turn that experience into something else. What can be terrifying and destructive becomes positive when you're able to move into the Waters of the Abyss and survive. You begin to act as a shaman in between worlds; not fully alive, but not dead either. You're just in the water, in between, able to go back and forth. It becomes a healing journey. The shaman doesn't work from a personal, human point of view. He works at the crossroads, bringing things back and forth. Le Grand Zonbi operates from an altered perspective, through which normal people must, in fact, seem like Zonbi as they go through their blind, habitual, patterned behaviors as though they were soulless slaves.

Worshiping the Lwa of le Grand Zonbi pulls the snake of knowledge and wisdom and Kundalini power through. It is the gift of freedom to look into the face of the Zonbi and experience it, and come out as a steed of God. As le Grand Zonbi rides us, we break into freedom.

C ALL ON LÈ MÒ when you wish to honor the Ancestors, or when you wish to communicate with a loved one who has died. Call on Lè Mò for overcoming fear of death, or for understanding of the Mysteries of death.

Lè Mò

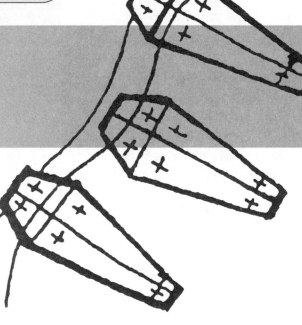

OFFERINGS

Flowers, basin of water, candles, marigold petals, foods and drinks that the Dead enjoyed while still living, *Vodou Visions* image of Lè Mò.

LITANY

"Pour les Morts. Pour ceux qui sont passés par la voile mystérieuse. Vous nous avez crées comme nous sommes. Nous vous devons la vie. Nous vous rapellons. Retournez d'en bas de l'eau. Acceptez nos offrandes. Entrez dans nos cœurs, dans nos bras, dans nos jambes. Entrez ici. Dansez avec nous!"

KREYÒL

"Pou Lè Mò. Sé gras à ou, nou la. Nou sonjé ou. Rétounin, soti an ba dlo-a. Aksepté ofran'n nou. Antré nan kè nou, nan bra nou, nan jam'm nou. Antré vin'n dansé avek nou!"

TRANSLATION

"For the Dead. For those who have passed through the mysterious veil. You have made us what we are. We owe you our lives. We remember you. Return from beneath the Waters. Accept our offerings. Enter into our hearts, our arms, our legs. Enter and dance with us!"

TRADITIONAL

Lè Mò are the Dead. They return through the Abysmal Waters to Ginen, ancestral home of Vodou, under the sea. The Dead have experienced the transforming Mysteries that surround the cycles of life and death. The Dead give advice and guidance from their watery realm. From their legions, the Lwa arise.

VISION

Wave upon wave of innumerable generations of the Dead appear flowing like a viscous tide. Yet each one of the Dead was so utterly precious to the lives that surrounded him. Within that sea of grief and tears, and the inevitable call to meet one's destiny, there is an endless surge of love. Our hands reach to the Dead, both in initial loss as the Dead are taken from us, but also to pull them back from the Waters of the Abyss.

All of this is beyond words. The Mysteries of death are held within silence. Intellectualization dishonors the powerful Mystery of love that rests within and transcends that of death. The Dead know all this and so do we, the living.

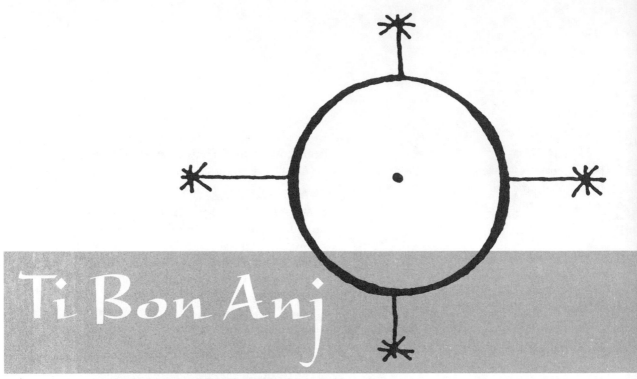

Ti Bon Anj

CALL ON THE TI BON ANJ when you are experiencing identity problems, when you wish to improve your self-image, or when you wish to align your actions with your True Will.

OFFERINGS

A talisman of your Will, your astrological birth chart, image of Ti Bon Anj.

LITANY

"Pour le Ti Bon Ange, Ange lumineux. Élément culturel de l'individualité. Zero est deux. Montrez-nous comment nous sommes. Montrez-nous notre volonté. Acceptez nos offrandes. Entrez dans nos cœurs, dans nos bras, dans nos jambes. Entrez ici. Dancez avec nous."

KREYÒL

"Pou Ti Bon Anj. Eléman kiltirel individialité. Zéro sé dé. Montré nou kouman nou yé. Montré-nou volonté nou. Aksepté ofran'n nou. Antré nan kè nou, nan bra nou, nan jam'm nou. Antré vin'n dansé avek nou."

TRANSLATION

"For the Ti Bon Anj, luminous cultural element of individuality. Zero is two. Show us who we are. Show us our Will. Accept our offerings. Enter into our hearts, our arms, our legs. Enter and dance with us."

TRADITIONAL

The Ti Bon Anj, "The Little Good Angel," and the Gwo Bon Anj, "The Big Good Angel," are the two aspects that make up the Vodoun concept of soul. The Vodoun soul is the reflected, metaphysical double of the body. The Ti Bon Anj is attached to the Gwo Bon Anj, and includes ideas of conscience, identity, and personality. The Ti Bon Anj is incapable of lying. I think of the Ti Bon Anj as corresponding to the Qabalistic concept of the Ruach, which is the aspect of soul that includes the intellect, the ego, and all that we think of as our identity. The Ti Bon Anj stays with the vehicle of the body during life. It is the objective, moral conscience that tells us how we should act and integrate experience. But we don't have to listen. Nothing is more frustrating than being able to recognize destructive behavior in yourself, and to go ahead and do it anyway.

VISION

The Ti Bon Anj is luminous, full of movement and light. A woman emerges from a ritual hut carrying a kanari, an earthenware jar that is said to hold a person's soul for safekeeping. The kanari holds the Gwo Bon Anj just as the body holds the Ti Bon Anj. The soul pours in and out at the time of possession. It seems precarious to trust one's soul to a kanari in the care of an Oungan. What if it broke or got lost? But the body is a precarious container as well. Upon death, the Ti Bon Anj rises beyond the clay and water of the body. During life, the objective Spirit, the Ti Bon Anj, protects the body and tells us the truth. The grace of the Angel walks through the land of shadows with us, and trusts and works with us in spite of how recklessly we live. When we are bad to ourselves, when we try to be who we are not, the Ti Bon Anj reflects back to us, the watcher within. It will not lie to us. Luminous, its eyes watch us, know us, and remind us of the truth of ourselves that is contained within the darkness of our earthenware jars.

CALL ON COURIR LE MARDI GRAS when you wish to enhance creative energy, or when you wish to increase masculine energy.

Courir le Mardi Gras

OFFERINGS

Goats' horns, chicken, masks or costumes from Courir le Mardi Gras. Horsehair or whip, any symbol of Capricorn, goat cheese. Courir le Mardi Gras image.

LITANY

"Courir le Mardi Gras, l'energie sans fin. Monde sans terminaison. Courir, courir le Mardi Gras. Mystérieux et terrible, Dieu se sacrifie. De l'innocence sacrée, tout est crée. Montrez-moi comment apprécier toutes choses. Acceptez nos offrandes. Entrez dans nos cœurs, dans nos bras, dans nos jambes. Entrez ici. Dansez avec nous!"

KREYÒL

"Dansé nan Madigra, san pran souf. Dansé, dansé nan Madigra. Koté Gran Mèt-la sakrifié prop tèt li. Montré mwen kouman poum kab aprésié bagay sou tè-a. Aksepté ofran'n nou. Antré nan kè nou, nan bra nou, nan jam'm nou. Antré vin'n dansé avek nou!"

TRANSLATION

"Run the Mardi Gras, endless energy. World without end. Run, run the Mardi Gras. Mysterious and terrible, God sacrifices himself. From sacred innocence, all is created. Show me how to appreciate all things. Accept our offerings. Enter into our hearts, our arms, our legs. Enter and dance with us!"

TRADITIONAL

Courir le Mardi Gras refers to a fairly bizarre Cajun tradition in southwestern Louisiana parishes. Dressed in masks, harlequin costumes, and pointy hats, riders go from house to house on Mardi Gras day. The owner of each house along the course throws a live chicken off the roof, while the riders race around, fighting for the chicken. Whoever catches the chicken breaks its neck and ties it to his saddle as a trophy. All the collected chickens are put into a gumbo that is prepared for the—by that point—drunken revelers.

VISION

A chicken is flung head-down from the rooftop. We are filled with a blind, unbreathing terror. Horses' hooves thunder around and below our awful collapse through unsheltering air. Their nostrils flare, and there is a glimpse of a crazed eye. Humans scream, hoot, and tear at once-glorious feathers. We hope to find meaning within brutal madness, or at least some spark of mercy or humanity.

The Christian myth: God gave his only son who died for our sins. Just once and it is done? Maya Deren says the Lwa themselves are in the sacrificial offering. When the offerings are sacrificed, they become the Lwa. Here the Divine makes the sacrifice of itself, enters into the flesh and suffers with us, in the same way that the Holy Guardian Angel suffers through our self-destructive behaviors with us. But the Divine lives simultaneously in the absolute, and so does not suffer blindly as we do. Does the Angel see the Angelic, beyond the madness and frenzy of the horses, or within the barbaric force of the riders?

Aleister Crowley, a notorious ceremonial magician who founded the Thelemic religion, advised getting rid of ruined forms, and transforming the rest. All over the globe Crowley's followers, Thelemites, offer up sacred elixir in frenzied devotion to the Egyptian hawk-headed Lord, Horus.

I offer life force to the Lwa. Will they receive it? I offer the unbridled energy of life. Ashé!

C ALL ON DELUGE whenever you are
about to undertake a technological
project, or when you wish to be washed
clean of toxins. Call on Deluge when you
wish to find balance and place within
Nature, and within the Waters.

Deluge

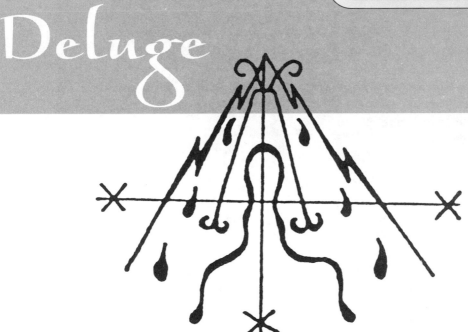

OFFERINGS

Floodwater, sticks that have been stripped by beavers, rocks from a levee, sand bags, Deluge image.

LITANY

"Quand il vient, le Déluge, je vais plonger dedans. Quand il arrive, le Déluge, tout va être nettoyé; tous va se dissoudre. Rien ne reste. Tous est dans les Eaux. Acceptez nos offrandes. Entrez dans nos cœurs, dans nos bras, dans nos jambes. Entrez ici. Dansez avec nous!"

KREYÒL

"Kan Délij´ nan vini, map plonjé la dan´. Kan délij´ nan vini, lap nétoyé tout´ bagay, lap fon´ tout´ bagay. Anyin pap rété. Tout´ bagay sé nan Dlo. Aksepté ofran'n nou. Antré nan kè nou, nan bra nou, nan jam'm nou. Antré vin'n dansé avek nou!"

TRANSLATION

"When the Deluge comes, I will dive in. When the Deluge comes, all will be cleaned; all will dissolve. Nothing remains. All is in the Waters. Accept our offerings. Enter into our hearts, our arms, our legs. Enter and dance with us!"

TRADITIONAL

New Orleans stands below sea level, and below river level. The Army Corps of Engineers has constructed an extensive levee system to guard the city from potential flooding from the Mississippi River or from Lake Pontchartrain. Pumping stations pump excess water out of the ground table whenever there is a serious downpour, and spillways release water into the Gulf whenever there is danger of flooding. Nevertheless, the city often floods in especially low-lying areas. And the Mississippi strives to move its course away from the city, farther west.

This scene depicts a particular location in uptown New Orleans where an electric tower marks a ritual site on the levee. It is a place of powerful Ashé, which aptly displays the confluence of scientific and mythic meaning.

VISION

Deluge represents technology versus the primordial force of Nature. We worship technology. We build electric towers to artificially illuminate the world. We build levee systems to contain the powerful force of life. We build roads and vehicles that devour the world's resources. We condition the air, irradiate fruits and vegetables, control the environment. What is repressed in one place explodes somewhere else. Relentlessly, the river moves, surges, overwhelms its banks. The towers fall; boundaries shatter. The Waters rush and take us. You do not pick the Lwa. The Lwa pick you.

The struggle between science and religion goes on. We worship science and make ourselves technological Gods.

There is life and the Will to control life. There is love, and there is the love supreme. There is the Will to live, and the Will to die. The Waters flow through life and death, reconciler of the opposites. Beyond the boundaries, all is undifferentiated.

The Water that we come from is the Water to which we return. Water upon Water. Deluge.

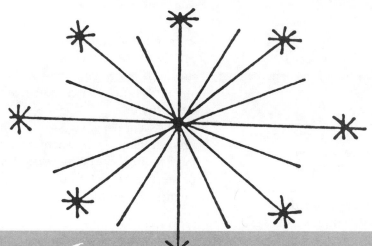

Zétwal

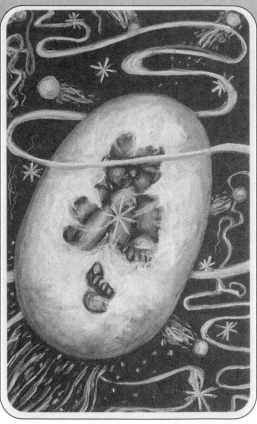

CALL ON ZÉTWAL when you wish to bring out your potential, or when you wish to realize your destiny.

OFFERINGS

Rhinestones, star fruit, star-shaped flowers, eggs painted with stars, candy eggs, Zétwal image.

LITANY

"Pour Z'Étoile, bébé dans l'oeuf. Ange qui garde le destin. Montrez-nous notre vraie volonté. Ange potentiel, source de l'espoir, pleurez sur nous avec votre lumière céleste. Acceptez nos offrandes. Entrez dans nos cœurs, dans nos bras, dans nos jambes. Entrez ici. Dansez avec nous!"

KREYÒL

"Pou Zétwal, bebe nan ze kap kontrolé destin nou. Montré nou vré volonté-a. Anj pouvwa, sous´ espwa, binyin-nou ak limiè sélès-la. Aksepté ofran'n nou. Antré nan kè nou, nan bra nou, nan jam'm nou. Antré vin'n dansé avek nou!"

TRANSLATION

"For Zétwal, babe in the egg who guards destiny. Show us our True Will. Angel of potential, source of hope, shower your celestial light upon us. Accept our offerings. Enter into our hearts, our arms, our legs. Enter and dance with us!"

TRADITIONAL

In Vodoun cosmology, the world is surrounded by waters above and below, which perfectly and eternally mirror one another. Zétwal, the star, charts the cosmic course of a person's destiny through the black waters of the night sky. Like shimmering starlight, the soul's meaning glistens through the passage of life experience.

VISION

Each particle of cool, astral light is a baby in an egg. Each egg is a double crossroads. One crossroad symbolizes the intersection of the physical with the invisible. The other extends that intersection through space and time. Danbala and Ayida Wèdo's World Egg is similarly etched with the double crossroads. Both of these images have to do with potential, which germinates through time in a vast, star-filled space. We are all searching though time for the meaning of our immortal souls.

Zétwal holds each of our destinies. It is the potential that lies within the course of our lives. To embrace destiny is to do gladly that which we must do. Zétwal is within and behind our experience, waiting for us to awaken to ourselves. The babe in the egg floats in its perfect course through the vast space of potential. It germinates silently as we constellate a personality, only to find that who we have become is who we always were meant to be.

Zétwal is our DNA of hope and of True Will. We move through a life of deep emotion in a world that more often than not engenders great pain and sorrow, to make ourselves a soul, the seed identity and central truth of which resides in Zétwal.

Magic Mirror

T HE MAGIC MIRROR calls up occult
power, lunar powers, magic, and sorcery.

OFFERINGS
Quicksilver, mercury, silver bowls of water,
mirrors, silver, purple, or indigo candles,
Magic Mirror image.

LITANY

"Miroir Magique, miroir cosmique. Surface de tension qui repousse et reflète les images, de l'illusion, et de la vérité. Reconsiliateur des eaux en bas et des émotions en haut, les Invisibles en bas, et les vivants en haut. Tout se reflète sur votre surface. Montrez-nous votre vraie image. Acceptez nos offrandes. Entrez dans nos cœurs, dans nos bras, dans nos jambes. Entrez ici. Dansez avec nous!"

KREYÒL

"Miwa Majik, Miwa Kosmik. Sifas kap montré imaj rêv ak réalité. Kap rékonsilié sak an-ro ak sak an-ba, Mò an-ba vivan an-ro. Montré-nou realité-a. Aksepté ofran'n nou. Antré nan kè nou, nan bra nou, nan jam'm nou. Antré vin'n dansé avek nou!"

TRANSLATION

"Magic Mirror, cosmic mirror. Surface of tension which pushes back and reflects images both of illusion and truth. Reconciler of the Waters below and the emotions above, the Invisibles below, and the living above. All is reflected on your surface. Show us your true image. Accept our offerings. Enter into our hearts, our arms, our legs. Enter and dance with us!"

TRADITIONAL

The Magic Mirror in Vodou is a metaphor for the cosmic world inhabited by the Invisibles. The Lwa are reflected upon the mirror, and are approached in ritual through mirror images and reversed gestures. The mirror is the glassy, reflective surface of the Abysmal Waters. They and the Waters of Life reflect each other on the mirror surface. The Gwo Bon Anj mirrors the body on the surface of the Waters. When the body dies, the soul sinks into the watery depths.

VISION

The Magic Mirror bobs into view, buoyed on turbulent waters. Two hands secure its otherwise precarious balance. The hands come from within the depths of the Waters where the Dead reside. In life, it is our image that reflects on the surface of the Mirror, but in death, we dive deeply below the surface. The body with its senses draws the soul into interaction with the world. The Gwo Bon Anj is drawn through the cosmic mirror into interaction with the world. The world and ourselves are reflected looking into the mirror. When we die, our Gwo Bon Anj enters back down into the Waters beneath the surface. By reaching in the mirror we stir up the reflective surface that divides below from above. We reach through the mirror to draw the Lwa from below.

The mirror is profoundly connected to the path of Madanm Lalinn. It is Lalinn who confers the power of the Magic Mirror. She is seen in the upper-right-hand, as a night-sky Goddess, who holds the crescent moon in her lap. The Marasa, as well, are appropriate patrons of the mirror, which—like the Twins—reflects that which is exactly opposite, but exactly the same. The images shown in the Magic Mirror are hieroglyphs that reflect true things, but that also have the magical power to transform.

We live, unfortunately, in a world that cares to look no deeper than surface appearance. Our world and our ability to imagine have become sick from attending exclusively to soulless surface illusion. We have forgotten that body, mind, spirit, and soul are all interconnected. Through Vodou, we experience our bodies as sacred spaces. We invoke into our bodies what cannot be seen on the surface because it must be reclaimed from the depths of the Eternal Waters. The Magic Mirror illustrates the illusion of appearance, and the truth of what is not apparent.

When you meditate with the Magic Mirror, make it your eyes that you see. Finally, our eyes must do more than just see the world. They must see into it.

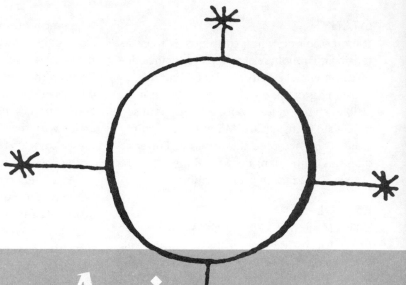

Gwo Bon Anj

ALL ON THE GWO BON ANJ when you seek the meaning of your life, when you wish to perceive yourself as a child of Spirit, or when you wish to see the sacred potential within others. Call on the Gwo Bon Anj when you are having a midlife crisis!

OFFERINGS

Egg painted as self-portrait, mirror painted as a self-portrait, white candle, Gwo Bon Anj image.

LITANY

"Pour le Gros Bon Ange, mon esprit, mon âme, ma psyche, mon moi qui ne meurt pas avec le corps. Mon double immortel, invisible, mais réel. L'ombre immortelle projetée dans l'invisible. Allez-vous devenir un Loa? Acceptez nos offrandes. Entrez dans nos cœurs, dans nos bras, dans nos jambes. Entrez ici, dansez avec nous!"

KREYÒL

"Pou Gwo Bon Anj-la, espri-moin, nanm moin, moin minm ki pa mouri lè kò moin mouri. Marasa immòtèl, invisib min réyèl. Lonbraj imòtèl ki projeté nan linvisib. Eské wap tounin youn Lwa? Aksepté ofran'n nou. Antré nan kè nou, nan bra nou, nan jam'm nou. Antré vin'n dansé avek nou!"

TRANSLATION

"For the Gwo Bon Anj, my Spirit, my soul, my psyche, my self, who does not die with the body. My immortal Twin, invisible but real. The immortal shadow, cast into the invisible. Are you going to become a Lwa? Accept our offerings. Enter into our hearts, our arms, our legs. Enter and dance with us!"

TRADITIONAL

The Gwo Bon Anj and the Ti Bon Anj are the two aspects of the Vodoun soul. When a person is born, they look out over the mirrored surface of the Waters. The mirror reflects back to them the image of their metaphysical double, or soul. This presiding Spirit, or Gwo Bon Anj, will live within you throughout your life.

If you read several books, or talk with several Oungan or Manbo, you are likely to hear differing, even contradictory definitions of which aspect of soul holds which functions. Some say that the Gwo Bon Anj is the part of the soul that remains by the grave when the body dies, and can be kept in a kanari jar. It can be put aside during possession, or stolen and trapped by a bòkò in the making of a Zonbi. Others place all those functions with the Ti Bon Anj. Gwo Bon Anj means "Big Good Angel." I understand it to be the immortal aspect of soul that survives death, goes into the Waters, and reincarnates into future generations. I see it as corresponding roughly to the Qabalistic concept of the Neschamah, the aspect of soul that relates to the over-soul, or greater self, and that is capable of becoming a Lwa.

VISION

The Gwo Bon Anj is the immortal twin of the time- and space-bound body. It carries within its spiritual fire the numinous meaning of the soul. Overwhelming and life-affirming love entices the soul to posit itself into the world. It is the magnetism of love that draws the soul back beyond the veil into the Eternal.

We are alone and isolated, but our twin, the Gwo Bon Anj, shapes our soul, and straddles the Abyss with us. The Gwo Bon Anj is born as a spiritual legacy from the love of the Mèt tèt. Globules of life spin off from a molten source. Babes suck their thumb in the traditional "sign of silence." When the body dies, the Gwo Bon Anj becomes the mystical babe, cast into the invisible. The amniotic sac is full of electric life energy. Warm, molten love.

The Gwo Bon Anj is a light shadow, cast across the silent expanse of the invisible.

Zétwal shows the babe that holds potential and that holds Will. The Gwo Bon Anj is the field of soul, in which the Will expresses.

What kind of world would it be if we all focused on the Gwo Bon Anj when we encountered each other? What if we thought of the Lwa that each might one day become when we look into the face of the Other?

CALL ON THE ANCESTORS to learn
about the history that is codified in
your blood. Call on them to reclaim and
embrace your legacy, and to connect
with your place in history.

The Ancestors

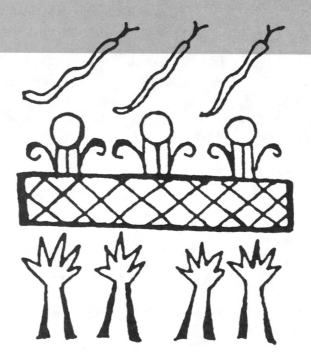

OFFERINGS

Foods your own family Ancestors liked, characteristic foods of your nationality, Ancestors' image.

LITANY

"Pour les Ancêtres qui nous ont précédés. Vous nous avez crées comme nous sommes. Nous vous conduisons jusqu'à l'avenir. Servez-vous de nos levres, nos yeux, de nos oreilles. Acceptez nos offrandes. Entrez dans nos cœurs, dans nos bras, dans nos jambes. Entrez ici. Dansez avec nous."

KREYÒL

"Pou Zansèt-yo ki té la anvan nou. Sé gras a-yo ké nou la. Nap pral ansam nan diréksion Laveni. Sèvi ak bouch-nou jé-nou, zorey-nou. Aksepté ofran'n nou. Antré nan kè nou, nan bra nou, nan jam'm nou. Antré vin'n dansé avek nou."

TRANSLATION

"For the Ancestors who preceded us. You made us as we are. We carry you into the future. Use our lips, our eyes, our ears. Accept our offerings. Enter into our hearts, our arms, our legs. Enter and dance with us."

TRADITIONAL

The Ancestors can be specific to you and your family, or they can be general—the venerated ones who came before—or they can be archetypal as they become Lwa. The Ancestors command respect and honor. In return, they give us the dignity of our inherited strengths and gifts. The Ancestors are the cultural roots of a spiritual or Divine tree. The Vodoun is rooted firmly in the rich soil of ancestor worship. Remember who you are, and where you came from. Carry that flame forward, beyond your own limited history.

VISION

Our Ancestors are irreplaceable. They were who they were. They made us who we are. But we carry them forward into the future. They see through our eyes, hear through our ears, touch through our hands, speak through our mouths. Our memory keeps them alive, and alters who they were. Ancestry is both fixed and fluid. Without ongoing human memory, the Lwa could not exist. Without the Lwa, there would be no ongoing generations of humans.

The Lwa riding the float are the Godforms Horus and Harpocrates. People beg for outward show, when what they really want is the inner reality. The Lwa are just as bound by the people and the aeon, and they have to remain on the float, over the heads of the people. We are absolutely bound to each other. Are the Gods real, or do we make them real through our worship of them?

Horus makes the occult gesture "the sign of the enterer." Harpocrates makes "the sign of silence." One is active and one passive. The rites and symbols that surround us, like the pageantry of Carnival in this vision, are active signals of the influence of our heritage. But there are submerged effects as well, in the collective unconscious. These promptings are deep within us. Hands reach in with profound longing for these racial memories. The ancestral Lwa are anxious to meet our need. This relationship between the living and the Dead can also be seen in the reaching hands in the image Lè Mò. Here the Spirits throw serpents to the living, which carry Ashé to them. Throughout time, the great mystery of ancestral bloodline undulates forward like the serpent on the side of the Mardi Gras float.

We owe our Ancestors respect and honor. We can best honor them by living lives of great value, by passing on our bloodlines, and by letting Ashé move through us, through our work, and into the future that we are creating.

Carnival

CALL ON CARNIVAL when you wish to put on the mask of the true self. Call on it to experience the fullness of your senses.

OFFERINGS
King cake, beads, doubloons, gold coconuts, Carnival "throws" of all sorts, costume sequins, ribbons and beads, candies, rum, cigars, Carnival image.

LITANY
"Pour Carneval: les Mystères de l'Esprit en chair et os, quand les Dieux se promènent dans les rues, et les Loa jouent avec l'humanité. Acceptez nos offrandes. Entrez dans nos cœurs, dans nos bras, dans nos jambes. Entrez ici. Dansez avec nous!"

KREYÒL

"Pou Kanaval: Mistè lespri-incané, lè Lwa-yo ap maché nan la ri. Aksepté ofran'n nou. Antré nan kè nou, nan bra nou, nan jam'm nou. Antré vin'n dansé avek nou!"

TRANSLATION

"For Carnival: the Mysteries of Spirit-in-the-flesh, when the Gods walk the streets, and the Lwa play with humanity. Accept our offerings. Enter into our hearts, our arms, our legs. Enter and dance with us!"

TRADITIONAL

It is interesting that New Orleans is a place of utter licentiousness and abandonment but at the same time of abiding and fundamental spirituality. Perhaps the flagrant debauch of Mardi Gras reflects some premonition of Gede's image, flashing across our awareness. For many, Mardi Gras means the freedom to enjoy, exhaust, display the mask of your true self now, while living fully in this moment, without excuse or apology. Bringing the Gods down here, into the gutter, with us. Our world, our streets, our bodies are the ebbós, the offerings: sacred, still, even while engaged in orgiastic and grotesque excess. Parades presided over by pantheons of forbidden Gods: Bacchus, Endymion, Oshún, Thoth, Isis, Babylon. What's up is down. Heaven earthed. Externalized in sequined, motley suits of berserk bodies and beings are phantasms of mind and soul. Carnival: filth, trash, spangles, drunks, and Gods.

VISION

Carnival means farewell to flesh, but has much to do with the Mysteries of Spirit-in-the-flesh. The body is the ultimate symbol of the Spirit incorporated moment by moment in living reality. The body transports the inner kingdom of heaven throughout the outside, material world.

To put on a Carnival mask is to enter into the perspective of the Lwa, who look out through the veil of their characteristic costumes from the source of their true self. Isis unveiled. The mask that is the true self. In putting on our Mardi Gras costume, we enter into the reverse of the mirror. Instead of the mirror reflecting back our image, we reflect our self as we want to be. The flambeaux offer light in the wild Carnival night. In the world we see as in a glass darkly.

Here all is magic and madness, and all fantasy takes on flesh. Dreams made real. We are made of dream. At Carnival, revelers participate carnally in the world's fantasy. There is no discrimination between one object and the next. Opposites interpenetrate. The world is intoxicated by the union of matter and spirit. The revelers become part of creation, and become creators of the world.

The world of Carnival is at its most corrupt and debauched, yet every last drunk sits at the feast and participates in communion. All is sacred; all is vile. Snakes of Ashé rain down on drunken, greedy hands.

Carnival is a time of complete license. The Bhagavad-Gita suggests that when the senses are given license, the sense object becomes an offering. Sensual perception is the sacrificial fire. This sacrificial fire burns everywhere. Carnival is an outpouring of Spirit. The Lwa are everywhere, in all things, in our very flesh. The word made flesh. Divine Presence become real. When we know it all as the play of the world dancer, Divine Presence becomes real, and we become Divine.

Tomorrow the flesh will be judged. But at Carnival, flesh and Spirit are one. There is no rule or authority on this day, so we dance in freedom, into the scandalous truth. As the dance unfolds, treasures are stumbled upon. Oh! There are the Lwa, dancing down at the crossroads, where meaning breaks through the boundaries of the mundane.

CALL ON THE BAWON when you wish to undermine social conventions. Call on them to help cope with unexpected change or chaos. Call on them for the humor to overcome difficulty or grief.

The Bawon

OFFERINGS

Rum, rum cakes, peppers, cigars, coins, the Bawon *Vodou Visions* image.

LITANY

"Pour les Barons, Cimetière, la Croix, Samedi—tous en noir, puissants, magiques. Venez au carrefour. Dansez, blaguez, vous qui êtes l'essence de la mort. Acceptez nos offrandes. Entrez dans nos cœurs, dans nos bras, dans nos jambes. Entrez ici. Dansez avec nous."

KREYÒL

"Pou Bawon-yo, Simitiè, Lakwa, Samdi, tou de nwa. Vini nan kafou-a. Dansé, bay blag ou min-m ki ésans lan mò. Akspté ofran'n nou. Antré nan kè nou, nan bra nou, nan jam'm nou. Antré vin'n dansé avek nou."

TRANSLATION

"For the Bawon, Simityè Lakwa, Samdi—all in black, powerful, magical. Come to the crossroads, dance, joke, you who are the essence of death. Accept our offerings. Enter into our hearts, our arms, our legs. Enter and dance with us."

TRADITIONAL

The Bawon are the chiefs and fathers of the Gede, the Gods of sex, death, and regeneration. The leader of the Bawon is generally Bawon Samdi. Other Bawon include Bawon Lakwa, Bawon Simityè, and Bawon Kalfou. Bawon possessions, like those of the Gede, often break into another Lwa's ceremony and disrupt them. They also often come in hordes. Perhaps they like being "en famille." Or perhaps they just thrive on chaos. They are obscene, grotesque, and comical. The Bawon are dapper and hilarious skeletons in the Gede's black and violet Masonic garb. While they are highly entertaining—always at someone's expense—they are also honest and wise.

The Bawon's Cross is the largest cross in the cemetery, usually located at the crossroads in the cemetery, and usually painted black and white. You must honor the Bawon first, feed them, and ask their permission before going to visit the tomb of a loved one.

The Bawon are syncretized with Saint Gerard. Bawon Samdi is sometimes syncretized with Saint Expedite. Their colors are black and violet.

VISION

The erotic moment is filled with both yearning and doom. The moment of erotic fulfillment contains within itself the foreboding of the loss of the love object, both because of the flattening out of desire and passion, and because sexual love leads to inevitable death. We lie to ourselves about both the love object, and this sorrowful sense of erotic doom. But the Bawon tell us that if we can learn to find humor in this otherwise most tragic of human experiences, we can transcend the human condition and enter into a mythic dance.

The Bawon, too, consume the knowledge of all who become the Dead, and so are very wise. They are most honest, and tend to reveal the embarrassing secrets of their Sèvitè. We can look through the Bawon's eyes to find truth in love and sexuality.

The Bawon, like all Lwa, respond to the passionate desire of the Sèvitè. The Lwa respond to erotic yearning. This erotic yearning can become a kind of spiritual eros that lifts the soul and psyche into union with the Gods.

The vision of the Bawon is alive and compelling in the same way that the Gede uprising in Haiti—when hundreds of possessed Gede descended on the palace of the president and demanded money before going away—compelled the president to give them money, and forced him to admit to sympathy with Vodou. The image of the Bawon is intensely powerful in itself. It contains emotional, psychic, and magical content that cannot translate into words, but plants itself in fullness, squarely in the psyche, and the hips and groin.

Danbala La flambo

C ALL ON DANBALA LA FLAMBO when you wish to increase shamanic flow of energy, or to raise Kundalini energy.

OFFERINGS

Dish of eggs and peppers, egg painted red, snakeskins lit on fire, "Tapas" (the element of body heat in yoga), white candles, Danbala La Flambo's image.

LITANY

"Pour Damballah La Flambeau, serpent de feu. Serpent de la nation Petro. Damballah La Flambeau, enroulez vos écailles brûlantes autour de nous. Touchez-nous, dragon, avec votre énergie. Acceptez nos offrandes. Entrez dans nos cœurs, dans nos bras, dans nos jambes. Entrez ici. Dansez avec nous!"

KREYÒL

"Pou Danbala La Flambo, koulèv di fé. Koulèv nanchon Petwo. Danbala La Flambo, antouré nou avek zékay ou. Manyin nou dragon, avek énègi-ou. Akseptè ofran'n nou. Antré nan kè nou, nan bra nou, nan jam'm nou. Antré vin'n dansé avek nou!"

TRANSLATION

"For Danbala La Flambo, fire snake. Snake of the Petwo nation. Danbala La Flambo, wrap your flaming scales around us. Touch us, dragon, with your energy. Accept our offerings. Enter into our hearts, our arms, our legs. Enter and dance with us!"

TRADITIONAL

Danbala La Flambo is the serpent father in his Petwo aspect. A fire snake, he is Danbala's generative force. The fiery energy of creation. André Pierre told me that Danbala La Flambo and Simbi of fire are one.

VISION

Danbala La Flambo moves through a field of flames as a red snake would move through grass. The crackling of flames matches the hissing of the serpent. The connection with the Kundalini serpent is apparent. But, more particularly, Danbala La Flambo expresses the power of Tapas, heat that burns out impurity. In the same way that Kundalini rising up the spine burns out impurities that can manifest as traumatic physical and psychic experiences, Danbala La Flambo encourages the fire of perception that rages through us and our minds. The fire of purification leads to serpent wisdom. Danbala La Flambo encourages us to take the plunge and allow our anger its proper place.

Appropriately placed and directed anger purges, purifies, burns clean, and seeks revolution.

Ayida Wèdo

CALL ON AYIDA WÈDO for hope and happiness. Call on her for security in a marriage, to keep it faithful and solid.

OFFERINGS

Rainbow-painted egg, basin of water with rainbow painted on bottom, azure blue and white candles, white desserts or those prepared with milk and powdered sugar, sweet coffee, the shed skin of a rainbow-colored snake, Ayida Wèdo's *Vodou Visions* image.

LITANY

"Pour Ayida Wèdo, l'arc en ciel, femme de Damballah, 'les eaux d'en haut,' la pluie, la profondeur marine, les sources qui nourrissent la race. Ayida Wèdo, Dieu la Mère. Acceptez nos offrandes. Entrez dans nos cœurs, dans nos bras, dans nos jambes. Entrez ici. Dansez avec nous."

KREYÒL

"Pou Ayida Wèdo, lakansiel, fanm Danbala, Dlo anlè, la pli, fon lan mè, sous kap nouri ras nou, Ayida Wèdo, Manman nou. Aksepté ofran'n nou. Antré nan kè nou, nan bra nou, nan jam'm nou. Antré vin'n dansé avek nou."

TRANSLATION

"For Ayida Wèdo, the rainbow, wife of Danbala, 'the waters from above,' the rain, the depths of the sea, the streams which nourish the race, Ayida Wèdo, God the Mother. Accept our offerings. Enter into our hearts, our arms, our legs. Enter and dance with us."

TRADITIONAL

Ayida Wèdo is the serpent wife of Danbala Wèdo. She is a water serpent with rainbow-colored scales, whose symbol, the rainbow, arches across the sky. Danbala Wèdo, the snake God, gave rain to the world. As the drops of water fell through the sky, they formed a rainbow of color. Danbala fell in love with Ayida, the rainbow serpent arched over the heavens. They married and joined as a double helix of snakes, giving birth to the human race. Ayida is the power of the sky, is the all-beneficent mother and protector of creation. Ayida is all the Waters above, the celestial Waters. As loyal wife of Danbala, she is rarely summoned without him. She is a very ancient, root Lwa. Together with Danbala, she represents fecundity. Her colors are azure blue and white. She is syncretized with Our Lady of the Immaculate Conception.

VISION

Ayida Wèdo comes down like rain. Ayida is the rainbow, the atmospheric water above the firmament that prisms light into color. She rains down on the earth, into streams and rivers, into the water table that nourishes the race. She is everywhere the water, prismatic like the rainbow.

Ayida Wèdo is strong and powerful. She is no frail girl. She dances with the serpent, Danbala, her husband. Ayida's head is the serpent's head, reflecting the reptilian serpentine nature of the Goddess. Together, she and the serpent form the series of rising and relaxing tensions that reflect the muscular movements of sexual union.

The Hindu texts, the Asuras, say that the universe is the visible form of conflict between the Gods and demons. The aggressive action of demons precipitates the response of the Gods. The Gods call on the feminine force to defeat the demons, for the Goddess is the greatest demon of all. In Paleolithic times, the serpentine image of the Goddess represented her affirmation of the ongoing cycles of life-death-rebirth. The advent of patriarchal religions, however, transformed the serpent Goddess into Leviathan, the demon she-monster of Nature that was the enemy of life and God. Here we see the Goddess in her full force, self-assured, in union with her God-husband.

She is the rainbow-prismed Waters that carry the undulating cycles of life.

Danbala Wèdo

CALL ON DANBALA WÈDO when you wish to receive the blessings of serenity and peace. Call on him when wisdom is needed.

OFFERINGS

All white foods, sweetened condensed milk, sweet coffee, snakeskins, Gummi snakes, egg on a mound of flour, basin of water, Danbala Wèdo's image.

LITANY

"Pour Damballah Wèdo, serpent sage, juste, éternel. Ancient père vénérable. Créateur, protecteur. Source de la sagesse de la vie. Patron des eaux du ciel et des rivières. Acceptez nos offrandes. Entrez dans nos cœurs, dans nos bras, dans nos jambes. Entrez ici. Dansez avec nous!"

KREYÒL

"Pou Danbala Wèdo, coulèv ki ganyin sagès, coulèv ki ganyin jistess, coulèv ki étènel. Asyen papa adoré. Créatè, protectè. Ki bay sagès lavi. Chef sièl la é toutt riviè yo. Aksepté ofran'n nou. Antré nan kè nou, nan bra nou, nan jam'm nou. Antré vin'n dansé avek nou!"

TRANSLATION

"For Danbala Wèdo, wise, just, eternal serpent. Ancient, venerable father. Protective creator. Source of life wisdom. Patron of the Waters of heaven, and of rivers. Accept our offerings. Enter into our hearts, our arms, our legs. Enter and dance with us!"

TRADITIONAL

Danbala Wèdo is the ancient sky father. He arches across the sky as a snake beside his rainbow wife, Ayida Wèdo. He is the origin of life, and the ancient source of wisdom. Danbala is absolutely beneficent, if somewhat aloof and abstract. His possessions begin with a dip into his sacred basin of water, and continue with the inarticulate undulations of a snake. He is covered with a white, undulating sheet during his possessions, and especially while he eats. Danbala's color is pure white, the color of the Ounsi's garb. He prefers white foods, milk, pudding, rice, and an egg perched on a mound of flour. He is syncretized with Saint Patrick, or with Moses, holding the Ten Commandments.

VISION

Danbala dips into water, then climbs a tree.

Water is the cool point of power. The creative force of Danbala first returns to water, from which comes all life. Danbala moves into the Tree of Life, where the Spirit dwells in secret wisdom. The roots reach down into the Waters of return, the branches reach up into Danbala's clear sky. Benign sky father, Danbala goes to the high branches, where he rests, removed from all that is earthly, removed from pettiness. In his sky, he assures and inspires us.

Danbala's tongue licks the top of our heads. A Tantric dewdrop drips inside the mind. All is consumed in white. Danbala is inarticulate, unapproachable. Do not supplicate him for favors: only ask his blessings.

The horse is inarticulate. The serpent does not speak in words. The secret wisdom is supernal, above and removed from the everyday. Yet it is there always, beyond word or question.

Danbala carries light and all power points of whiteness on his scales. His body undulates and light shimmers into obscurity; purity within confusion. The whiteness of possession into the darkness of the material.

Numinous, Danbala.

His sharp teeth crush the shell of the egg, his sacred food. He swallows the yolk of creative Mystery whole. World without end. Danbala nourishes on the egg of creative potential. Cover him with a white sheet while he eats, for his Mysteries are secret.

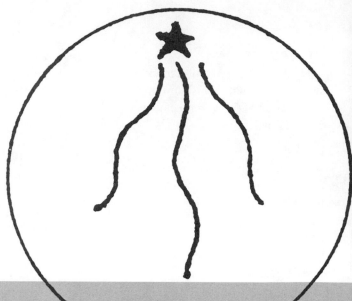

Olodumare

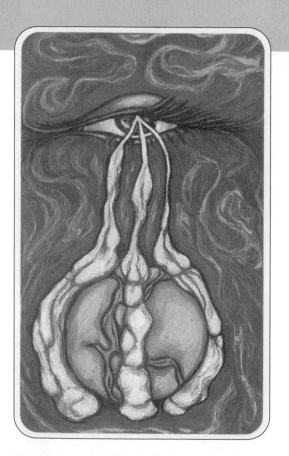

CALL ON OLODUMARE as you
would the supreme God. Call not
for favors, but simply to know that
Olodumare exists.

OFFERINGS

Anything that symbolizes God to you, "Ambrosia" (oranges and bananas with coconut), chocolate (God must like chocolate), figs or fig branch, white candles, image of Olodumare.

LITANY

"Pour Olodumare, au dessous de nous, vous nous avez crées. Ancient triple Orisha, créateur du monde. Tout ce que nous connaissons est l'ombre du baiser de votre conscience. Acceptez nos offrandes. Entrez dans nos cœurs, dans nos bras, dans nos jambes. Entrez ici. Dancez avec nous."

SPANISH

"Para Oludumare arriba de nosotros así, su nos has creado. Oricha viejo y triuno, creador del mundo Lodo que conocemos es el beso de tu consciencia. Accepta nuestros ofrecimientos. Monta en nuestros corazones, nuestros brazos, nuestras piernas. Monta y baile con nosotros."

TRANSLATION

"For Olodumare, above us, you have created us. Ancient, triune Orisha, creator of the world. All we know is the shadow of the kiss of your conscience. Accept our offerings. Enter into our hearts, our arms, our legs. Enter and dance with us."

TRADITIONAL

In Santería, Olodumare is God Almighty, Eternal, omnipotent, omniscient, without beginning or end. Olodumare is the creative essence of the world, and is immanent within all the world. Olofi, the creation, is an aspect of Olodumare, as is Olorun, the act of creation. Olorun is Olodumare's act, Olofi is what Olodumare acted upon. While Olodumare is the Supreme Will of the world, he is distant, abstract, or removed from it. There is a gulf between Olodumare and the world. This gulf is traversed by the Orisha powers.

VISION

Olodumare's triune aspects pour onto the earth in three rivers of tears. We walk through the vale of tears to experience soul making. The sorrows, losses, pains of physical life cause us to look to Olodumare for meaning. We look into Malkuth (the earth sphere) to apprehend the clarity of Kether (the archetypal). Throughout the vision, the great eye of Olodumare is utmost clarity. An overwhelming presence. The tears flow into the waters of the world. Visions pour out through his unknowable knowing from before the time of creation, of all time and all things. Olodumare encompasses the Ashé of all things: all things and all acts are but tear streams from Olodumare's unblinking eye.

It is said that Olodumare is beyond human comprehension and experience, but it is clear that he is in all that we are, in every breath and moment of being. We are immersed in Ashé, immersed in Olodumare.

Nan Nan Buklu La Flambo

CALL ON NAN NAN BUKLU LA FLAMBO to flame the fires of ancestral memory, to heat and temper inherited prime material. Call on her to fire the Will.

OFFERINGS

Hot herbal teas, fiery medicinal herbs, herbs burnt in a cauldron, Nan Nan Buklu La Flambo's image.

LITANY

"Pour Nan Nan Bouclou La Flambeau, agent de la volonté. Feu spirituel. Elle qui assure la continuité de l'univers, et de l'individu. Acceptez nos offrandes. Entrez dans nos cœurs, dans nos bras, dans nos jambes. Entrez ici. Dansez avec nous."

KREYÒL

"Pou Nan Nan Buklu La Flambo ki sé volonté. Se'li ki asiré continuité l'ininvè ak moun. Aksepté ofran'n nou. Antré nan kè nou, nan bra nou, nan jam'm nou. Antré vin'n dansé avek nou."

TRANSLATION

"For Nan Nan Buklu La Flambo, the agent of Will. Spiritual fire. She who insures the continuation of both the universe and the individual. Accept our offerings. Enter into our hearts, our arms, our legs. Enter and dance with us."

TRADITIONAL

Originally in Dahomey, Nananbuluku was the ancestral grandparent of the Gods Mawu and Lisa. She was both Mother and Father, and therefore was an androgynous Supreme Being. Nananbuluku was a remote God who transformed into Nan Nan Buklu or Nan Nan Belecou in Haiti, an herbal Lwa. In its La Flambo aspect, Nan Nan Buklu's Ashé reaches back to its Divine Ancestor's progenerative fires.

VISION

Nan Nan Buklu La Flambo's rites are fiery and magical. The flames on her vèvè resemble the Hebrew letter shin, which represents the creative fire of the Divine. Nana Bukuu in Fon and Dahomey traditions is the creatrix, blowing spiritual fire through a pipe into the third eye of human heads. The pipe is like the magical wand that directs and sublimates Will. The flame's spark vivifies and animates the human spirit. We all have a spark of Ashé, the life energy of God, inside us. It is present both in the individual and the entire universe. We experience it as magical Will, our one true purpose in incarnating. When we develop our Will so that it resonates with Universal Will, we connect back to the Divine, the Godhead.

Nan Nan Buklu La Flambo is a female Lwa, but we have placed her Qabalistically in the sphere of Chokmah on the Tree of Life, a male sphere of power. She manifests as a male, blowing life force or creative fire through a pipe. The phallic symbolism is obvious. These gender crossings are only confusing if we insist on restrictive and rigid gender roles.

Gran Ibo

CALL ON GRAN IBO to whisper secret wisdom to you, and to acquire knowledge of the magical and medicinal properties of herbs.

OFFERINGS

Canary food, seeds, swamp plants, especially those with healing properties, blue-gray candles, *Vodou Visions* image of Gran Ibo.

LITANY

"Pour Gran Ibo, l'ancienne du marais qui connaît la langue des plantes. Gran Ibo, qui marche sur les points du soleil en semence. Avec un canari pour attribut magique. Acceptez nos offrandes. Entrez dans nos cœurs, dans nos bras, dans nos jambes. Entrez ici. Dansez avec nous."

KREYÒL

"Pou Gran Ibo ki konpran langaj plant-yo. Gran Ibo kap maché ak youn kanari chajé ak maji. Aksepté ofran'n nou. Antré nan kè nou, nan bra nou, nan jam'm nou. Antré vin'n dansé avek nou."

TRANSLATION

"For Gran Ibo, ancient woman of the swamp who understands the language of plants. Gran Ibo who walks on the points of the sun within the seed. With a canary for magical attribute. Accept our offerings. Enter into our hearts, our arms, our legs. Enter and dance with us."

TRADITIONAL

Gran Ibo resides in the swamp. She is privy to the ancient wisdom of the swamp, which leaves traces of its language in the root, the flower, the bug, the leaf, the beast, and the bird. She knows her way through the perils that hide in the gnarled roots of the cypress stands. Her energy imbues the healing plants of the swamp. The canary is her main symbol. It is said that canaries lead the soul to the astral realm.

VISION

The Ibo have to do with the rhythm of language.

Gran Ibo can be felt in the rhythm of the swamp, the issuing of life, and the reabsorption into death. The plants, the trees, the water, and the wildlife throb with intelligence and communicate without words. Often when the Ibo possess a person, they talk in grunts and mumbles. There is no actual articulation. Gran Ibo turns away from the outside world and gives her attentive ear to the teeming interior world of the swamp. Her canary symbolizes the flight between the thoughts of the Gods and the humans who receive and interpret, or misinterpret, their meaning.

Gran Ibo's canary whispers to her of rituals offered in her honor, of prayer that asks for admittance into the rhythms of the intelligence of the swamp.

Nan Nan Buklu

CALL ON NAN NAN BUKLU for knowledge of root treatments, and to enhance the healing properties of such treatments. Call on her to help heal the rift between Spirit and matter.

OFFERINGS

Medicinal herbs, sigil for healing, symbols of the womb, herbal healing teas, mandrake root, Nan Nan Buklu's image.

LITANY

"Pour Nan Nan Bouclou, Loa racine, mère ancienne, source des Jumeaux, la matrice du monde. Amenez la reconciliation entre la Nature et l'Esprit. Acceptez nos offrandes. Entrez dans nos cœurs, dans nos bras, dans nos jambes. Entrez ici. Dansez avec nous."

KREYÒL

"Pou Nan Nan Buklu, Lwa rasin, manman Marasa, matris lé mon. Rekonsilié la Nati ak espri yo. Aksepté ofran'n nou. Antré nan kè nou, nan bra nou, nan jam'm nou. Antré vin'n dansé avek nou."

TRANSLATION

"For Nan Nan Buklu, root Lwa, ancient Mother, source of the Twins, womb of the world. Bring about reconciliation of Nature and Spirit. Accept our offerings. Enter into our hearts, our arms, our legs. Enter and dance with us."

TRADITIONAL

Nan Nan Buklu is an ancient, root Lwa, who reaches back to the sources of the pantheon of African Spirits. As the first androgynous Grandparent who gave birth to the first Twins, Mawu and Lisa, she/he is the source of all the Gods. Over time, she became less prominent, and in Haiti is primarily a Lwa of healing herbs. She may have become associated with Ayizan to some degree, as Ayizan expresses many of the same Mysteries of the ancient, maternal source who opens the path for all the other deities.

VISION

There was a time before time when there was just the Mother. Nan Nan Buklu is from the moment just before life splits into differentiated opposites. Nan Nan Buklu is ancient and vast. Her womb births all life. She gave birth to the Twins, the first Ancestors. Nan Nan Buklu precedes the opposites of life and death; Spirit and matter. The Twins are that which is born, lives, and dies. Nan Nan Buklu is the continuity of life that goes on and on.

The Twins appear as two men who exchange a mandrake root. The mandrake is in the shape of a human. Nan Nan Buklu's vèvè is in the shape of the human as a five-pointed star, or pentagram. The two men are twins, opposites who share one soul. Nan Nan Buklu is the one center that they share. She is the one life before Spirit and Nature split into antagonistic camps. Here the mandrake root is a magical, medicinal herb that has the power to heal the rift between Spirit and matter.

Healing can occur when we return to the root knowledge that life and death are not divided, but are one. Spirit and Nature are one. Nan Nan Buklu is there, ancient Mother, when we return to her, as she was there before any of this world was born.

C ALL ON OLOFI when you want to
feel connected with the earth, or
when you need grounding. Call on Olofi
when you need to balance Ashé.

OFFERINGS

Kombucha mushroom tea, medicinal herbs,
foods that grow in the earth, such as potatoes and yams, symbols of your creativity,
Olofi's image.

Olofi

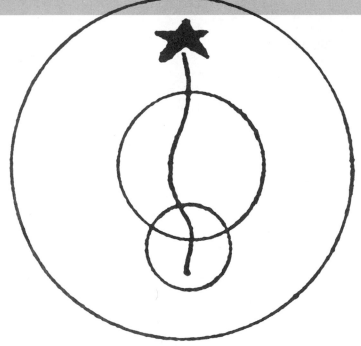

LITANY

"Pour Olofi, Dieu, Père des Orishas, patron de la terre, l'imminence de la nature. Nous sommes vos enfants. Nous vous cherchons dans le monde. Acceptez nos offrandes. Entrez dans nos cœurs, dans nos bras, dans nos jambes. Entrez ici. Dansez avec nous!"

SPANISH

"Para Olofi, Dios, Padre de las Orichas, patrón de la tierra, escencia en la naturaleza. Somos tus minos. Te buscamos en la tierra. Accepta nuestros ofrecimientos. Monta nuestros corazones, nuestros brazos, nuestras piernas. Monta y baile con nosotros!"

TRANSLATION

"For Olofi, God, Father of the Orishas, patron of the earth, immanence within Nature. We are your children. We look for you within the world. Accept our offerings. Enter into our hearts, our arms, our legs. Enter and dance with us!"

TRADITIONAL

Olorun, Olodumare, and Olofi are triune aspects of God. Olofi is Ashé in action. Olofi is creation. Olofi created the Orisha by breathing his Ashé into stones. Olofi breathed his Ashé into mud figures that he and Obatalá fashioned, giving life to humans. Humans, the Orishas, and God all lived together in harmony, but the Orishas wanted more of Olofi's Ashé. Olofi felt too closely identified with the earth, and with human need, so he left the earth and he separated his realm from the human. It is important that humans not ask too much from Olofi.

VISION

Olofi is one of the emanations from Olodumare. She is the emanation that stayed with Olodumare's creation as patron of the earth, and Father of all the other Orishas.

Olofi appears as a pregnant woman. Our presuppositions concerning gender are not so rigid as we imagine. Once there is a sepa-ration into male and female roles, we encounter myths such as Adam and Eve's fall from grace, with its attendant notion of original sin. But Olofi is complete unto its own nature. She is eternally pregnant with the earth, eternally engaged with creation, eternally engaged with life. In urban American culture, awe and surrender are associated with shame, weakness, and vulnerability. But Olofi is immanent within all of Nature, within the world, within ourselves. Olofi offers hope and connectedness. We are not alone, we are not separate from any of the rest of the earth, from the peoples of the earth. Olofi is within all of us, within all things.

It requires a change of perspective to see Olofi. We become so bound to the material that we can neither see within it to Olofi's indwelling presence, nor beyond it to register that all of the earth is contained within Olofi's belly. We experience life as it comes to us, alone. Life seems full of pain and loss and death. It seems futile to look for soul meaning in such an insignificant fate. Yet the cycles of time and the ongoing passage of generation upon generation, birth, life, and death, tell the mystery of ongoing life, ongoing creation—Olofi.

Olofi is unspeakably beautiful, powerful, and big. Her face is turned in profile because humans cannot see the full face of Olodumare. Olofi is the link between the material earth with its struggling creation, and the Divine. Look within the world for that link.

As the earth within Olofi's belly turns, cycles of destruction and regeneration succeed one another. After the destruction of life on the planet, Nature indomitably and instinctively starts to grow again. When it seems like the end of the world, in times of destruction or plague, Olofi offers mysterious medicinal herbs from her fertile earth. She offers the hope of cyclical change.

Olofi is pregnant with dreams that she births into the world.

Gede La Flambo

Call on Gede La Flambo when you seek heightened sexual energy.

OFFERINGS

Black rooster, pepper, strings of peppers, peppered food and drink, goat, black crosses, walking cane on which white symbols have been painted, gravedigger's tools, cinnamon candies ("red hots"), cigars, Gede La Flambo's image.

LITANY

"Pour Guedeh La Flambeau, Guedeh Gé-Rouge, de la passion brûlante, de la sexualité magique, de la verité transformative. Guedeh La Flambeau, passionnée, erotique, obscène. Le prophète de nos excès. Acceptez nos offrandes. Entrez dans nos cœurs, dans nos bras, dans nos jambes. Entrez ici. Dansez avec nous!"

KREYÒL

"Pou Gede La Flambo, Gede jé rouj, chalè pasion, maji fè lan-mou, fè bagay. Gede La Flambo, pasyoné, érotik, sé profèt eksè nouyo. Aksepté ofran'n nou. Antré nan kè nou, nan bra nous, nan jam'm nou. Antré vin'n dansé avek nou!"

TRANSLATION

"For Gede La Flambo, Guedeh of the red eye, of enflamed passion, of magical sexuality, of transforming truth. Gede La Flambo, passionate, erotic, obscene. The prophet of our excesses. Accept our offerings. Enter into our hearts, our arms, our legs. Enter and dance with us!"

TRADITIONAL

Gede La Flambo is flaming death and regeneration. He is the essence of the fires of the cremation ground, where physical matter is transformed into spiritual substance. He is erotic to the point of embarrassing, and he is outrageously crass. His gestures are obscene, his jokes are off-color. His banda dance is a low, nasty, hip-grind that mimics sexual intercourse. Gede La Flambo is the burning moment of orgasm, during which the self is fused into Spirit. He is "the little death" and he is Death. He doesn't wait for an invitation. If he is provocative and embarrassing, it is because in his office of death, sex, and regeneration, he is beyond all social taboos. With his nasal speech, his laughter, and his explicit sexual grind, he reminds us of what drives us.

Gede La Flambo is syncretized with Saint Gerard. His day is Saturday. His colors are black and purple and white.

VISION

This is the path of the power of sex magic. The figure of Gede La Flambo compels, transfixes, commands. As the Gede often invade the ceremonies of other Lwa, Gede La Flambo invades his Sèvitè sexually. Here he grabs his Sèvitè off the ground and forces her into a wild, erotic dance. His dark glasses hypnotically reflect the flashing tongues of flame that spark off him. His flaming tongue explores pleasure, and enflames passion. Gede La Flambo cannot be handled. He is ravenous. Let him eat.

Recently, the connection between sex and death has been most glaringly experienced through the AIDS plague. A moral judgment has been placed on those who suffer from the disease, as if they asked for this viral punishment through their sexual excesses. A cruel and aloof society has wanted AIDS sufferers to die quietly, without complaint. But they have not been silent. Instead their anger, honesty, and activism have demanded universal compassion and recognition for their situation. This is Gede's empowering dance. Gede La Flambo defies nice morality. He speaks the truth. His dark glasses reflect the flame of truth into the face of social morality and conventional human façade.

We must find the strength to look into this reflection, for the truth is revolutionary.

CALL ON MANMAN BRIJIT to ensure a just judge and a favorable outcome to a court case. Call on her for correct understanding of death and regeneration.

Manman Brijit

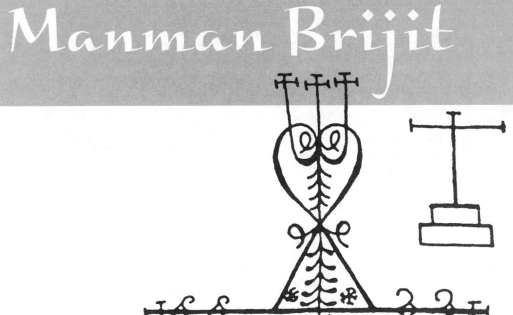

OFFERINGS

Stones from cemetery, placed in a pile, nettles, cotton (to stuff nose, eyes, ears, and mouth of the dead), flowers, black and violet candles, wood of an ash, peanuts, wheat flower, cornmeal and raw rum, Manman Brijit's *Vodou Visions* image.

LITANY

"Pour Manman Brigitte, femme de Baron Samedi, mère de tous les Guedehs. Maîtresse des Cimetières et mère de tous les morts qui y reposent. Grande Brigitte, juge et avocate éminente. C'est pour vous cet autel de pierres. Acceptez nos offrandes. Entrez dans nos cœurs, dans nos bras, dans nos jambes. Entrez ici, dancez avec nous."

KREYÒL

"Pou Manman Brijit, fan'm Bawon Samdi, manman tout Gede-yo. Métrès Simitiè ak tout mò yo. Gran Brijit jij, avoca. Lotel roche sé pou-ou. Aksepté ofran'n nou. Antré nan kè nou, nan bra nou, nan jam'm nou. Antré vin'n dansé avek nou."

TRANSLATION

"For Manman Brijit, wife of Bawon Samdi, Mother of all the Gede. Mistress of the cemetery and Mother of all the dead who rest there. *Grande* Brijit, eminent judge and lawyer. This altar of stones is for you. Accept our offerings. Enter into our hearts, our arms, our legs. Enter and dance with us."

TRADITIONAL

Manman Brijit is the wife of Bawon Samdi, and the Mother of the Dead. She lives with the Gede in the cemetery, where altars are built for her out of a pyramid of rocks. She wears the shroud cloth of the Dead, wrapped around her shoulders. Her eyes, ears, and nose are stuffed with cotton, and her jaw is tied shut with a cloth. When she possesses someone, she lies down like a corpse.

As death is the final judge, so is Manman Brijit considered to be a supreme judge and lawyer. In my neighborhood, the women with whom I work call on "Mother Bridgit." Most of their sons are in prison, put there by a legal system that presupposes guilt in African-American teenage males. They love their sons, and they want to help them. What can they do in a society that is stacked against them? They call on Mother Bridgit. She is their equalizer.

Manman Brijit is said to hold the same powers as her husband. If the first person buried in a new cemetery is a woman, that cemetery is said to belong to Manman Brijit. If the first buried is a man, then that cemetery belongs to Bawon Samdi.

VISION

The skeleton within us is not calcified, but dances instead. Manman Brijit is the Mother of the Dead. She is a wise judge and lawyer. In death we may be luckier than in life, for in death our Mother is wise and powerful to protect us. This is not always the case in life.

We are all devotees of Manman Brijit, for we are all born into her when our bodies are buried in the womb of her earth. She sits in judgment of us, as death is the final judgment of our time on earth.

While Kali is the active Mother of Death, Manman Brijit is meditative, silent, internal. Her mouth, eyes, ears, and nose are stuffed with cotton. Her jaw is pulled shut with cloth, and her shoulders are wrapped in the cloth of death. The corpse is silent within the earth. The focus is turned inward. Manman Brijit sits, absorbed in deepest meditation. We offer her candles to draw out her attention. Our older Mother, she absorbs us into silence.

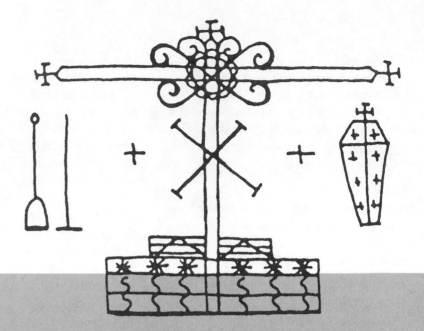

Gede

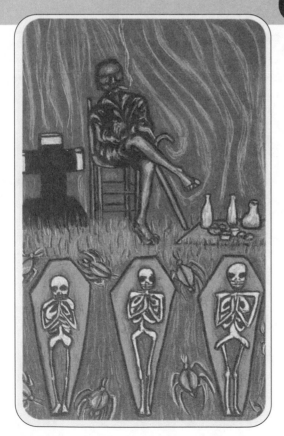

C ALL ON GEDE when there is a serious, even life-threatening illness that
needs healing, or when you have difficult
questions that need sound, reliable, and
honest answers. Call on Gede when you
need help with grieving, to welcome the
Dead to the Waters of the Abyss, and
when you want to enhance sexual potency, or heal sexual repression. Call on
him to protect young children.

OFFERINGS

Peppers, pepper sauce, pepper soaked in rum, cigars, hot Creole food, black roosters, black cock feathers, sunglasses with one lens, top hat, pieces of marble from a cemetery, crosses, graveyard dust, black and violet candles, Gede's *Vodou Visions* image.

LITANY

"Pour Guedeh, Loa obscène de la mort, et de la sexualité. Père de tous les Morts qui habitent aux cimetières. Guedeh, qui marche sur les points mercuriels en bas de carrefour. Mangez, mangez ce soir, vous qui avez tellement faim. Acceptez nos offrandes. Entrez dans nos cœurs, dans nos bras, dans nos jambes. Entrez ici. Dansez avec nous."

KREYÒL

"Pou Gede, Lwa seks, Lwa fè bagay, Lwa lan mò. Papa tout Mò ki abité nan simitiè. Gede kap maché an ba kafou. Manjé, ma swè-a, ou-minm ki gran gou. Aksepté ofran'n nou. Antré nan kè nou, nan bra nou, nan jam'm nou. Antré vin'n dansé avek nou."

TRANSLATION

"For Gede, obscene Lwa of death and of sexuality. Father of all the Dead who live in the cemeteries. Gede, who walks on the mercurial points of the crossroads. Eat, eat this evening, you who are so hungry. Accept our offerings. Enter into our hearts, our arms, our legs. Enter and dance with us."

TRADITIONAL

Gede is the Lwa both of death and sexuality. He lives in the cemetery, at the bottom of the largest cross, or a cross that stands in the central crossroads in a cemetery. He rules the Dead. He is the Father of all the Dead. Gede usually is pictured as a skeleton dressed in dapper clothing, with black tails and a top hat. He wears white gloves, carries a cane, and smokes a cigar or pipe. Gede wears dark sunglasses that have only one lens. Sometimes this is said to symbolize that he sees in two worlds. Sometimes it is said that it more crassly represents the power of his one-eyed phallus. Gede is vulgar, even obscene. He is cocky. He tells off-color jokes, often at the expense of his followers. If he picks on you, you may have to pay him to go away. But Gede always tells the truth, and can be counted on when the situation is difficult. He is the patron of young children. In spite of his association with death, Gede is also the Lwa who is most often called upon for healing when there is an illness. Gede is death, but also he is procreation and regeneration. Gede often breaks in uninvited to the ceremonies of the other Lwa. He is gluttonous, hoarding food under a table or behind a wall, where he devours it. Death is always hungry. Gede's dance is graphically sexual, with grinding hips and pelvis. Sometimes he even humps the drums. He is the great equalizer who laughs at our human egos. Gede's colors are mauve or violet and black. He is syncretized with Saint Gerard.

VISION

Gede appears as some nasty, degraded old drunk at a bar. But Gede is not degraded. He is simply above all notions of morality. He laughs at morality. He laughs at our secrets because death renders our secrets laughable.

Gede feels us up all through our lives. He is a hungry and mysterious lover who plays erotically with us throughout life and waits, cockily, for each of his lovers to join him. Here he sits in his traditionally outrageous attire, top hat, tails, walking stick, and sunglasses, lord of the buried cities of the Dead. His Sèvitè have brought him bountiful offerings, but he remains ravenous. Neither of his appetites can be appeased. He remains isolated, for his is the final great Mystery from which we all shy away.

Oyá

CALL ON OYÁ when you need to express, dispel, or direct anger or rage. Call on her to empower yourself with the warrior spirit and when you wish to stir up a storm to cleanse the world and to blow up the truth.

OFFERINGS

Graveyard dust, statues of Saint Theresa, or Our Lady of Candelaria, eggplants that have been cut into nine pieces or that have been dressed in torn orange skirts, orange, purple, or wine-red candles, nightshade vegetables, such as potatoes or yams, orange rags, fabricated lightning bolt, Oyá's *Vodou Visions* image.

LITANY

"Pour Oyá des vents, des éclairs, des tempêtes. Oyá qui danse sur les tombeaux dans ses jupes dechirées. Dansez pour nous, Oyá! Faîtes tourbillonner vos jupes, chavirer nos esprits à la folie, ou au génie. Nettoyez le monde avec vos orages; faîtes le renaître avec les vents de vos jupes. Acceptez nos offrandes. Entrez dans nos cœurs, dans nos bras, dans nos jambes. Entrez ici. Dansez avec nous!"

SPANISH

"Para Oyá de los vientos, del relampagueo, y de los tempestades. Oyá, quien baile encima de las tombas con las faldas rotas. Echa abajo nuestras mentas con genio o con locura. Limpia el mundo con tus tempestades. Destruyelo de nuevo con los vientos de tus folda. Accepta nuestros ofrecimientos. Monta nuestros corazones, nuestros brazos, nuestras piernas. Monta y baile con nosotros!"

TRANSLATION

"For Oyá of the winds, of lightning, and storms. Oyá, who dances on tombs with her torn skirts. Overturn our minds with genius or madness. Clean the world with your storms, destroy it anew with the winds of your skirts. Accept our offerings. Enter into our hearts, our arms, our legs. Enter and dance with us!"

TRADITIONAL

Oyá is the Santería Goddess of wind, of storms, and tempests. She is often associated with destruction, and is seen holding lightning bolts in her hands. She wears torn orange rags that cover her from head to feet. She possesses the power of fire. Often associated with death, Oyá is sometimes said to live in the cemetery. Others say that she lives in the market and only goes into the cemetery after her sister, Yewá, has finished eating the dead bodies there. Oyá's colors are usually given as orange or dark blood-red. Her collares beads are usually striped red, black, and white. She likes eggplant, as well as hens and goats. Her number is nine. Oyá is one of the warrior Orishas. She is an extremely aggressive feminine force. As such, she is Shangó's favorite consort, because she can go into battle with him. Oyá and Yemayá are enemies, and cannot be fed together because legend has it that Yemayá once lived in the cemetery and Oyá in the ocean. Yemayá tricked Oyá into trading homes, and Oyá has never forgiven her for the favor. Oyá is syncretized with Our Lady of Candelaria, or with Saint Theresa.

VISION

Oyá dances on the edge that divides life and death, madness and genius, interior and exterior, the self and the Divine. She lives by the gates of the cemeteries. She is neither of the topside nor the underworld, but the passageway between both. Oyá gives us genius or insanity, and to dance with Oyá is to dance on the slender separation between the two. We all like to feel the security of acceptance. We want to perceive that we are at the center of things. We're afraid to be on the fringe, lest we trespass into solitude and rejection. But when we're in the middle of something, we can't see clearly. Only on the edge can we review the situation and redefine it. An edge is the border of change.

Oyá dances on a tombstone. Her torn orange skirts rise up, and tempests squall from her dark, hidden womb. She rearranges the things of the world, disturbing their normal place and order so that deeper meaning and insight might arrive. Oyá is the storm of destruction that moves us to seek more deeply for meaning, for our truer and stronger selves. Whenever I call on Oyá, the wind blows. The storms come with lightning and mayhem and chaos, with madness, with the electric flash of purity. She burns and blows and leaves fresh possibility in a world that is shaken and wet and torn apart. She is dynamic. Hers is the magical energy of the vortex, the volcano, the whirling dervish who spins and spins. Hers is the plump, purple, bizarre, and formidable night vegetable, the eggplant. As Oyá's orange skirts lash out against the purple night sky, they show us the fury of madness and they blow the world clean. Oyá is the alchemical wind at your back. If it is there, you must face and endure the demon Goddess. If it isn't there for you, nothing you can do will bring on the storm. Come to me, Oyá! Spin your skirt and blow the winds of life to me. Catch me in your demon wind.

Out of chaos, the creative.

Agwe La flambo

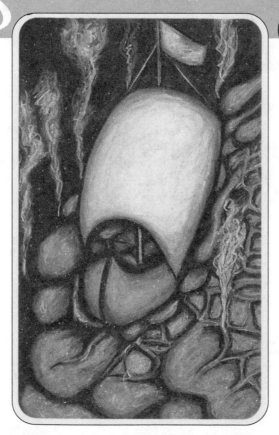

Call on Agwe La Flambo for safe passage through tumultuous emotions and stormy relations. Ask him for acceptance of change.

OFFERINGS

Small boat set on fire, hot sauce, pumice, basalt, Agwe La Flambo's image.

LITANY

"Pour Agwé la Flambeau, qui marche sur les points humides et chauds du feu de l'eau. Qu'est-ce qui brûle sous la surface? Qu'est-ce qui confère la puissance pour la vapeur de votre temple? Amenez votre barque, *Immamou*; passez sur la lave turbulente de l'océan fondu. Acceptez nos offrandes. Entrez dans nos cœurs, dans nos bras, dans nos jambes. Entrez ici. Dansez avec nous!"

KREYÒL

"Pou Agwe La Flambo, kap mashé sou pwen mouyé ak pwen cho nan dlo. Ki sa kap boulé an ba dlo? Ki sa ki bay pouvwa vapè nan tanp-ou? Minnin *Immamou*, bato-ou, pasé sou lan mè kap boulé. Aksepté ofran'n nou. Antré nan kè nou, nan bra nou, nan jam'm nou. Antré vin'n dansé avek nou!"

TRANSLATION

"For Agwe La Flambo, who walks the wet, hot points of fire of water. What burns beneath the surface? What empowers the steam of your temple? Bring *Immamou*, your boat; pass over the turbulent lava of the molten ocean. Accept our offerings. Enter into our hearts, our arms, our legs. Enter and dance with us!"

TRADITIONAL

Agwe La Flambo is the fire aspect of Agwe. While Agwe would not traditionally be included in the Petwo nation, Agwe La Flambo might be considered as the admiral at the helm of his ship, giving the order to shoot the big cannons, or, in modern times, deploying depth charges and torpedoes.

VISION

The floor of the temple is molten lava. Agwe La Flambo's boat sails over the lava into the temple. As each Sèvitè is consecrated, they become members of the boat's crew.

Agwe La Flambo carries messages from the deep self that erupt up from the earth. Molten symbols erupt into the conscious mind. Recognizing these thoughts causes change and total destruction to the old way of being. In the myth of the fall, humankind becomes conscious, and in so doing finds itself banished from the paradise of innocence. It isn't necessary to place blame for the event, however. Adam and Eve had to evolve. Humankind had to attain consciousness. Lava flows encroach inevitably. You can't stop them. The old is inevitably burned away. Change must occur. Evolution is compulsory.

Water and fire combine to form steam, which powers engines and Agwe La Flambo's boat. The moist, hot breath blows on the sails and empowers us if we elect to ride on his boat.

If we don't take in the messages of the deep self as they are poured out, molten, from the earth, then they harden to the stone of the material world or turn to volcanic basalt, which only reflects our own image to us. We see only the surface, as opposed to the depths.

Labalèn

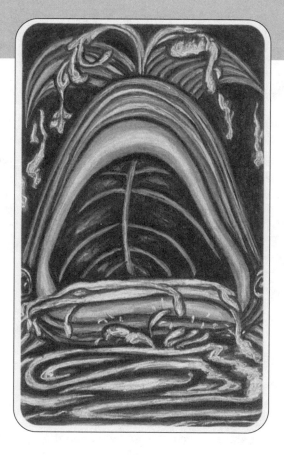

CALL ON LABALÈN for protection, nurturing, and a sense of safety. Call on her to bring up fertile images from the deep waters of the psyche to surface consciousness.

OFFERINGS

Seawater, baby octopus, ambergris, fish, algae, plantain, spirulina, Labalèn's image.

LITANY

"Pour La Baleine, mère de l'océan qui transporte les secrets d'en bas jusqu'à la surface, enceinte de la vie et des Mystères de la profondeur. Protégez-nous, La Baleine. Acceptez nos offrandes. Entrez dans nos cœurs, dans nos bras, dans nos jambes. Entrez ici. Dansez avec nous."

KREYÒL

"Pou Labalèn, manman la mè ki poté sécrè sòti dépi nan fon lamé. Ansènt avek mistè fon lamè. Pwotéjé nou, Labalèn. Aksepté ofran'n nou. Antré nan kè nou, nan bra nou, nan jam'm nou. Antré vin'n dansé avek nou."

TRANSLATION

"For Labalèn, ocean Mother who carries secrets from the bottom to the surface, pregnant with the Mysteries of the depths. Protect us, Labalèn. Accept our offerings. Enter into our hearts, our arms, our legs. Enter and dance with us."

TRADITIONAL

Labalèn is a whale, whose body swims gracefully through the sea. She represents maternal nurturing, although she is sometimes said to be Lasirèn's lover or husband instead of her mother. Sometimes Labalèn is referred to as the same Lwa as Lasirèn, but perhaps in a more distant or remote aspect. Labalèn is Jupitarian in her expansiveness. She is the great, protective womb of the sea.

VISION

*"Protégez-moi, mon seigneur.
Ma barque est si petite
Et votre mer si large."*

*"Protect me, Father.
My boat is so small
And your ocean so large."*

Mother of the sea, Labalèn rides on the surface of the water. Her huge body encompasses and protects us. She moves from the surface of the waters to the great depths, traversing the axis of the crossroads.

Her great mouth is open to consume us. The arched bone in the roof of Labalèn's mouth looks like the vaulted ceiling of a cathedral. She is both womb and mouth. The mouth eats. The act of eating caused the fall. The sex act consummates the fall. Labalèn is about to eat us. We are born into the body where we eat or are eaten. Is this the act of Eucharist or of sacrifice? In magical work, speech is sexualized. The mouth gives forth prophesy. The emptiness within the mouth connects to the visionary space in which dreams arise. The word gestates out of imagination and becomes flesh.

Labalèn is huge. All body. Yet within her is emptiness. She travels from the surface to the depths, where imagination is dark and fertile. She dives after images, diving deep into the waters of the psyche. She filters the waters of the imaginative sea through her for nourishment. She eats all and therefore is Mother of us all. She is pregnant and vast, yet empty. She is cumbersome, yet she flows between body and imagination, speech and silence. She is poetry in motion. Grace.

SAILORS CALL ON AGWE for safe passage over the sea, and for protection for their ships.

IMMAMOU

Agwe

OFFERINGS

Sea grass, an oar, white lamb and white chickens, champagne, cakes, barque laden with food and drink, seashells, seawater, washed ocean stones, Agwe's image.

LITANY

"Pour Agwé des Eaux, roi de la mer. Agwé Main-Forte, mari de la Sirène. Avec la conque marine nous appellons le vent pour que le bateau/temple *Immamou* puisse hisser la voile [Rigaud]. Acceptez nos offrandes. Entrez dans nos cœurs, dans nos bras, dans nos jambes. Entrez ici. Dansez avec nous."

KREYÒL

"Pou Agwe, wa lamè. Agwe Mén Fò, mari Lasirèn. Nap souflé nan lambi pou nou rélé van yo pou *Immamou* pran lamè. Aksepté ofran'n nou. Antré nan kè nou, nan bra nou, nan jam'm nou. Antré vin'n dansé avek nou."

TRANSLATION

"For Agwe of the Waters, king of the sea. Agwe of the mighty hand, husband to Lasirèn. With the seashell we call the wind in order that the boat/temple *Immamou* set sail [Rigaud]. Accept our offerings. Enter into our hearts, our arms, our legs. Enter and dance with us."

TRADITIONAL

Admiral Agwe is king of the sea, husband of Lasirèn, and guardian of seafaring vessels. A white lamb, white chickens, and a painted wooden barque are prepared for Agwe, filled abundantly with food and drink and offered at sea, over the symbolic location of the "island beneath the sea." Agwe eats as the barque submerges into the waves. His conch shell horn summons the winds that catch the sails of Agwe's boat *Immamou*. Agwe is considered to be an ideal husband, strong and sustaining like the sea.

Agwe is syncretized with Saint Ulrich.

VISION

The wind fills Agwe's sails. The rigging of his cathedral creaks and strains, brings us all we could need from his abundant ocean.

The drums pulsate and undulate with the body of the ocean, which is like a serpent's body. The wind hits the sails and the tempo changes. There is danger, and Agwe guides us through to smooth sailing.

The ocean is complex, teeming with life, teeming with the souls of the Dead. Filled with beauty, suffering, danger, and joy. The people on the boat offer their bodies' blood (as salt water) and suffering as sacrifices to Agwe. They give a barque laden with food in offering back to Agwe, to be reabsorbed by the water. There is that which is born, lives, and dies, and that which goes on and on.

The ocean is the psyche, soul, deep emotion, erotic yearning. The wind is the air, intellect. Here we experience erotic psyche. Our erotic yearning for union with the ocean of Divinity seduces the realm of the spiritual. This erotic yearning is both sexual and spiritual. It is the magical shell of Agwe that calls the winds that bring *Immamou*, Agwe's boat, which is his temple.

Obatalá

CALL ON OBATALÁ for purity, peace, serenity, wisdom, and clarity. Call on him to cool off hot situations and to calm the pace of life, so that clear judgments can be made. Call on him for favorable legal judgments.

OFFERINGS

Rice, water, coconut, bread, bananas, cotton, cocoa butter, cascarilla, white cornmeal, milk, white candles, escargots, white sugar, snail shells, white foods, white flowers, aluminum, white gold, Obatalá's image.

LITANY

"Pour Obatalá, ancient roi des Orishas. Homme et femme, sage et profond, Obatalá, qui marche sur les points frais et blancs. Ami des escargots et des invalides. Obatalá du ciel. Je vous vois dans les nuages. Je vous appelle des montagnes. Acceptez nos offrandes. Entrez dans nos cœurs, dans nos bras, dans nos jambes. Entrez ici. Dansez avec nous."

SPANISH

"Para Obatalá, Rey viejo de las Orichas. Hembra y varon, sabio y profundo, Obatalá quien anda en puntos blancos y frescos. Amigo des caracoles y de los desvalidos. Obatalá de los cielos, te veo en las nubes. Te suplico desde las montañas. Accepta nuestros ofrecimientos. Monta nuestros corazones, nuestros brazos, nuestras piernas. Monta y baile con nosotros."

TRANSLATION

"For Obatalá, ancient king of the Orishas. Male and female, wise and profound, Obatalá, who walks on cool, white points. Friend of snails and invalids. Obatalá of the sky. I see you in the clouds. I call you from the mountains. Accept our offerings. Enter into our hearts, our arms, our legs. Enter, and dance with us."

TRADITIONAL

Obatalá is the first and the head Orisha in Santería. He is both male and female. He is the cool sky Orisha, and the Orisha of justice, clarity, and purity. His color is white, and he is referred to as "the chief of the white cloth." Obatalá is cool and moist, kind, wise, and of good humor. Obatalá once drank palm wine while molding humans from clay. He was careless in his drunken state, and made deformed figures. All the misshapen, disfigured people in the world were caused by Obatalá's oversight. Obatalá made all handicapped people his children, but to this day he should never be offered palm wine as an ebbós.

Obatalá's sacred animals include the wise and regal elephant, white doves, and snails, which give off a slick, cool trail that is supposed to be excellent for cooling the head. Obatalá rules the head, and his children must be careful to keep theirs cool and calm. Obatalá is said to own all heads, and so cannot be "received" by anyone. Obatalá's clarity of thought and vision, combined with his cool reason and wisdom, makes him the perfect judge. He lives on the mountaintop, and it is most effective to bring his offerings there.

He is syncretized with Our Lady of Mercy. His color is white. His ceremonial implement is a horse's tail, the handle of which is encrusted with cowrie shells. His day is Sunday.

VISION

Obatalá likes to stay near the altar, the heart of the temple. When I see his faithful at Obatalá's celebrations, I find him situated in the person's heart. It is the sincerity in the hearts of his children that calls Obatalá.

Obatalá appears like beautiful white clouds moving through the sky. Obatalá's dove, a pure carrier of Spirit, flies free to the heavens. Obatalá can also come up through the feet as a snail that leaves its cool, moist, iridescent trail as it slithers up the spine. He/she is in the small, moist, insignificant things that people step on or around, but don't notice. Obatalá leaves a snail's path through the world. He/she is in all the moist, life-giving things of the world, the primordial earth that cools to allow life to start. Obatalá is in the moist vapors, clouds, cool body fluids, the skin that ventilates, the cooling breath. His whiteness appears in creatures of the night and things of the earth that see no light, like grubs. We look in all the wrong places for Obatalá. We yearn for Obatalá's kindness and gentility. We long for his/her wisdom and justice, but instead we focus on all our hardships and suffering, all the injustice in our lives. Meanwhile, there is Obatalá, looking back at us in all the places and parts of our life that we ignore. Snail-like, she/he moves on cool and moist points, kind, wise, and just. Overhead, his white dove flies with a heightened perspective on all our petty problems. From above, our problems become insignificant like little snails.

Obatalá is experienced as a cool and cleansing bath, and recommends magical baths to cool and cleanse the Spirit. She/he is a blessing that soothes our lives.

Unlike most patriarchal sky Gods who are seen as more pure and holy than the female earth Goddesses, Obatalá is not divided into gender. Obatalá offers us the wholeness of Spirit.

WHEN YOU must do battle, it is good to have Ogou La Flambo at your side.

Ogou La flambo

OFFERINGS

Iron, bullets, 151-proof rum set on fire, red rooster, blood, Ogou La Flambo's image.

LITANY

"Pour Ogou La Flambo, qui marche sur les points de Mars enflammés. Ogoun La Flambeau, Dieu guerrier fâché, chef des champs de bataille brûlants, gorgé de sang. Donnez-nous votre courage, votre puissance terrible. Acceptez nos offrandes. Entrez dans nos cœurs, dans nos bras, dans nos jambes. Entrez ici. Dansez avec nous!"

KREYÒL

"Pou Ogou La Flambo, kap maché nan difé planèt Mas. Ogou La Flambo, Lwa la gè. Prété nou fos kouray ou ak pouwa ou. Aksepté afran'n nou. Antré nan kè nou, nan bra nou, nan jam'm nou. Antré vin'n dansé avek nou!"

TRANSLATION

"For Ogou La Flambo, who walks on the points of flaming Mars. Ogou La Flambo, God the angry warrior, chief of the burning fields of battle, gorged with blood. Lend us your courage, your terrible power. Accept our offerings. Enter into our hearts, our arms, our legs. Enter and dance with us!"

TRADITIONAL

Ogou La Flambo, aflame with rage, drunk with blood and carnage, is the blind force of destruction. His is a rage that takes no prisoners. He is the principle of war that keeps man at his fellow man's throat. He inspired the Haitian slave uprising in 1804 that led to Haiti's independence from France. His is the might that crushes oppression. He lends his shoulder to mankind for endurance and survival.

Ogou La Flambo is syncretized with Saint Jacques, also called Ogou Sen Jak, and Saint James. His color is red.

VISION

Here is Yahweh of the battlefields, destroying. The battlefield is bathed in flames and blood, carnage, and stench. Ogou La Flambo loves his battle. Spinning, dancing through rivers of blood that consume the Dead and the dying, he revels in the ballet of destruction. He hacks an open path with his sword. Ogou is the force that guards your arm in battle. His power enables you to slay your enemies.

The drumming stops. Noises from the street seep into the temple. Shouts, car doors, banging metal. A symphony for a kick-ass urban Lwa. War in the streets. The cities are burning.

War is a battle between factions. Opposites in opposition. Ogou La Flambo is the transpersonal, archetypal factor that emerges once the opposites within the limited, personal ego are slain. His flames burn up all that is nonessential and factioned within his personality. Essential material can be brought forth out of the battle with the self.

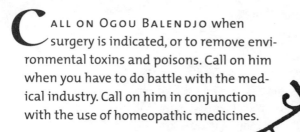

CALL ON OGOU BALENDJO when surgery is indicated, or to remove environmental toxins and poisons. Call on him when you have to do battle with the medical industry. Call on him in conjunction with the use of homeopathic medicines.

Ogou Balendjo

OFFERINGS

Iron nails, soaked in water, healing bath salts dissolved in water, homeopathic medicines, hypodermic needle, medicinal tea, Ogou Balendjo's *Vodou Visions* image.

LITANY

"Pour Ogoun Bahlin'dio, Loa qui guérit avec le fer. Pour vaincre la maladie, accompagnez-nous dans notre lutte. Guérrissez-nous. Donnez-nous la santé. Acceptez nos offrandes. Entrez dans nos cœurs, dans nos bras, dans nos jambes. Entrez ici. Dansez avec nous."

KREYÒL

"Pou Ogou Balendjo, Lwa kap géri avek fè. Konbat maladi. Edé nou nan batay kont maladi. Géri nou. Ban nou la santé. Aksepté ofran'n nou. Antré nan kè nou, nan bra nou, nan jam'm nou. Antré vin'n dansé avek nou."

TRANSLATION

"For Ogou Balendjo, the Lwa who heals with iron. Conquer illness. Accompany us into battle against disease. Heal us. Give us the victory of health. Accept our offerings. Enter into our hearts, our arms, our legs. Enter and dance with us."

TRADITIONAL

Ogou Balendjo walks the wet points of the Ogou Mysteries, under the influence of the moon and Venus. He is Ogou Badagri's brother. The God of the Ogoun River in Africa is named Bahlindjo. Ogou Balendjo protects his serviteurs from being harmed by poison. Balendjo is also a doctor or healer, especially a healer of children. He is syncretized with Saint James Minor or Saint George.

VISION

Ogou Balendjo is a medic, surrounded by battle, trying to heal fallen warriors amidst the pounding of drums. The immensity of the job is staggering.

The Ogou are political and militaristic. Ogou is the patron Lwa of the United States. It is interesting that the United States is currently politicized around the health profession. Issues surrounding health insurance, AIDS, the NIH's insistence that chemotherapy is something other than poison, and the anger of the gay community are all factors contributing to an atmosphere of revolution right now. The history of mankind is fraught with bloody revolution, but perhaps the healing crisis in the United States will result in a healing revolution.

The water aspect of Ogou, the warrior, is as a healer. Medicine is often made of small doses of poison. Homeopathic medicine extracts the essence of disease in order to heal. Here Ogou's characteristically destructive tendencies are employed to kill disease.

Ogou Feray

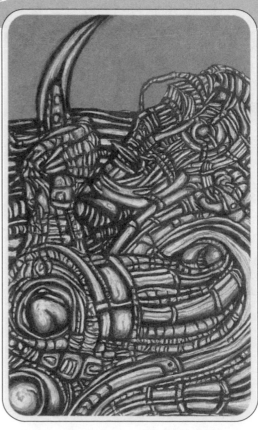

CALL ON OGOU FERAY to give you strength in battle. Call on him to strengthen you, and to help you endure.

OFFERINGS

Machete or saber, iron, toy soldiers, grenade, red candles, 151-proof rum (make pathway of rum from vèvè to offerings, and set on fire), Ogou Feray's image.

LITANY

"Pour Ogoun Ferraille, qui marche sur les points de Mars. Maître de la forge, Dieu de feu. Guerrier, héros. Protégez-nous, pénétrez-nous de votre puissance. Acceptez nos offrandes. Entrez dans nos cœurs, dans nos bras, dans nos jambes. Entrez ici. Dansez avec nous."

KREYÒL

"Pou Ogou Feray, kap maché sou planèt Mas. Mèt foj-la. Solda. Brave. Pwojété nou. Ba-nou pouwa ou. Aksepté ofran'n nou. Antré nan kè nou, nan bra nou, nan jam'm nou. Antré vin'n dansé avek nou."

TRANSLATION

"For Ogou Feray, who walks on the points of Mars. Master of the forge. Warrior, hero. Protect us, infuse us with your power. Accept our offerings. Enter into our hearts, our arms, our legs. Enter and dance with us."

TRADITIONAL

Ogou Feray is both the heroic warrior and the master of iron and the iron forge. He moves with the power of Mars. Ogou's might is characteristically indicated by his machete, with which he imparts the warrior's strength and endurance to his serviteurs. Ogou Feray is a hot aspect of the Ogou, a member of the Nago nanchon. He likes to be ceremonially honored with pomp and circumstance. He likes to appear gloriously attired in full-dress, military regalia, and he likes his libations to be poured with 151-proof rum instead of water.

VISION

Ogou Feray slaps himself together out of junkyard metal. Huge slabs of iron slap together with a tremendous sound. Slapping, screeching, crashing, and slamming together. Ogou the God is born out of the birth pains and groans of this metal. He is made of the fruits of industry. Therefore, he is appropriate as the patron Lwa of Western civilization and imperialism. Here he is a futuristic, iron, cyber-God. He is half being, half machine, with a rolling mechanical eye.

Ogou the warrior purifies through destruction. Ogou is the forger of iron. The aeons of human suffering in war forces us into being strong as metal. Ogou fans the fire of the forge. The fearsome bloodletting of war purifies the human race. When Ogou's force deteriorates into politics, the force is corrupted. In the fierce and bloody battlefield, his force is pure.

C ALL ON OGGÚN when you are
going into battle, when you need
protection from criminals, when you are
about to embark on a journey, especially
by train or car, when you need strength
to endure a tremendous amount of
work, when you are about to undergo
surgery, when you need energy to transform a situation that is stuck, or when
you need a job.

Oggún

OFFERINGS

Spicy foods, 151-proof rum, gin, vodka, dark cigars, red palm oil, roosters, male goats, a machete, a rake, a spade, an awl, a pick, and a hoe, three large railroad spikes in a cauldron, a small bag of salt, palm wine, roasted yams, bullets, knives, a sword, a single chain link, Oggún's *Vodou Visions* image.

LITANY

"Pour Oggún, guerrier, patron de ferraille et des travailleurs. Venez sur votre cheval blanc. Venez avec votre épée. Protégez-nous. Acceptez nos offrandes. Entrez dans nos cœurs, dans nos bras, dans nos jambes. Entrez ici. Dansez avec nous."

SPANISH

"Para Oggún, guerrero. Patrón del hierro y de los trabajadores. Venga encima tú caballo blanco. Venga con tú espada. Defiendanos. Accepta nuestros ofrecimientos. Monta nuestros corazones, nuestros brazos, nuestras piernas. Monta y baile con nosotros."

TRANSLATION

"For Oggún, warrior. Patron of iron and of workers. Come on your white horse. Come with your sword. Protect us. Accept our offerings. Enter into our hearts, our arms, our legs. Enter and dance with us."

TRADITIONAL

One of the warrior Orishas in Santería, Oggún is the God of iron and all metals. He is in charge of employment, and protects all those who work with iron, including construction workers, steelworkers, jewelers, blacksmiths, miners, knife makers, surgeons, and butchers. He is the God of modes of transportation, particularly of cars and trains. He is also the God of vehicular accidents, and of train wrecks. He protects against criminals. His is the sacrificial knife that is the first object to touch the blood of the animal sacrifices, making Oggún the first to consume the offering in a ceremony. Oggún is the fierce force of violence, the God of war, and the raw power embodied in the slaughter. But he can also be called upon to mediate disputes, or to be a diplomat. He has a profound sense of justice, and is the ferocious hand of punishment that rights human wrongs. Often solitary, and sometimes described as somewhat brutish, Oggún is a relentless hard worker, and he is the strength of endurance that helps us carry our load. He is also able to create with iron, and with his vital energy. Therefore, he often can empower creativity. Oggún's sexuality is vitally intense. He is hopelessly in love with Oshún.

Oggún is syncretized with Saint Peter, and the warrior saints. His number is usually three or seven. His colors are black and green. His day is Tuesday.

VISION

Oggún rides up on a beautiful, powerful white horse. The horse is Oggún's Sèvitè, possessed by the God. Oggún gives his horse strength. The horse gives Oggún stature, as well as providing a vehicle for Oggún's strength.

Oggún becomes two cavalry cops, riding shoulder to shoulder at the end of Mardi Gras day. They clear everyone and everything off the street. They are an irresistible authority. It is an odd juxtaposition between the carefree revelers and the cold, hard hand of authority. Our dreams and innocent play run up against the earthly reality of Oggún. He tempers humans. He forges them into iron. Trial by fire. He makes us strong.

If you look at the two shields as hats, and the two forelocks of the horses as pony tails, you will see two young girls facing the cops. Oggún is said to take advantage of weakness. To become strong, we must know our own weaknesses. We must face them, and forge them into strengths.

It is Oggún who fights for justice. Oggún confronts us when we are untrue to our word, or when we fall off our path.

CALL ON LEGBA LA FLAMBO to open the door to the Flambo pantheon. Call on him to increase masculine potency, and to make devotion to the solar-phallic Mysteries.

Legba La flambo

OFFERINGS

Pepper in rum, grilled foods, pipe tobacco soaked in rum, Tabasco sauce, flashing powders, Legba La Flambo's *Vodou Visions* image.

LITANY

"Pour Legba La Flambeau, Dieu le soleil, le phallus ancien de la Volonté, principe de la vie; énergie primordiale, le cordon qui relie l'univers avec son origine divine. Maître des magies du carrefour. Acceptez nos offrandes. Entrez dans nos cœurs, dans nos bras, dans nos jambes. Entrez ici. Dansez avec nous."

KREYÒL

"Pou Legba La Flambo, Lwa soley, zozo nan tan lontan ki sé fòs Volonté. Princip lavi, manman enèji. Kod ki maré nou ak Lwa yo. Mèt maji kalfou. Aksepté ofran'n nou, nan bra nou, nan jam'm nou. Antré vin'n dansé avek nou."

TRANSLATION

"For Legba La Flambo, God the sun, ancient phallus of the Will. Principle of life, primordial energy. The link that connects the universe with its primordial origin. Master of the magics of the crossroad. Accept our offerings. Enter into our hearts, our arms, our legs. Enter and dance with us."

TRADITIONAL

Legba La Flambo is God, the sun. Sometimes bonfires are lit for Legba, and his horses walk in the fires, under his protection. This is Legba as Logos, the creative word of God.

It is said that Kalfou, or Bawon Carrefour, the midnight sun, or the moon to Legba's sun, is the Petwo Legba. While Legba opens the door to the crossroads, Kalfou's magical Will darts and flashes across from known to unknown. It is a perilous crossing for the identified self. But Legba La Flambo offers exploding powders that reveal the flash of the Spirit.

VISION

Hands possessed on the drums! Legba La Flambo enters as a lightning bolt into the necks of the serviteurs. The hairs of Legba La Flambo's beard and head are white with electricity. Each hair is a lightning bolt. His body is so charged with electricity that his hands flash with exploding powders. He is the fire of the sun, the red, radiant solar disk that destroys and burns, and the eye of Siva, destroying the world into perfection. He is the holy, ancient phallus, creating, creating, indiscriminately creating.

Spinning, Legba spins the dancers. Chaos and creation. He is the pleasure of creation. His pleasure climbs within him, and explodes into the sun. Legba La Flambo laughs and laughs. He is the joke that leads to the truth. He is the ecstatic pleasure that leads us back to God the sun. He tells us to take power instead of fearing it and the destruction that can sometimes accompany it.

Legba La Flambo, seated in the fire of the sun, contains the mystery of the Father and the Sun/Son. His lightning bolts are the Holy Ghost.

CALL ON SILIBO NOUVAVOU when you want to feel purified, or when you take a cleansing bath. Call on her when you want to consolidate your magical ability and knowledge.

Silibo Nouvavou

OFFERINGS

Pond water, sunflower seeds, rhinestone necklace (necklace of stars), fireball candies, tea lights floating in a bowl of water, mirrors painted with suns and stars, Silibo's *Vodou Visions* image.

LITANY

"Pour Grande Shi-Lih-Bo Nouvavou, Loa vierge de la purification. Initiée par le soleil, qui prend ses bains dans les feux du soleil. Loa des rivières et des petits lacs. Vous êtes la puissance de la magie. Acceptez nos offrandes. Entrez dans nos cœurs, dans nos bras, dans nos jambes. Entrez ici. Dansez avec nous!"

KREYÒL

"Pou Gran´ Silibo Nouvavou, Lwa vièj pirifikasion kap bènyen nan difé soley. Lwa riviè ak lëtan. Ou sé pouvwa maji. Aksepté ofran'n nou. Antré nan kè nou, nan bra nou, nan jam'm nou. Antré vin'n dansé avek nou!"

TRANSLATION

"For Grand Silibo Nouvavou, virgin Lwa of purification, initiated by the sun, who bathes in the fires of the sun. Lwa of rivers and ponds. You are the power of magic. Accept our offerings. Enter into our hearts, our arms, our legs. Enter and dance with us!"

TRADITIONAL

Grand Silibo Nouvavou governs streams and ponds. Silibo is a virgin Lwa who purifies or bathes herself in the sun. She confers omniscience, and unites the magics of Vodou.

VISION

Silibo Nouvavou appears as a powerful woman, enjoying the full pleasure of her strength, certain in the full measure of her self-knowledge. She bathes in the fiery ocean of the sun. The image of the woman cloaked in the sun is an image that is threatening to many men, but empowering to women. Silibo is a virgin Lwa who is both initiated and purified by the sun. She is virgin in the sense of being an unwed, independent maiden, belonging to herself only, like the sacred prostitutes of Aphrodite, unmarried, but not sexually inexperienced. She is not the shamed, evil, biblical woman, but rather the one who is unsoiled by her choices, equal to any man, and free.

The sun is the solar-phallic presence: the masculine God. Silibo is initiated through union with him, but she remains pure, guiltless, and loving toward herself. The vision is intensely sexual. Silibo is pleasure and potency. She is the Shakti of the Hindus, the Shekinah of the Hebrews, Babylon of Revelations, glorified. In all, she is the feminine power of the Divine.

As Silibo bathes in the fiery sexual waters of the sun, she cleanses herself. As the fire of the sun mingles with the waters of Silibo's rivers and ponds, it is transformed into steam, which is used for power and energy. Hers is the transformative power of magic. She steams the world.

Legba

CALL ON LEGBA when you need guidance for an important decision, when you are about to set out on a journey, or when you need to improve communication, especially with Spirit.

OFFERINGS

Pipe tobacco, rum, three pennies, bones at a crossroads, or, on Legba's altar, a walking stick. Legba's image.

LITANY

"Pour Legba, qui garde la porte. Dieu le soleil, la rayonnement de la création, père et patron. Mystère des carrefours, source de communication entre le visible et l'invisible. Legba, phallus cosmique, poteau-mitan qui s'étire du soleil à la racine. Acceptez nos offrandes. Entrez dans nos cœurs, dans nos bras, dans nos jambes. Entrez ici. Dansez avec nous."

KREYÒL

"Pou Legba, gadien pòt Lwa soley. Papa ak patron. Mistè kafou, sous rélasion visib ak envisib. Poto Mitan ki monté jis nan siè-la. Aksepté ofran'n nou. Antré nan kè nou, nan bra nou, nan jam'm nou. Antré vin'n dansé avek nou."

TRANSLATION

"For Legba, who guards the door. God the solar Father, the radiance of creation, Father and patron. Mystery of the crossroads, source of communication between the visible and the invisible, the center post which stretches from the sun to the root. Accept our offering. Enter into our hearts, our arms, our legs. Enter and dance with us."

TRADITIONAL

The guardian of the crossroads, Legba opens the door that divides the spiritual and physical worlds. Legba is called on first in a Vodou ceremony to allow the other Spirits to pass through his door. He is old and lame from traveling through the world with his children. Legba is seen as a benevolent father figure, but he can be a trickster as well. He can open doors, but he can close them, too. Because of this trickster aspect, Legba has been transposed in New Orleans folklore into a kind of bogeyman. If children aren't well behaved, they are warned that "Papa Legba will get you!" The legendary blues singer Robert Johnson claimed that he paid Legba three dollars at the crossroads so that he could have a successful singing career.

Legba wears Masonic black clothes, and he carries a walking stick. He sits, as the sun, at the top of the crossroads. He is syncretized with Saint Lazarus, who is crippled and walks with a cane, Saint Peter, the gatekeeper of heaven, or with Saint Anthony. Legba likes rum, a good cigar, and the color red. Often bones are placed on his altar.

VISION

Light is creation. Legba is the radiance of the sun, the solar-phallic source of the world. But the sun radiates light continuously into the physical world. Legba not only fathers the world, he participates in his own ongoing creation. Legba is old and crippled; he has been worn by walking through his world. Legba opens the door between the internal and external worlds. Here he tells stories that open the door. The stories stay in the world, as gifts of participation from Legba. But the stories are old and crippled, like Legba himself. We have to look through them to find the original radiance. These stories come to us as fairy tales, as great texts of religion, as folk tales. Encoded within them is the invisible. The sun behind Legba is black. The stories may be gnarled and twisted, but within them truth may be found: "The sun at midnight is ever the sun."

Legba is the crossroads. His old, gnarled stick touches the ground and forms a crossroad where the spiritual penetrates and exchanges with the horizontal plane of the physical. Where the axis crosses, Legba opens the door. Old and crippled as he is, he knows the ordeals a person will face once he opens the door.

CALL ON ELEGGUÁ for luck, to
improve communications, to
guard the door to your home, to open
opportunities and roads.

Elegguá

88

OFFERINGS

Smoked fish, smoked possum, coconut, cigar smoke, white candles, toys, candy, sweets, rum, red palm oil, Elegguá's image.

LITANY

"Pour Elegguá, qui garde la porte. Elegguá, Esprit fourbe qui garde le seuil. Amenez mon message. Portez les mots, enfant qui joue dans le soleil. Acceptez nos offrandes. Entrez dans nos cœurs, dans nos bras, dans nos jambes. Entrez ici. Dansez avec nous."

SPANISH

"Para Elegguá, quien guarda la puerta. Elegguá, espiritu engañador quien guarda el umbral. Traiga mi mensarje, lleva mis palabras, Santo Niño quien juega en el Sol. Accepta nuestros ofrecimientos. Monta nuestros corazones, nuestros brazos, nuestras piernas. Monta y baile con nosotros."

TRANSLATION

"For Elegguá, who guards the door. Elegguá, trickster spirit who guards the threshold. Bring my message. Carry my words, child who plays in the sun. Accept our offerings. Enter our hearts, our arms, our legs. Enter and dance with us."

TRADITIONAL

Elegguá is the Divine messenger who carries messages between humans, the Orishas, and God. He is the opener of the doors and paths to opportunity. He is honored first in Santería ceremonies, and he opens the door for all the other Orishas to enter. Elegguá shuts the door on the ceremony if he is not happy. He guards the door to the home, and he is often found in a cabinet by the front door of a house. Elegguá is a trickster who can close the doors and miscommunicate messages as easily as he can open them. He is particularly harsh with his children when they are negligent, although he is a child himself. People who have received an Elegguá warrior head usually sprinkle water on it, or pour three libations before it to "cool" the head. He is received as one of the warriors, and he is symbolized usually by a cement, coconut, or seashell head with cowrie shells for eyes and mouth. A short metal blade protrudes from the head and represents the power of his Ashé. Do not fail to wash and feed Elegguá every Monday, and rub him with red palm oil. He can bring you luck, choices, and opportunities. But he can punish and humiliate you as well, if you displease him. While Elegguá controls fate, he expects a person to make wise decisions concerning her own destiny.

Elegguá is syncretized with Saint Anthony, and El Niño del Atoche. His colors are red and black. His number is three. His day is Monday.

VISION

Elegguá appears in the aspect of a little girl associated with Grand Silibo, the woman cloaked with the sun. In this aeon, she is the counterpart to Horus, the crowned and conquering child-warrior.

Elegguá opens the door. You can come in, but you may not get back out. Be careful what you wish for, because you just might get it. What is he hiding behind that door? The darkness frightens us because Elegguá opens the door to pure psychic energy. Like the Heyoka guides—the contrary trickster Spirits of Native American spirituality—everything inside that door is upside down and backward. Elegguá is a trickster who can turn us out. If we fear Elegguá and dread what we encounter, our messages will be circumvented, doors will close against us, our world will turn upside down. If we learn to play with Elegguá, if we accept every experience as an opportunity, the door is opened to all boons. It is open to Spirit; to the freedom of the child. Elegguá spins out solar radiance to each of us.

Inside the door, Elegguá plays in the rays of the sun.

Ezili La Flambo

SINGLE MOTHERS should call on Ezili La Flambo for her patronage. Call on her to work through rage and repression. She can find work for you when you need it. Call on her when you need to "tough out" a broken heart.

OFFERINGS

Omelet with corn and peppers, red candle carved as a woman holding a heart, pepper jelly; red jewelry, honey with cinnamon and pepper, corn sprinkled with gunpowder, raw liquor (tafin), sweet and spicy incense, Ezili La Flambo's *Vodou Visions* image.

LITANY

"Pour Erzulie La Flambeau, enflammée de la passion. Erzulie de la jalousie et de la vengeance qui adore le feu, et qui marche sur les points de l'araignée. Mère maïs, inspiration à la révolution, danse de la destruction et de la furie. Acceptez nos offrandes. Entrez dans nos cœurs, dans nos bras, dans nos jambes. Entrez ici. Dansez avec nous."

KREYÒL

"Pou Ezili La Flambo, fanm pasioné. Ezili jalouzi ak révanj ki rin men difé, kap maché sou zaréyin. Manman mayi, enspirasion révolision. Aksepté ofran'n nou. Antré nan kè nou, nan bra nou, nan jam'm nou. Antré vin'n dansé avek nou."

TRANSLATION

"For Ezili La Flambo, enflamed with passion. Ezili of jealousy and vengeance, who loves fire and walks on the points of the spider. Corn mother, inspiration to revolution, dance of destruction and of fury. Accept our offerings. Enter into our hearts, our arms, our legs. Enter and dance with us."

TRADITIONAL

Ezili La Flambo is the Petwo aspect of the love Goddess. She is more commonly called Ezili Dantò, and she is the bitter enemy of Ezili Freda. Ezili La Flambo is characterized by her rage and jealousy. Her vèvè symbolizes her heart pierced by a dagger. She is the patron of unwed mothers, and she fiercely protects her Sèvitè. She is willing to roll up her sleeves and get her hands dirty in order to do hard work for her children.

When the Petwo Ezili's rage and violence are particularly pronounced to the point of drawing blood, she transforms into Ezili Je Rouj, Ezili of the red eyes. Her possessions can be alarming, as with clenched hands and restricted, paralytic gestures she struggles with her inarticulate rage and frustration. Malevolent and man-eating, she is the terrible corn mother of terrifying demeanor.

Dantò, however, is one of the best-known

Petwo Lwa. Unlike Freda, who is dreamy, coquettish, and prone to weeping, Dantò is practical, gives luck, and is a beautiful, strong, black woman.

Ezili La Flambo's animal is the black Haitian pig. She is syncretized most often with Mater Salvatoris, the Black Madonna, whose facial scars were left from a fight with Ezili Freda. She is also syncretized with white Madonnas and children, such as Mount Carmel, who is Our Lady of Prompt Succor, as well as with Our Lady of Lourdes.

VISION

Ezili La Flambo spins and dances wildly with two daggers. She slams her feet down, crushing corn beneath her. Her spinning fury courses through the body. Consciousness shrinks before her, because she is so intimately recognized.

We walk into relationships with vulnerable hearts, wanting the passionate touch of love. Instead, we move from affection to obsession to possession, restriction, and rage. Ezili La Flambo comes in with vengeance and jealousy. She spins into destruction and fury. But she is also the corn mother. She spins with daggers on the corn. In smashing it, she transforms the corn into the substance of nourishment. It also becomes the cornmeal that is used for making the vèvès that call the Gods. Petwo Ezili's rage inspires revolution. As she chafes and rages at restriction, she rattles our cages. She shows us where we must break free into power.

Ezili La Flambo whips up the courage within to renew. She brings change and growth into life despite the diminishing and deadening restraints of social programming. Hers is an act of love that destroys and transforms what was, and empowers growth. Use her rage to revolutionize the quality of your love. Fight to protect your innocence, and your ability to act from your own truth.

Lasirèn

MUSICIANS SHOULD CALL ON LASIRÈN for musical inspiration. Call on Lasirèn when you wish to seduce or when you wish to be seduced. Devotees of Lasirèn should call on her for luck or riches. Sailors call on Lasirèn for safe passage over the ocean.

OFFERINGS

Mirror, comb, cigarettes, shells, perfume, sweet wine, pink rose petals, pearls, seaweed, fish, saltwater, mermaid dolls or images, statues, jewelry, sacred songs, blue sea glass, Lasirèn's image.

LITANY

"Pour La Sirène, enchanteresse, Reîne-chanterelle. Femme d'Agwé. Demi-poisson, demi-femme, qui connaît les Mystères de l'eau, et des ondes. Chantez pour nous la musique sacrée. Enchantez en chantant. Acceptez nos offrandes. Entrez dans nos cœurs, dans nos bras, dans nos jambes. Entrez ici. Dansez avec nous!"

KREYÒL

"Pou Lasirèn. Rèn shantrel. Madan Agwe, mwatyé pwason, mwatyé fan-m. Ki kon mistè nan dlo. Shanté pou nou. Aksepté ofran'n nou. Antré nan kè nou, nan bra nou, nan jam'm nou. Antré vin'n dansé avek nou!"

TRANSLATION

"For Lasirèn, enchantress. 'Rèn Shantrel' [lead choir member]. Wife of Agwe, half fish, half woman, who knows the mysteries of water and waves. Sing the sacred music for us. Enchant by chanting. Accept our offerings. Enter into our hearts, our arms, our legs. Enter and dance with us!"

TRADITIONAL

"La Sirène" means "mermaid" in French. Lasirèn is the wife of Agwe, and an aspect of Ezili. She rules under the sea. Her power is in the depths of the ocean. Some say Labalèn is her mother, some say Labalèn is her husband, or that she is the same Lwa as Lasirèn.

Lasirèn is an enchantress, and the patron Lwa of song and music. She calls out with her trumpet, and entrances with her siren's song. Lasirèn is a beautiful sorceress. Half woman, half fish, she swims in the archetypal Waters between Ezili Freda's beauty and Dantò's passionate violence. Lasirèn bestows luck on her devotees, but be careful! Her beauty and seductive song can lure you to a watery death. Some say, too, that she steals babies and takes them down into her ocean kingdom.

Lasirèn is usually syncretized with Saint Martha or Saint Philomene. Her colors are all hues of ocean blues.

VISION

Half fish, Lasirèn is the perfect metaphor for women, who are deeply connected with tellurian nature. "Fish" is a derogatory term for women. The Siren's song is an enchantment that deters sailors from their course of action. Women are seen as erotic temptresses who sway noble and purposeful men from their True Will. In Vodou, the sensual is not separate from the spiritual. They are one undulating wave of desire. The mermaid is half human, half fish. Lasirèn's song does not wrap us in a fake and fatal glamour; hers is a song that calls to Spirit. Lasirèn undulates in the rhythm of sacred song. Spirit is tangled in her long, flowing hair. When women are mistrusted and misjudged, their song becomes the Siren's song, which leads men into perilous obsession. When they are trusted, honored, and respected, their song is powerful and sweet, and unlocks the mystery of the Divine in Nature.

Labalèn swims in the distance, carrying Spirit in her belly, across the Waters, drawn by the mermaid's song.

CALL ON EZILI for matters of the heart, love, and beauty. When a lover is wanted, call on Ezili to enhance your ability to attract love. Call on her as well when you are disappointed by failed dreams, or when you want to bring your expectations into alignment with reality.

OFFERINGS

Ezili's colors are white, pink, and pale blue. She likes perfume—especially atomizers of Anaïs-Anaïs—pastries, white cake, lace, hand mirrors, Orangeat (a sweet liqueur), images of the Virgin Mary, especially Mater Dolorosa, grenadine, jewelry, rice cooked in cinnamon milk, bananas fried in sugar, mild cigarettes, champagne or white wine, and fruit, espe-

Ezili freda Daomé

cially white grapes. Sometimes a small wooden boat is hung for her from the ceiling of the Ounfò. Ezili's *Vodou Visions* image.

LITANY

"Pour Erzulie Freda Dahomey, qui marche sur tous les points du luxe. La Maîtresse de l'amour, reîne de la beauté, la source du rêve de l'impossible perfection. Belle Erzulie, coquette qui vit dans l'air de l'élégance. Donnez-nous des rêves à foison. Entendez nos prières, Maman. Acceptez nos offrandes. Entrez dans nos cœurs, dans nos bras, dans nos jambes. Entrez ici. Dansez avec nous!"

KREYÒL

"Pou Ezili Freda Daomé, kap maché tou patou nan richès. Metrès lanmou la rèn la boté, sous rèv pèféksion. Ezili bel fanm, kon'n abiyé. Ba nou anpil rèv. Tandé la priyè nou, manman. Aksepté ofran'n nou. Antré nan kè nou, nan bra nou, nan jam'm nou. Antré vin'n dansé avek nou!"

TRANSLATION

"For Ezili Freda Daomé, who walks on all luxurious points. Mistress of love, Queen of beauty, the source of the impossible dream of perfection. Beautiful Ezili, coquette who lives in the atmosphere of elegance. Give us the abundance of our dreams. Listen to our prayers, Mother. Accept our offerings. Enter into our hearts, our arms, our legs. Come and dance with us!"

TRADITIONAL

Ezili Freda Daomé is the Vodou Goddess of love and beauty. She walks in an atmosphere of luxury and elegance. A fair-skinned mulatto, Ezili loves all trappings of refinement and wealth: lace, gold, mirrors, jewelry, and perfume. Ezili is the force that allows mankind to dream of a more perfect life. Slaves saw the abundance of the colonists' homes and lives, and since they knew that they could not attain that wealth, they transferred their dreams of wealth and leisure to Ezili in the heavenly realms. Ezili personifies an unattainable and virgin ideal. She comes to her horses as the coquette, dancing elegantly, flirting, disdaining the other women, displaying her beauty and riches. She inevitably leaves her horses in inconsolable tears, because reality always falls disappointingly short of her dreams.

Ezili's color is white or pink. She is symbolized by a heart-shaped vèvè, and often by a little boat that hangs from the ceiling of an Ounfò. She likes sweets, pastries, champagne, and lace. She is syncretized with the Virgin Mary, and with Mater Dolorosa, the Mother of Sorrows, who is surrounded by baubles and jewels.

VISION

There is a strong connection between Ezili, mirrors, and water. Ezili's tears are the source of the waters of the world: the waters of birth, and the sea of death. She often dances with Gede. Love, which defies death, dances with death. It is love that leads inevitably to the Waters of the Abyss, the Waters of return.

Ezili looks into mirrors and dreams of perfection. It is this dream that leads to her dissatisfaction and disappointment, and which brings on the tears that are the source of the Waters of the Abyss. The mirror is Maya, or illusion. The water is Psyche, or soul. Ezili's little boat that rides on the surface of the water symbolizes worldly things. The water that supports the boat is Psyche, and the depth and substance of Ezili. In all Ezili's primping and luxury is concealed Psyche, the soul of the world. We can look through the surface of the water to see profoundly into the depths that teem with life to create a true dream self.

In the mirror, Ezili is Nuit, the Egyptian Goddess whose body arches across the sky, and her worldly things are the stars of Nuit's body. In the waters, she is Kali, dancing with death.

Oshún

CALL ON OSHÚN to bring love, beauty, and luxury into your life. Call on her during pregnancy to ensure the healthy development of the fetus. Call on her to bless fresh waters. Artists should call on her to inspire the creation of works of beauty.

OFFERINGS

Yellow flowers, river water, honey with cinnamon sticks (taste before giving to Oshún, as someone tried to poison her once), white wine, mirrors, gold or brass bells, jewelry, fans, peacock feathers, honey cakes, kola nuts, omelettes with shrimp and watercress, amber resin, amber and coral beads, cowrie shells, yellow cloth, yellow candles, small boats, oranges, pumpkins, Oshún's *Vodou Visions* image.

LITANY

"Pour ma mère, Oshún, reîne des rivières, des lacs, des cours, des chutes d'eau. Belle Oshún, la puissance féminine, la beauté érotique, la reîne de la sensualité. Près de la cascade, ma mère Oshún se repose souvent. Aie Yeou! Entendez nos prières, Oshún. Acceptez nos offrandes. Entrez dans nos cœurs, dans nos bras, dans nos jambes. Entrez ici. Dansez avec nous."

SPANISH

"Para mi madre, reina de los ríos, lagos, arroyos, y de las cascadas. Mama Cachita, hermosa y linda, poder feminino, balleza erotica, reina de la sensualidad. Cerca de la cascada, mi madre descansa mucha. Ay Heou! Escucha nuestros ruegos Ochún. Accepta nuestros ofrecimientos. Monta nuestros corazones, nuestros brazos, nuestras piernas. Monta y baile con nosotros."

TRANSLATION

"For my Mother, Oshún, Queen of rivers, lakes, streams, waterfalls. Beautiful Oshún, feminine power, erotic beauty, Queen of sensuality. Near the waterfall my Mother Oshún often rests. Aie Yeou! Listen to our prayers, Oshún. Accept our offerings. Enter into our hearts, our arms, our legs. Enter and dance with us."

TRADITIONAL

Oshún is all flowing sensuality. The Santería Orisha of love, erotic feminine beauty, and luxury is also the Spirit of fresh or sweet water: rivers, streams, ponds, lakes, and waterfalls. In her love of all things beautiful, she is patron of art. Oshún has many lovers among the Orishas. She has lured Oggún, been married to Orúnmila, seduced Ochosi, and is the youngest wife of Shangó. She is flirtatious, coquettish, and jealous. She is easily bored with confinement of any kind. Emotional and sensitive in the extreme, she does not take well to insult or injury. Nor is she forgiving. But if she is fond of you, she will bathe and adorn you in all the best that life has to offer: wealth, love, beauty, beautiful clothes and jewelry. Oshún is also the consummate witch! She knows many spells and ebbós, which are often placed in one of her sacred foods, the pumpkin.

Oshún is syncretized with Our Lady of Caridad del Cobra, the patron of Cuba, or Our Lady of Charity. Her color is yellow, her number is five, her celebration day is September 8, her metal is gold or brass, her collares are strung in groups of five yellow beads, separated by one coral bead.

VISION

Oshún is a coquette who dolls herself up and flirts in the surface of the mirror. But if you entice her to respond to you, her powerful waters come flowing from deep within. Her waters flow like rich, delicious honey, fresh and sweet over the world. This is a formula of feminine magic—to conform one's waters to rocky cliffs as waterfalls do, or to basins in the earth as lakes do. In this way, the waters that love and hug the earth reflect through relation the truth of each other. We love in the other what we recognize reflected back to ourselves. Oshún gives love and art. Through art, we seek the truth of beauty. Through love, we seek to respond to the Divinity reflected in the other. Oshún is powerful and beneficial. Offer prayers to her for the waters of love to flow into your life and sweeten it. Oshún's waters rush over waterfalls, cascade into pools of deep meaning, and carry the transformative power of love.

Oshún lifts her skirts to display the place of Mystery within her from which honey water flows out through the world.

CALL ON SIMBI LA FLAMBO
when you wish to do magic!

Simbi La flambo

OFFERINGS

Yams tied up in red metallic ribbons. Yam casserole with peppers, mango chutney, rainwater collected during an electrical storm, electronic components and computer parts, printed e-mail transmissions, yams cooked in hot sauce, snakeskins soaked in rum, vial of mercury, Simbi La Flambo's image.

LITANY

"Pour Simbi La Flambeau, prêtre des Mystères psychopompes. Simbi La Flambeau, magicien de feu, énergie-serpent, maître des Mystères tantriques. La puissance de la Volonté qui transforme tout ce qu'il veut. Acceptez nos offrandes. Entrez dans nos cœurs, dans nos bras, dans nos jambes. Entrez ici. Dansez avec nous!"

KREYÒL

"Pou Simbi La Flambo. Majisien difé. Enèji koulèv. Mèt mistè. Pouvwa volonté ki chanjé tou sa li vlé, tou sa li manyin. Aksepté ofran'n nou. Antré nan kè nou, nan bra nou, nan jam'm nou. Antré vin'n dansé avek nou!"

TRANSLATION

"For Simbi La Flambo, priest of psychoceremonial Mysteries. Simbi La Flambo, fire magician, serpent energy, master of Tantric Mysteries. The power of Will that transforms all it touches, all it desires. Accept our offerings. Enter into our hearts, our arms, our legs. Enter and dance with us!"

TRADITIONAL

Simbi La Flambo is the Petwo Simbi in his purest form, a slithering, licking, moving, mercurial fire. He is the energy of all that flows. Simbi La Flambo is the fiery charge of electricity and the transformative energy of magical change. Simbi La Flambo is also fiery medicine, rushing through the blood to cure.

Simbi La Flambo can be hard to handle. He can communicate through heated arguments, debate, and fiery ordeal.

He is syncretized with the Magi.

VISION

Simbi La Flambo works the Tantric Mysteries. He is the alchemical marriage of conjunctio: the union of opposites, heated and transmuted in the furnace of desire. He is the fire of Will, directed through the body of the snake. How can humans swim through Simbi La Flambo's flames? Through love. Through union. Through love under Will.

Simbi La Flambo walks the mercurial points. He is quicksilver. He darts and flashes through the world. His tongue is a flame that licks us through the magic of experience and stimulates us to pursue our true Will. Fire purifies, transforms, and bathes. It transforms the merely human and renders it able to contain the archetypal. As Simbi La Flambo swims through a sea of fire, the human ego is integrated with the immortal, transpersonal soul.

The rider and Simbi La Flambo are united and fused as the earthly fires of the ego, encountering the frustration of desire, are transformed into the spiritual fires of the Gods.

ALL ON SIMBI DLO for protection of streams, springs, and all fresh-waters. Call on his communication skills when negotiating between two parties.

Simbi Dlo

OFFERINGS

Cock feathers, yams, river rocks, mangoes, snakeskin in basin of water, *Vodou Visions* image of Simbi Dlo.

LITANY

"Pour Simbi de l'eau, serpent tellurien qui se soulève d'en bas de l'eau, qui nous amène la connaissance de la profondeur. Acceptez nos offrandes. Entrez dans nos cœurs, dans nos bras, dans nos jambes. Entrez ici. Dansez avec nous."

KREYÒL

"Pou Simbi Dlo, ki soti an ba dlo pou ba nou la konesans fon la mè, ak la rivyè. Aksepté ofran'n nou. Antré nan kè nou, nan bra nou, nan jam'm nou. Antré vin'n dansé avek nou."

TRANSLATION

"For Simbi Dlo, tellurian serpent who rises from below the waters, who leads us to knowledge of the depths. Accept our offerings. Enter into our hearts, our arms, our legs. Enter and dance with us."

TRADITIONAL

Simbi Dlo, or "Simbi in two waters," is the best known of the Simbi. While Simbi is generally considered a Petwo Lwa, he is actually a Kongo Lwa who straddles the nations between Petwo and Rada. Simbi Dlo's domain extends through the freshwaters upon the earth, as well as the Abysmal Waters of the soul.

Simbi Dlo is particularly guardian of freshwater, springs, lakes, and pools. He is known to kidnap children who swim in his springs. They must serve him for a few years but, when he returns them to their homes, he rewards them with psychic abilities.

VISION

Simbi is tellurian Nature, the underworld beneath the topside world. There, in shadows, we encounter our depths. We fear Simbi's wild eyes, his bite. But his poisonous venom can be medicinal. He slithers through submerged regions where dreams, talent, and magic lie. Simbi bites down on a mouthful of water and transforms it into serpents that slither in a thousand directions. From our shadow side, a thousand impulses communicate our depths to our topside consciousness. If we allow ourselves to eat or integrate these impulses, we gradually transform the depths into konesans.

C ALL ON SIMBI for healing, to improve communications, and to keep your computer trouble-free.

Simbi

OFFERINGS

Yams, a Magic Mirror, green snakeskins, light green candles, mangoes, turtle shells, river rocks, mercurial incense, mercury, Simbi's image.

LITANY

"Pour Simbi, serpent/psychopomp qui marche sur les points magiques mercuriels. Serpent qui entre, sort comme un trait parmi les illusions. Magicien qui reflète ce qui est au dessous dans ce qui est en bas. Acceptez nos offrandes. Entrez dans nos cœurs, dans nos bras, dans nos jambes. Entrez ici. Dansez avec nous!"

KREYÒL

"Pou Simbi, kap maché sou pwen majik planèt Mèku. Majisien kap montré sa ki an lè nan sa ki anba. Aksepté ofran'n nou. Antré nan kè nou, nan bra nou, nan jam'm nou. Antré vin'n dansé avek nou!"

TRANSLATION

"For Simbi, serpent/psychopomp, who walks on the magical points of Mercury. Serpent who darts between illusions. Magician who mirrors forth that which is above in that which is below. Accept our offerings. Enter into our hearts, our arms, our legs. Enter and dance with us!"

TRADITIONAL

Simbi is the magical serpent of Vodou. He is lord of the freshwater rivers, streams, rainfall, and all things that flow, like electricity and electronics. He is the mercurial serpent that carries communications—the perfect patron Lwa of e-mail! His vèvè depicts the flow of energies around and through the crossroads. Simbi slithers across the crossroads, guides the possessed through the dangerous no-man's-land between the moment of loss of consciousness and the taking on of a Lwa during the crisis of possession. Perhaps this is one of the reasons that he is associated with clairvoyance. Simbi's magic extends to the realm of botanicals, the leaves of which he uses for healing.

Simbi is syncretized with the Three Wise Men. His colors are gray or light green. His animal is the tortoise.

VISION

Flashes of light and magic! Simbi, the magician, stands in the balance between good and evil, between that which is above and that which is below. Simbi makes the traditional gesture of the magician: one hand reaching up to the power of superconsciousness, the other directing that power out into the material world. He stands between the opposites, reconciles them, balances them, redirects them, and transforms them, as if by magic. He is the channel that directs the current of Will from the unlimited light above into the concentrated flash of light below. His channeling is reflected in the tubular body of the snake or the magical wand or the phallus.

His is the mercurial-phallic power, rather than the solar-phallic power. His is the quality of quicksilver, and here the magical energy darts out as numerous little green messenger snakes. Thought arises in the mind and runs in a thousand directions, a thousand thoughts. Concentrating one thought, one word, one Will, the magician makes himself the courier of the magical power of change. As his eye or purpose becomes single, he is flooded with light. It is the flash of the Spirit.

Simbi delights in this play of magic. It is fun to work with and direct the energy of change, the power of Will. Simbi is a master of magic. He darts and flashes through the dark. It is his work and his joy. Run the mercurial points with Simbi!

Shangó

CALL ON SHANGÓ for the courage needed to work though fear and to face personal transformation. Call on him for personal power and for justice. Drummers call on him to inspire drumming and dancers call on him for inspiration through dance. Call on him for passionate procreation.

OFFERINGS

Bananas, red apples, bitter kola nuts, red palm oil, sarsaparilla, thunderstones (elongated, smooth stones that are said to be formed by thunderbolts), rams, roosters, rum, sugarcane, icon of Santa Barbara, red candle, cascarilla (crushed eggshell), Shangó's *Vodou Visions* image.

LITANY

"Pour Shangó, roi sage et beau, seigneur du tambour et de la danse, puissance du tonnerre. Nous vous glorifions, Shangó, de la hache double, maître de la guerre et de la magie. OBAKOSO! Caboé, caboé, caboé. Cabiosilé o! Acceptez nos offrandes. Entrez dans nos cœurs, dans nos bras, dans nos jambes. Entrez ici, dansez avec nous."

SPANISH

"Para Changó, rey guapo y sabia, señor del tambor y del baile, poder del trueno. Le alabamos, Changó, del hacho doble filo, maestro de la guerra y del magia. El Rey no se murio! Bienvenidos, bienvenidos, mi Señor.

Accepta nuestros ofrecimientos, monta nuestros corazones, nuestros brazos, nuestras piernas. Monta y baile con nosotros."

TRANSLATION

"For Shangó, wise and beautiful King, lord of drumming and dance, power of thunder. We praise you, Shangó, of the double ax, master of war and of magic. The King does not die! Welcome, welcome, welcome, my Lord! Accept our offerings. Enter into our hearts, our arms, our legs. Enter and dance with us."

TRADITIONAL

Shangó is the son of Yemayá, but was also a historical King, the fourth chief of Oyo in eastern Nigeria. Shangó was quick to anger and tempestuous, which may account for his association with the power of thunder and lightning. Myth indicates, however, that he acquired those powers from his wife, Oyá. There are numerous tales about Shangó, but many include versions of his dealings with his brothers or generals, Gboonkaa and Timi. Most say that he plotted to turn the two against one another, or plotted to turn people against them so that he could preserve unrivaled power and dominion for himself in his kingdom. He was so full of remorse and shame over his actions that he hanged himself. Differing accounts say that Oyá found him or that his body had disappeared when his followers went out to find him. Either way, it is common to say, "Obo ko so!" ("The King did not hang!"). Shangó transcended humanity and became an Orisha.

Shangó is lord of fire and his energy is powerful, violent, and transformative. His is the courage that leads people through fear in order to transform their experience. If a person is resistant to change, Shangó's initiations can strike like lightning. Shangó is a God of male sexual power and masculine beauty. He has had many wives among the Orishas. In Yoruba custom, women kneel and lift their breasts in their hands in ritual ges-

ture to Shangó. He is the patron of dance and of drumming. Shangó's powers also preside over magic, and his initiates, filled with Shangó's force, perform feats of magic at his festival.

Shangó's devotional necklaces alternate red and white beads. He is syncretized with Santa Barbara. Palm trees are sacred to him. His ceremonial objects are the double-handled ax and the seeree, a small gourd that is used as a rattle.

In Haiti, Shangó is associated with Ogou, and is called Ogou-Shangó.

VISION

The power of thunder drives Shangó's vision. Shangó, an Orisha who is acquainted with the experience of death, is the magical link between the human and the Divine. He reaches up with his double ax to receive the influx of Ashé, which he dispenses outward into the calabashes that are held by the women devotees. Shangó is master of magic, and in the symbolism of his ax pouring life into the vessels of the women is expressed the sexual Mysteries that power magic.

Shangó is King. His violent temper and the ferocious power of his state send men to war. They bleed from the vessels of life force that are their bodies. Women bleed from their wombs. They give the sons of their wombs to the Kings that they might spend them in battle. This is the great sorrow of women who must deal with war. So women weep, men fight and die, and the kingdom continues.

The King does not die. His power is carried in the women's calabashes onward into new transformations. While Shangó's force destroys through his storming rages, he also imparts the courage to procreate in the hopes of transcending the human condition. He holds his double-handled ax above his head. The passionate lover balances the fearsome dictator. Shangó's heart drums the rhythmic embrace of love and Will.

C ALL ON MASA LA FLAMBO for tempering, and for safe passage through trials by fire. Call on them for purification, and for detoxing.

Masa La Flambo

OFFERINGS

Basalt (volcanic glass); well water with peppers; highly caloric and spicy foods; lunar foods such as rice cakes and crescent breads, sprinkled with hot sauce. Masa La Flambo's image.

LITANY

"Pour Masa La Flambeau, Mystères qui marchent sur les points de la lune, qui marchent entre les points sur lesquels marchent les autres Mystères, qui transportent le feu liquide d'un Loa à l'autre. Loas de transfert magique. Nous nous baignons dans le bain de feu magique. Montrez-nous le puits de feu intérieur qui est la porte de l'Hounfor. Acceptez nos offrandes. Entrez dans nos cœurs, dans nos bras, dans nos jambes. Entrez ici. Dansez avec nous."

KREYÒL

"Pou Masa La Flambo, mistè kap maché sou la lin. Kap transmèt difé youn Lwa bay youn lòt. Lwa transfè maji. Nap binyin nan youn benye difé ki sé pòt Ounfò-a. Aksepté ofran'n nou. Antré nan kè nou, nan bra nou, nan jam'm nou. Antré vin'n dansé avek nou."

TRANSLATION

"For Masa La Flambo, Mysteries who walk on the points of the moon, who walk between the points on which the other Mysteries walk, who transport liquid fire from one Lwa to another. Lwa of magical transfer. We bathe in your magical bath of fire, which is the door of the Ounfò. Accept our offerings. Enter into our hearts, our arms, our legs. Enter and dance with us."

TRADITIONAL

Masa La Flambo particularly embodies the Masa Mysteries' rulership over magical baths. Here are the Masa's fire baths that burn in the furnace of alchemical, molten change and transformation. Masa La Flambo strikes a strong image in the imagination, carrying the fire-filled pots that are used in the Boulé-zen from one point of Mystery to another. The Boulé-zen are the ceremonies in which earthenware pots filled with offerings and oil are heated. The Boulé-zen heats up both the offerings and the Lwa, increasing their power. Their furnace is a fiery well of magic fire. Theirs is the molten core of the earth and the fires of the imagination. As masters of these fire baths, they are able to give passage through their beings from one point to another. They carry the life force within their Mysteries.

VISION

Masa La Flambo pour calabashes of molten substance into a furnace. Particles of fire flare up and are consumed into the air like images of Maya, the Hindu concept of illusion, in the astral light. You can't fix your eyes on Masa La Flambo. They dart and flit between fiery points. Life force is fleeting. We cannot hold on to life; we can only savor its precious flame.

Masa La Flambo traditionally rule wells. The fire Masa are symbolized by the alchemical athanor in which dross metal is tempered and transformed into gold. They are also symbolized by the molten pools within volcanoes, which erupt as creative and destructive liquid fire; creative as in the symbolism of ejaculating sperm—destructive as fiery lava that consumes the land. These are Kali's cremation fires, which burn in the well of her womb. Ogou Feray forges his iron in these furnaces. Masa La Flambo burn off the imperfections and excesses of the dross self to leave the precious, tempered self in its stead. Tapas, or body heat, burns off toxins to leave the treasures of the soul.

Madanm Lalinn

Call on Madanm Lalinn for astral vision, for enchantments, for all lunar magic.

OFFERINGS

Mica, candles, honey, croissant rolls, sweet liqueur, images of the moon, rice cakes, white cakes, mirrors in a bowl of water, Madanm Lalinn's *Vodou Visions* image.

LITANY

"Pour Madame La Lune, puissance lunaire, puissance de l'imagination. Créatrice des images, des fantaisies, des folies. Luminescence gentille qui reflète la clarté du soleil. Madame, qui s'enveloppe dans le mystère de l'enchantement. Encorselez-nous dans vos marées! Acceptez nos offrandes. Entrez dans nos cœurs, dans nos bras, dans nos jambes. Entrez ici. Dansez avec nous!"

KREYÒL

"Pou Madanm Lalinn, ki ganyin pouvwa nan lalinn, ki ganyin pouvwa imaginasyon, ki kréyé toutt imaj, ki kréyé gwissans é lafoli, ki bay mwayen pou wè limiè soley. Youn Madanm ki ganyin mistè é kibel. Mété nou nan foss lanm ou. Aksepté ofran'n nou. Antré nan kè nou, nan bra nou, nan jam'm nou. Antré vin'n dansé avek nou!"

TRANSLATION

"For Madanm Lalinn, power of the imagination, creator of images, of fantasies, of folly, gentle reflection of the sun's light. Madanm, who surrounds herself with glamour. Intoxicate us with your tides. Accept our offerings. Enter into our hearts, our arms, our legs. Enter and dance with us!"

TRADITIONAL

Madanm Lalinn is the glamorous and luminous lady of the moon. She influences the tides and dreams.

VISION

Madanm Lalinn walks in on cool points. She is moist. Water, water everywhere. Her colors wash in like astral frescoes painted on translucent flakes of reflective mica: white and pearlescent, then shimmering into color.

The vision is all about reflection and imagination: reflection on surfaces; reflection of the sun's light; reflection of the astral into the physical; reflective Magic Mirrors, which work with reversed images. In Vodou, we give offerings with the left hand so they can reverse into the realm of the Invisibles. This world is a reflection of the astral. It is a reflection of spiritual truth, through a glass, darkly. Through Lalinn's Magic Mirror we cross back into the truth, which is the false play of astral images: Maya.

Madanm Lalinn's image does not show in the water's surface, because I am her reflection in visioning her. People looking into her image are her reflection.

Reflection as a mental state is a condition of passive receptivity, which allows inspiration of Spirit to enter into the imagination. It is important to note that Lalin is Madanm (Mrs.), not Mademoiselle (Miss). She is not innocent or naïve. The realm of the imagination warrants our serious respect. She draws her finger through the moon's reflection, slicing it. Acts of the creative imagination can be violent, like the very act of pencil scratching into paper, or brush hitting canvas. The world of sorrow or pain causes us to reflect, to think. These reflections lead to creative acts. They cut below the surface, and are soul-deep. Madanm Lalinn cuts through the surface reflection to the dark depths in which our creative genius lurks, to where the substance is, to the creative and imaginative dark waters of the soul.

Our imagination must not be deceptive or idle. Our creative acts must be honed till they are a match for our experience of the truth, or we will descend into madness and folly, which are also Madanm's domain.

Masa

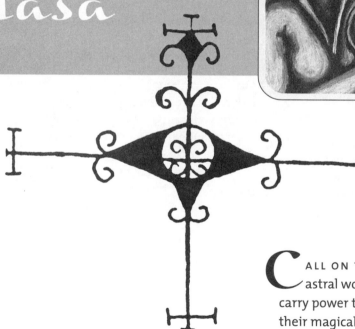

CALL ON THE MASA to charge all astral workings. Call on them to carry power to all your work. Call on their magical vessel to explore the astral realm.

OFFERINGS

Well water, libation bottles, mirrors, bath salts, herbal medicinal baths, honey cakes (lunar), rice cakes (lunar), crescent rolls (lunar), Masa's *Vodou Visions* image.

LITANY

"Pour Masa, qui marche sur les points de la lune, tout en amenant l'eau d'un Mystère à l'autre. Maître de l'eau. Emportez-nous dans votre barque magique vers la lune. Nous nous baignons dans vos bains magiques alimentés par vos puits puissants. Acceptez nos offrandes. Entrez dans nos cœurs, dans nos bras, dans nos jambes. Entrez ici. Dansez avec nous."

KREYÒL

"Pou Masa, kap maché sou la lin kap poté dlo bay Lwa-yo. Mèt dlo. Mété nou sou bato ki pral nan la lin. Nap benyen nan benyen majik ou poté banou. Aksepté ofran'n nou. Antré nan kè nou, nan bra nou, nan jam'm nou. Antré vin'n dansé avek nou."

TRANSLATION

"For Masa, who walks on the points of the moon while carrying water from one Mystery to another. Master of water. Take us on your magic boat to the moon. We bathe in your magic baths, which are supplied by your wells of power. Accept our offerings. Enter into our hearts, our arms, our legs. Enter and dance with us."

TRADITIONAL

The Masa are masters of the Waters. They particularly carry the Waters between the power points that constellate other Lwa. The Masa are conduits that transport Ashé; they are magical in nature, lunar, astral, unfixed. Their magic is experienced in the moment of change, of transferal, of exchange. Like shamans, they move through negative space—the in-between—to transport power to the positive points of the Lwa. The Masa are also the wells that hold the Waters, and the libation jug that pours water onto the ground of the Ounfò, linking it to the astral power of the Mysteries. From their Waters, magical, lunar vessels are born to transport the Waters throughout the heavens, issuing into the world.

VISION

Masa dances between the points of other Lwa in unfettered joy. She is the astral light and water. To dive into her water is to dive into the realm of the imagination with its fluid images and fluid states of mind. Masa's Waters are healing baths. The imaginative realm is eternal, beyond space and time. In the imagination, we are free to experience the joy of Divine humanity. The astral light is there, everywhere, within interior realms. Masa's crescent boat is always waiting to take us to the moon—realm of visions, of poetry, of intoxicating inspiration. Indeed, Masa's wells are ancient sources of inspiration.

Magicians teach that the physical world is based on astral images. The astral images are blueprints for mundane reality. If we can learn to dance creatively with the images of imagination, we can change our circumstances by changing ourselves. Look in between the forms of physical reality; it is there that Masa flows.

Here Masa rubs a magic calabash. Like Aladdin's lamp, it secretes magic. From her calabash flow her inspiring Waters that are wells of spiritual wisdom, hidden within the desert of material life.

Masa's boat is a crescent moon. Its sails are powered by imagination. It is the duty of seers and visionaries—the poets, artists, musicians—to carry Masa's transformative powers between the points; to remind us always of the transformative power of the imaginative realm that exists eternally between the points of temporal reality.

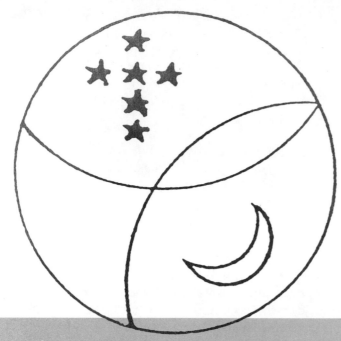

C ALL ON YEMAYÁ for protection, peace, benevolence, and wealth. Call to her when you need nurturing or to secure the devotion of family. Call to her whenever you are by the ocean.

Yemayá

OFFERINGS

Seafood, seaweed, seashells, watermelon, flowers, blue and white beads, blue candles, mirrors, fruits, especially melons and grapes, coconut milk, sugarcane syrup, plantains and fried pork rinds, coconut cakes, light cigarettes, seven coins, silver boat filled with offerings, tied with blue and white ribbons, and set to float on the ocean waves, Yemayá's *Vodou Visions* image.

LITANY

"Pour ma Mère, Yemayá, Mère et maîtresse de l'océan. Mère des Orishas, gardienne des enfants, reîne des ondes. Je suis la fille de l'océan, la fille des ondes, la fille de l'écume. Yemayá, Mère de l'océan, oh ma Mère Yemayá, descendez et conseillez-moi. Acceptez nos offrandes. Entrez dans nos cœurs, dans nos bras, dans nos jambes. Entrez ici. Dansez avec nous."

SPANISH

"Para mi Madre, Yemayá, Madre y dueña del mar. Madre de las Orichas, protectora de la niñez, reina de los ondas. Soy la hija del mar, hija de las ondas, hija de las espumas del mar. Yemayá, Madre del mar. Ay, Madre mia bajate a mì, y dame consuelo y alivio. Accepta nuestros ofrecimientos. Monta nuestros corazones, nuestros brazos, nuestras piernas. Monta y baile con nosotros."

TRANSLATION

"For my Mother, Yemayá, Mother and mistress of the sea. Mother of the Orishas, guardian of children, queen of the waves. I am the daughter of the ocean, the daughter of the waves, the daughter of the seafoam. Yemayá, Mother of the ocean. Oh, my Mother, Yemayá, descend and counsel me. Accept our offerings. Enter into our hearts, our arms, our legs. Enter and dance with us."

TRADITIONAL

Yemayá is the Santería Goddess of the ocean and saltwater. She is the absolute, maternal feminine. She wears a cowrie shell headpiece and a beautiful, full dress of ocean blue. Her song and her dance sway and undulate like the waves and tides. She spins and spins, often looking into a mirror. Yemayá is Mother to many of the Orishas. Sometimes she is said to be Oshún's Mother, sometimes her devoted sister. But it is accepted that Oshún often hands her children over to Yemayá once they are born, for Yemayá to nurture and raise. Yemayá is proud and protective of her children.

Yemayá has seven aspects, including Olokun, the mermaid/siren/sorceress who dwells on the dark bottom of the sea. Yemayá brings abundance and wealth from the sea. Hers is the peace, comfort, and benevolence of the Mother, but she can be dangerous to her children, who, if they become obsessed with their Mother, walk out into a watery, entranced death. Yemayá's powers include the typhoon and tidal wave. Her usual tranquillity can equally erupt, overwhelm, and destroy. She should be approached with love, but also with awe and honor.

Yemayá is syncretized with Our Lady of Regla, and La Diosa del Mar, the Star of the Sea. She is patron of Brazil. Her color is blue, her number is seven, and her collares are strung alternately with seven blue and seven white beads.

VISION

Yemayá is dark in blues and pregnant with the saltwaters of birth and life. She nurtures all life.

Yemayá holds us as her children in her arms. Knowing ourselves as her children, we can receive her protection and nurturing. Yemayá is full with the oceans of the world. She is big, proud, powerful. Her waves crash inward with colossal power. If you can get in sync with her rhythms, you can flow with all her power behind you, empowering you. Or, if you swim against her tides, her surf will crash over you and drown you.

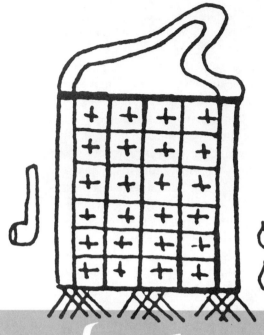

CALL ON AZAKA LA FLAMBO when you need to churn the creative soil of the imagination. Call him when you are creatively stuck.

Azaka La Flambo

OFFERINGS

Corn with hot sauce, corn cakes cooked with jalapeño peppers, burlap sacks filled with pipe tobacco, barbecued corn nuts, tafia rum, kleren, Azaka La Flambo's image.

LITANY

"Pour Azaka La Flambeau, qui enflamme la terre mise en sillons. Azaka La Flambeau, qui fume sa pipe magique. Mari/Sorcier, et principe fécondateur des plantes. Acceptez nos offrandes. Entrez dans nos cœurs, dans nos bras, dans nos jambes. Entrez ici. Dansez avec nous!"

KREYÒL

"Pou Azaka La Flambo, kap fimen pip magik-li. Papa pitit', bòkò ak nouriti plant'. Aksepté ofran'n nou. Antré nan kè nou, nan bra nou, nan jam'm nou. Antré vin'n dansé avek nou!"

TRANSLATION

"For Azaka La Flambo, who enflames the power of earth. Azaka La Flambo, who smokes his magic pipe. Husband/Sorcerer and fertilizing source of the plants. Accept our offerings. Enter into our hearts, our arms, our legs. Enter and dance with us!"

TRADITIONAL

Azaka, the minister of agriculture, is in his fire aspect as Azaka La Flambo. He is ravenous and devours his food whenever he can get it, like a feral animal. He is said to be Gede's brother but lacks Gede's sophisticated, satirical performance. Rather, Azaka La Flambo is a simple peasant with a vast hunger for food and for sex. For all of that, he is a very hard worker and helps peasants to shoulder their many burdens.

VISION

Azaka La Flambo works with the fire of creative imagination. He smokes his pipe and, from the puffs of smoke, figures appear. These figures are fertile, creative, fecundating.

Azaka La Flambo does not dig for what is deep in the earth. Rather, he works with what the earth has thrown up, like lava. The imaginative mind takes what material comes up from the dark, unseen depths, creating images from it. It is said that humans tell stories so that we can tell ourselves who we are. We make ourselves through our own myths. Azaka La Flambo smokes the tobacco he has grown in the rich earth. Images grow in the meeting of fire and earth. The mythic stories give meaning to our most basic, essential human experiences. Man, woman. The envisioning of family and future. The weaving of story line in smoke. The planting of seed in the earth.

Azaka La Flambo churns the dark earth for family histories and creates the stories of self in his magic smoke.

CALL ON GRAN BWA when you want to connect with your ancestral roots or when you want to connect with the spiritual home of Vodou.

Gran Bwa

OFFERINGS

In a basin of water, offer Gran Bwa leaves, roots, branches, or flowers. Other offerings include goat cheese, skin that has been shed by a red-tail boa, water bugs, a drawing of the Qabalistic Tree of Life, a tree sapling (which can be planted as part of the ritual), and Gran Bwa's image.

LITANY

"Pour Grand Bois, qui marche sur tous les points magiques de l'arbre. Les branches boivent la lumière du soleil, pendant que les racines boivent les Eaux dans la terre. Maître de l'île en bas de l'Eau où retournent les Morts, d'où retournent les Loa. Grand Bois, donnez-nous le pouvoir de l'asson. Acceptez nos offrandes. Entrez dans nos cœurs, dans nos bras, dans nos jambes. Entrez ici. Dansez avec nous!"

KREYÒL

"Pou Gran Bwa, kap maché nan nam pyé bwa. Bransh bwa valé limyè soley-la alòské rasin ap sousé te-a. Mèt zilé-a an ba dlo, koté Mò-yo alé ak koté Lwa-yo sòti. Banou pouvwa asson. Aksepté ofran'n nou. Antré nan kè nou, nan bra nou, nan jam'm nou. Antré vin'n dansé avek nou!"

TRANSLATION

"For Gran Bwa, who walks on all the magical points of the Tree. The branches drink the light of the sun, while the roots drink the Waters within the earth. Ruler of the island beneath the Waters, to which return the Dead, from which return the Lwa. Give us the power of the rattle. Accept our offerings. Enter into our hearts, our arms, our legs. Enter and dance with us!"

TRADITIONAL

Gran Bwa is the master of Ginen, the magic island below the sea, and patron of the forests. His vèvè looks like a cross between a human and a tree. It is reminiscent of the Tree of Life and of the Divine man. Gran Bwa's roots extend into the earth, his branches and leaves reach up through the air into the light of the sun. His magic courses between Gede's Abysmal Waters and Legba's solar radiance. The Dead return to Gran Bwa's island. Ancestral roots belong there, and from Ginen arise the Lwa. Gran Bwa's magical animal is a red serpent. He is syncretized with Saint Sebastian, who is often depicted tied to a tree. Gran Bwa likes to be offered branches and flowers.

VISION

The translucent white fingers of Gran Bwa's forest undulate beneath the Waters. Gran Bwa appears as a red serpent in the tree branches, undulating as well. Everywhere is movement and shimmering. Everywhere there are tiny gemlike bugs that contain the souls of the Dead and the Lwa. The Waters of the Dead are teeming with life. All is luminous, reflecting spiritual presence within the magic forest.

Gran Bwa, the red serpent, slithers up a white tree trunk. The tree is the symbolic glyph of the Qabalah. Gran Bwa's trees are under water, reflecting in a strangely silent and submerged way the forest of the topside world. "As above, so below, as below, so above, but after a different manner." The branches of a tree reach into the sky; the roots grow deep into the earth. The sap connects it all like blood, like the presence of Spirit. According to initiatory tradition, the serpent path takes us back up the Tree from Malkuth, where Gran Bwa resides, to Kether, the realm of Danbala, the serpent God. Gran Bwa, the red serpent, is warm with blood, the magic sap of life. The Tree draws life from submerged areas into the light of the sun.

CALL ON AZAKA to bring in a good crop and to bless the fields. Farmers, especially, but also all workers and laborers should call on Azaka to help them carry their workloads. Call on Azaka whenever there is hard work to be done.

Azaka

OFFERINGS

Corn, Indian corn, corn nuts, corn bread, to-bacco, burlap or straw bag with corn, pop-corn, herbs, cornmeal, cereal, rum, garden tools, Azaka's image.

LITANY

"Pour Azaka, Loa de la Terre. Cousin simple des paysans qui travaillent dans les champs. Azaka de la terre mise en sillon, des produits des champs, de la moisson. Acceptez nos of-frandes. Entrez dans nos cœurs, dans nos bras, dans nos jambes. Entrez ici. Dansez avec nous."

KREYÒL

"Pou Azaka, Lwa la Tè. Kouzin peyizan kap travay la tè. Azaka Lwa travay la tè ak rekolt. Aksepté ofran'n nou. Antré nan ké nou, nan bra nou, nan jam'm nou. Antré vin'n dansé avek nou."

TRANSLATION

"For Azaka, Lwa of the Earth. Simple cousin of the peasants who work in the fields. Azaka of the ploughed earth, of the fruits of the field, of the harvest. Accept our offerings. Enter into our hearts, our arms, our legs. Enter and dance with us."

TRADITIONAL

Azaka is God's minister of agriculture. He is the Lwa of the cultivated fields and patron of farmers. He is an extremely hardworking Lwa who helps the peasants shoulder their heavy burdens. Azaka is a peasant himself, a good-natured but simple country cousin. He dresses in blue denim with a red scarf, a straw hat and a tasseled macoute, or woven straw bag, over his shoulder. He smokes a pipe and carries a machete. He is Gede's brother and, like Gede, has a ravenous ap-petite. He tends to devour food during his possessions. He has Gede's appetite for sex, too. Azaka has been likened to a Vodoun Pan—a bit crass and appetent perhaps, but full of germinating life force. What Azaka lacks by way of Gede's urban sophistication, he makes up for with sincerity of character, with generosity, and with his willingness to help out. Azaka carries roasted corn kernels in his macoute, which he shares with all his Sèvitè when he arrives.

Saint Isadore, with his bag and dark blue robe, is syncretized with Azaka.

VISION

Azaka sows the seeds and works the earth. Skeletons grow in rows, like corn, which Gede—Azaka's brother—cuts down with a scythe. The dust of their bones forms the ground that Azaka plows. Gede sneers at Azaka's work. The skeletons' grins mock his ef-fort. Azaka just works on in simple accep-tance. From Azaka, we can learn about the richness of daily labor. Daily digging. Daily blessings from Azaka. Over his able shoulder is the rainbow of promise that someday his hard work will reach fruition.

Azaka does not care that he is disregarded and goes unhonored. Perhaps if we gave more credit to the fruits of the field and less credit to the weaponry of death, we would feel ourselves better nourished. Azaka is sim-ple goodness and the goodness to be found in hard work.

Ochosi

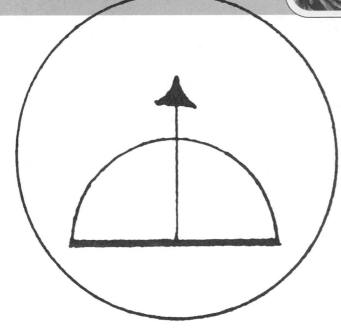

CALL ON OCHOSI for help with trials, for a successful hunt, or for knowledge of the ways of the forest. Call on him for knowledge of botanical healing and magic.

OFFERINGS

A bow and arrow, fruit, candy, venison, game birds, milk, honey, and cornmeal, mixed. Ochosi's *Vodou Visions* image.

LITANY

"Pour Ochosi, Orisha des chasseurs, et des animaux des forêts. Lancez votre flèche, Ochosi, à mon étoile secrète. Ajustez bien en haut, aux destins qui brillent dans la nuit. Acceptez nos offrandes. Entrez dans nos cœurs, dans nos bras, dans nos jambes. Entrez ici. Dansez avec nous."

SPANISH

"Para Ochosi, Oricha de los cazadores y de las animales del bosque. Fusila tú saeta, Ochosi a mi estrella secreta. Apunta arriba, Ochosi al destinidad que brilla en la noche. Accepta nuestros ofrecimientos. Monta nuestros corazones, nuestros brazos, nuestras piernas. Monta y baile con nosotros."

TRANSLATION

"For Ochosi, Orisha of hunters and forest animals. Let go your arrow, Ochosi, at my secret star. Aim high, Ochosi, at the destinies that shine in the night. Accept our offerings. Enter into our hearts, our arms, our legs. Enter and dance with us."

TRADITIONAL

One of the warriors, Ochosi is Orisha of the hunt, and the forest. He is patron of hunters. His is the life of the loner, although he does maintain a relationship with Oggún and Obatalá. He uses his exceptional hearing and sight to hunt for game. He has acquired knowledge of the magical use of forest herbs from Osain, Orisha of herbs. He sometimes helps to carry out Obatalá's justice. As a result, he has become the owner of jails and prisons.

His symbols are the bow and arrow. He is syncretized with Saint Sebastian or Saint Norbert.

VISION

The forest forms in its fullness of color, sound, and smell. It is full of animal and vegetal energies and hunters, all in a kind of chaotic conspiracy.

Ochosi is active in the earthy realm of Malkuth that implies a return to the origins of archetypal Kether. There is a connection here with Sagittarius, the archer of the zodiac, who totally ignores the earth aspect in his high aspirations. Sagittarians often aim at higher powers and philosophies, ignoring the suffering body. They search for something so high that they fail to respect or acknowledge the needs of the body. You have to discover the beauty and delight of the earth, or you miss the Mystery of incarnation.

Ochosi's arrow resembles my own magical wand and is shot from the heart—not at animals, but at the stars. A silence of glittering indigo space and stars shimmers down, back into the forest to inspire the conspiracy of destiny.

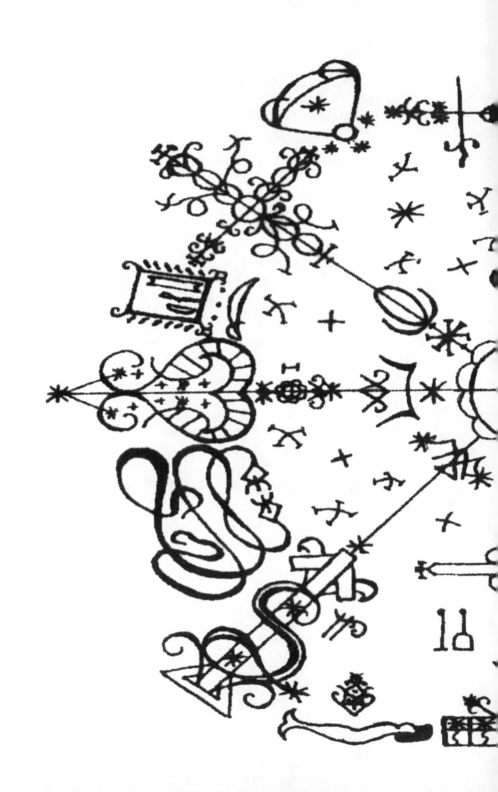

Oungan

THE OUNGAN are the high priests of Vodou, who have accepted themselves and taken up their power. An Oungan can "work with both hands," i.e., can work with both malevolent and benevolent powers, or can work with all the nations of Lwa, or can work predominantly with the one particular nation to whom their nature seems most well suited. The Oungan are syncretized with the Kings of a traditional tarot deck. Drums are the magical implement or weapon. We are in the realm, suit, and element of fire. The Santero is the counterpart of the Oungan in Santería.

*

Petwo Oungan

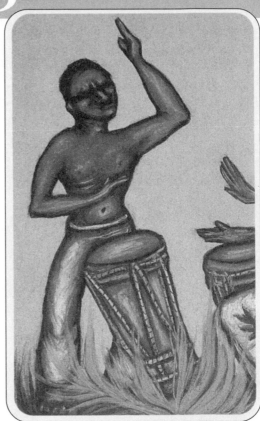

CALL ON PETWO OUNGAN for mastery of Petwo rites and rhythms. Call on him to "heat up" your energy.

OFFERINGS

Pieces of paper on which are written things you wish to transform and then are burned on the altar. Fiery incense, bottles of hot sauce wrapped in metallic red ribbons, drumsticks set on fire, red candles, pepper oil mixed with 151-proof rum set on fire, image of the Petwo Oungan.

LITANY

"Pour l'Houngan Petro, qui marche sur les points de feu en feu. Maître des rythmes Petros—revolutionnaires, magiques, solaires. Jouez pour nous les rythmes brûlants des Dieux. Acceptez nos offrandes. Entrez dans nos cœurs, dans nos bras, dans nos jambes. Entrez ici. Dansez avec nous."

KREYÒL

"Pou Oungan Petwo, kap maché sou difé. Mèt rit Petwo—révolisionè, majik. Joué misik Lwa-yo pou nou. Aksepté ofran'n nou. Antré nan kè nou, nan bra nou, nan jam'm nou. Antré vin'n dansé avek nou."

TRANSLATION

"For the Petwo Oungan, who walks on the points of fire of fire. Master of Petwo rhythms—revolutionary, magical, solar. Play for us the fiery rhythms of the Gods. Accept our offerings. Enter into our hearts, our arms, our legs. Enter and dance with us."

TRADITIONAL

The Petwo rites are fiery in temperament, revolutionary, magical, and practical. They are considered spontaneous, informal, but dangerous. The Petwo Lwa, whom the Oungan must direct, are aggressive, fast, and hot. They are hard to handle, and demanding, but they work hard for their Sèvitè. Through them, the Petwo Oungan offers fierce protection to his Sosyete.

Red is the color. Fire is the element. The Petwo nanchon is syncretized with the Wand suit of a traditional deck.

VISION

Petwo Oungan offers himself up for transformation. The magical energy of change brews in the Ounfò. The floor flames, and flames flare out of the mouths of the drums. Each tongue of fire is a Spirit. Old ones dance among the dancers. Heat. Magic. Change.

The Petwo Oungan burns in the Spirit of the Flambo. He becomes the center of solar radiance, spewing out molten gas from himself. The Flambo play hardball. The Petwo Oungan must master his energies, master his rhythms. He must become liquid fire or be burned out by the overpowering Lwa. The Petwo Oungan's spine is fused in the furnace of the Gods.

The Gods make us strong. They give us ordeals of fire that strengthen us, but they also help us to shoulder the pain. In Tantric magic, overwhelming passion is given over to the Gods, who can handle it. The Petwo Oungan gives the pain of transformation to his Gods. Humans are uncomfortable with revolution, are reluctant to accept change. The pain of destructive fire gives over to a new way of being. The Petwo Oungan himself is the offering made to the Gods. He aligns himself with the cosmic, magic fire of transformation. Instead of being destroyed by fire, he aligns himself magically with it, directs it into the rhythms, the flames of which radiate out like tongues of Spirit from his drum.

Go into a ritual for the Petwo Oungan expecting to feel magically empowered by transformation of the self. Whom do you want to become?

CALL ON THE KONGO OUNGAN to help you reflect before reacting. Call on him for mastery of the Kongo rites and rhythms.

Kongo Oungan

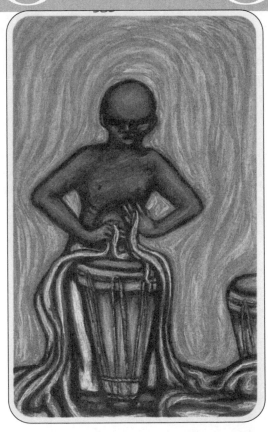

OFFERINGS

Drums, orrisroot, transcribed Kongo rhythm patterns, red sanders incense, Kongo Oungan image.

LITANY

"Pour l'Houngan Congo, qui marche sur les points de l'eau de feu. Docteur magique, guérissez-nous. Acceptez nos offrandes. Entrez dans nos cœurs, dans nos bras, dans nos jambes. Entrez ici. Dansez avec nous."

KREYÒL

"Pou Kongo Oungan, kap maché sou dlo. Bòkò, géri nou. Aksepté ofran'n nou. Antré nan kè nou, nan bra nou, nan jam'm nou. Antré vin'n dansé avek nou."

TRANSLATION

"For the Kongo Oungan, who walks on the points of water of fire. Magical doctor, heal us. Accept our offerings. Enter into our hearts, our arms, our legs. Enter and dance with us."

TRADITIONAL

The Kongo nation originated in Angola and in the Congo basin of Africa. The Kongo rites are said to be composed of beautiful dancing and singing and are marked by a particular grace. The Kongo Spirits are cheerful, bright, and sociable. They are flowing, like the water element that is syncretized here from traditional tarot. The Kongo drums are similar to the Petwo drums, with the exception of the double-headed timbal drum, which suggests the reflective nature of water of fire. Interestingly, it is the master drummer who plays the timbal battery.

VISION

The hands of the Oungan strike the drumhead. Rhythm pours out, flowing through the Waters of the world. This is the path of water of fire. Fire purifies; water consecrates. The water of the body is the blood. The blood is the life, and the life is Spirit. The heart pumps the blood in the rhythm of life. The Oungan's heart is purified with the fire of passion. His blood flows, consecrating his body with the presence of Spirit. The Oungan in New Orleans Vodou is referred to as "Doctor." The Oungan is a doctor who heals the rift between matter, man, and Spirit. If our blood flows in the purifying rhythms of the Waters, our hearts can open to the flash of Spirit.

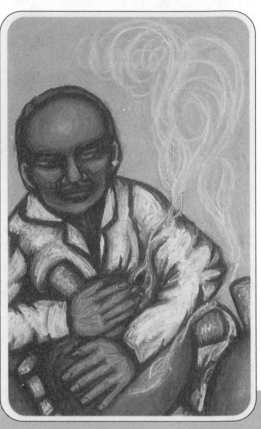

Rada Oungan

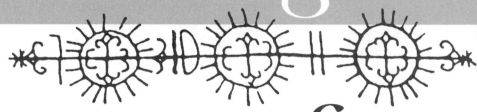

CALL ON THE RADA OUNGAN to distill True Will from intellectual dialogue. Call on the Rada Oungan for mastery of the Rada rites.

OFFERINGS

Cinnamon candy, cinnamon-scented candles, spicy incense (ling aloes), burned over and in Rada drums. Rada Oungan image.

LITANY

"Pour l'Houngan Rada, qui marche sur les points de l'air de feu. L'Houngan Rada, maître des rythmes qui traversent l'air, jusqu'aux oreilles des Dieux. Enseignez-nous le tambour divin. Acceptez nos offrandes. Entrez dans nos cœurs, dans nos bras, dans nos jambes. Entrez ici. Dansez avec nous."

KREYÒL

"Pou Rada Oungan, kap volé nan lè-a. Rada Oungan sèl mèt misik kapral nan zorey Lwayo. Apran-nou bat tanbou. Aksepté ofran'n nou. Antré nan kè nou, nan bra nou, nan jam'm nou. Antré vin'n dansé avek nou."

TRANSLATION

"For the Rada Oungan, who walks on the points of air of fire. Rada Oungan, master of the rhythms that travel through the air to the ears of the Gods. Teach us Divine drumming. Accept our offerings. Enter into our hearts, our arms, our legs. Enter and dance with us."

TRADITIONAL

The Rada Oungan is master of the Rada rhythms and pantheon. The Rada nation is strongly associated with Africa, and is exemplified by formal, elegant, benevolent, and balanced rites. There are three Rada drums used in ceremony, the Maman, the Segon, and the Boula. The drumheads are pegged to the conical wooden bodies of the drums. One drumstick is used with the Maman and the Segon, while two are used with the Boula. The use of sticks is said to make Rada drumming more formal and ordered than the Petwo, which uses two hands. The Rada nation is syncretized with the element of air. The Rada Oungan walks the path of air of fire.

VISION

The Rada Oungan arrives in a state of possession. The tranced whites of his eyes are mesmerizing. His powerful arms enter into, and empower, the drumming. It's difficult to experience possession while drumming, but this is the mastery that this Oungan embodies. Fire is the element of Will. The Rada Oungan is air of fire, or the intellectual aspect of Will. We want our Will to give us license to do whatever we want, but actually the development of Will requires extreme discipline, reflected in this path by the ability to maintain rhythm while possessed. Our True Will will be in harmony with the Divine Will of the world.

The intellect has many voices, many arguments. How do we hear the one voice, the True Will? The Oungan's eyes are turned inward. He listens to an inner voice. This is the voice of patriarchy. Like Yahweh speaking in a still, small voice. Like Yahweh speaking in a place that is no place. The Rada Oungan is in that space of internal quietude that is no place. The drum is made to speak. It is the word of the True Will. It is the word that creates a God. It is the rhythm that calls the Gods.

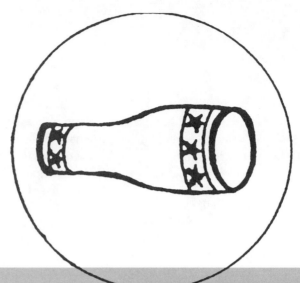

Santería Santero

CALL ON SANTERÍA SANTERO for mastery of the earth plane, and for mastery of Santería rites and rhythms.

OFFERINGS

Any favorite foods of your Santero, or of your Santero's Orisha, herbs, drums, Santería Santero image.

LITANY

"Pour Santería Santero, qui marche sur les points de terre de feu. Santería Santero, courageux, puissant, doué de sagesse. Chuchotez à nous les secrets des Dieux cachés dans les rythmes des tambours. Acceptez nos offrandes. Entrez dans nos cœurs, dans nos bras, dans nos jambes. Entrez ici. Dansez avec nous!"

SPANISH

"Para el Santero, quien anda en los puntos de la tierra del fuego. Santero valiente, poderosisimo, sabio. Cuchicheanos los secretos de los Dioses que se estan escondido en los ritmos de los tambores. Accepta nuestros ofrecemientos. Monta nuestros corazones, nuestros brazos, nuestras piernas. Monta y baile con nosotros!"

TRANSLATION

"For the Santería Santero, who walks on the points of earth of fire. Santería Santero, courageous, powerful, knowledgeable. Whisper the secrets of the Gods to us, hidden in the rhythms of the drums. Accept our offerings. Enter into our hearts, our arms, our legs. Enter and dance with us!"

TRADITIONAL

A Santería priest must go through several levels of initiation before becoming a Santero. The elekes, or necklaces, must be given to the initiate; the Warriors, Los Guerreros, must be given; and the sacrifices must be made as well as the Asiente or Hacher Santo, which "crowns" the initiate and "seats" the Orisha. Upon "making saint," the Santero becomes known as the child of his presiding Orisha. Olofi determines before birth which Orisha will be a child's parent. It is the Orishas who open the path and draw the initiate down it, to eventually be made a Santero. The role and practices of Santeros are strictly governed by tradition. In all of their work, both with the Orishas and with their extended family of Godchildren, the Santeros strive to preserve the purity and honor of their religious traditions.

The Santería Santero represents fire of earth. The Santero centers his Will in the rich earth of tradition.

VISION

The Santería Santero is all about rhythms. He works with the healing vibration of herbs. He resonates between the rhythms of the Gods and the rhythms of humans. He maintains the rhythmic balance between mastery and service, power and humility. He is empowered by the influx of spiritual power, yet is humble. He is not particularly moral or particularly kind. He is knowledgeable, honest, courageous, and he sees the true rhythm of Spirit within the world, within us all.

Courage is from the French *cœur,* meaning heart. To live the spiritual life and commit to maintain meaning requires living from the heart. The Santero's power of self is huge, from the heart, and pulses with the spiritual rhythms of love.

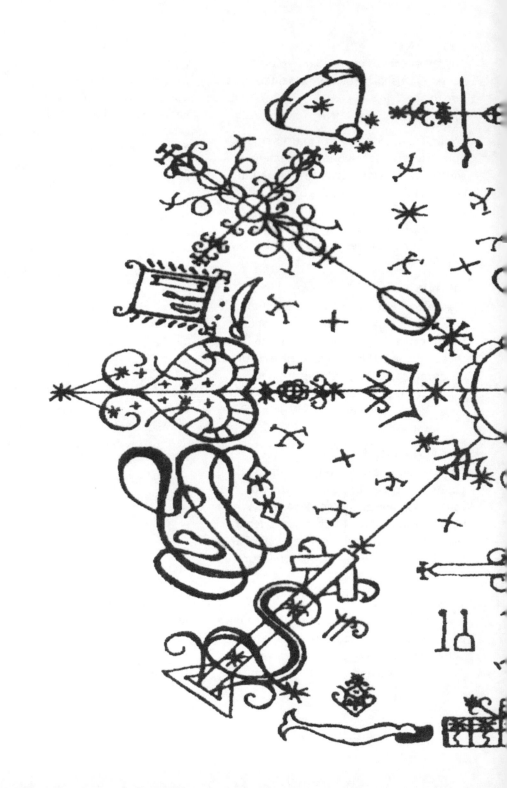

Manbo

THE MANBO are Vodou's high priestesses, who have come through the
Couché initiation to be accepted by
Spirit. They have taken up their role as
spiritual leaders. The Manbo are equal in
power, function, and authority with the
Oungan. In the symbolism of the tarot,
the Manbo correspond with the Queens.
They are syncretized with the element
water. Their magical weapon, or ceremonial implement, is the serpent.

No particular Manbo is intended here.
Nor is it intended for any human Manbo
to be worshiped. This is the quintessential archetype of the Manbo as it is revealed through the elements, or nations.

The Santera is the Manbo's counterpart in Santería.

*

C ALL ON THE PETWO MANBO to confer secrets of sex magic and to charge
magical elixirs. Women call on her for sexual confidence and assertiveness. Men call
on her to attract a magical sex partner.

Petwo Manbo

OFFERINGS

Red rose wrapped in snakeskin, snakeskin in water, red candies, red peppers in water, opopanax incense, Petwo Manbo's image.

LITANY

"Pour la Petro Mambo, qui marche sur les points de feu de l'eau, l'extase de la passion, plaisirs d'amour, initiatrice du pouvoir du serpent. Acceptez nos offrandes. Entrez dans nos cœurs, dans nos bras, dans nos jambes. Entrez ici. Dansez avec nous."

KREYÒL

"Pou Manbo Petwo, kap maché sou dlo. Pasion, ekstaz, plézi lanmou. Aksepté ofran'n nou. Antré nan kè nou, nan bra nou, nan jam'm nou. Antré vin'n dansé avek nou."

TRANSLATION

"For the Petwo Manbo, who walks on the points of fire of water. Ecstasy of passion, pleasure of love, initiatress of the serpent power. Accept our offerings. Enter into our hearts, our arms, our legs. Enter and dance with us."

TRADITIONAL

The Petwo Manbo represents fire of water, presides over the magical sexual elixirs, and walks the hot points of emotion and passion. Her red serpent is the Kundalini serpent of Tantric Yoga. Love under Will is the nature of her formula.

VISION

The fire snake drinks the erotic moistures of the priestess. The river flows with blood. Kundalini rises.

The priestess delights in the pleasure of sexual union. She makes no apologies. She is the pure power of sex, which is the magical blood that flows through her. This sort of priestess is threatening to most people, which, in turn, inspires her to defiance and anger. It takes extraordinary strength and magical ability to handle the snake, to exchange the fire breath with him.

Kongo Manbo

CALL ON THE KONGO MANBO for the blessing of the Waters. Call on her for clairvoyant abilities, especially for working with the crystal ball and for the ability to enter into trance states.

OFFERINGS

Blue candies, benzoin incense, blue beads, holy water, Kongo Manbo's image.

LITANY

"Pour la Congo Mambo, qui marche sur les points de l'eau en l'eau. Puissance de l'eau. Gardienne de l'eau de l'Hounfor. Enseignez-nous. Acceptez nos offrandes. Entrez dans nos cœurs, dans nos bras, dans nos jambes. Entrez ici. Dansez avec nous."

KREYÒL

"Pou Manbo Kongo, kap maché sou dlo. Mèt dlo. Gadien dlo nan Ounfò. Apran' nou. Aksepté ofran'n nou. Antré nan kè nou, nan bra nou, nan jam'm nou. Antré vin'n dansé avek nou."

TRANSLATION

"For the Kongo Manbo, who walks on the points of water of water. Power of water. Guardian of the water of the Ounfò. Teach us. Accept our offerings. Enter into our hearts, our arms, our legs. Enter and dance with us."

TRADITIONAL

The Kongo Manbo governs water of water. Here is the element of water, the realm of emotion, intuition, and psychism, in its essen-tial state. This is the Manbo who looks into the mirrored surface of the Waters, and draws through the reflection of the Gods. The Kongo Manbo easily allows her own identity to float off in order to reflect the image of Spirit.

VISION

The Kongo Manbo rushes in with the roaring, resounding sound of the numberless Dead, who float in the Waters of the Abyss. Hers is the power of water, not the wishy-washy, submissive quality usually associated with the Queen of Hearts. The Kongo Manbo's waters extend throughout the world. Her heart pumps the waters of the world. She is the Queen of Cups. Each drop of water of the ritual libations provides a sacred entrance to her greater waters. The Manbo in ritual moves within the power of these waters, where the Dead and Spirits rest, where the Mysteries of death and sex reside. Implied is the sexual formula of the high priestess who adapts herself fluidly to the partner she is with. Her body is the gateway between outer reality and the watery realms of imagination and magic. She is the reflective mirror that uses tremendous magnetic force of water to draw you through the mirror surface to the interior depths.

Rada Manbo

PRIESTESSES should call on the Rada Manbo when they need empowering, and when they need support in carrying the burden of their work. Priests should call on the Rada Manbo when they need to develop forbearance, when they wish to give support to their partner, and when they are feeling insecure, or overshadowed by their partner. Call on her to reveal lies.

OFFERINGS

Spanish moss, camphor, myrrh oil, rainwater, the Rada Manbo image.

LITANY

"Pour la Mambo Rada, qui marche sur les points de l'air de l'eau. L'intelligence de l'eau. Enseignez-nous comment diriger le pouvoir du serpent. Acceptez nos offrandes. Entrez dans nos cœurs, dans nos bras, dans nos jambes. Entrez ici. Dansez avec nous!"

KREYÒL

"Pou Manbo Rada, kap volé nan siel, kap maché sou dlo. Apran´ nou sèvi ak pouvwa koulèv-la. Aksepté ofran'n nou. Antré nan kè nou, nan bra nou, nan jam'm nou. Antré vin'n dansé avek nou!"

TRANSLATION

"For the Rada Manbo, who walks on the points of air of water. Intelligence of water. Teach us how to direct the power of the serpent. Accept our offerings. Enter into our hearts, our arms, our legs. Enter and dance with us!"

TRADITIONAL

The Rada Manbo governs air of water, where intellect is applied to emotions. She can sometimes indicate the brutally revelatory nature of the Vodou Mysteries, whose honesty can cut through intellectual rationalizations and emotional manipulations.

VISION

The Rada Manbo is powerful, self-assured, satisfied—and armed! She is crowned with the serpent. She has mastered the serpent power. Such a woman is often met with aggression and disapproval from men, but she is to be balanced with gentility and softened. More often, masterful high priestesses are isolated and shunned. How many powerful Manbo attract weak, controlling, and oppressive men? The Rada Manbo slices off the head of her oppressor. She is obviously enjoying her power. She is satisfied by her relationship with Spirit.

The Rada Manbo inspires fear in the serviteurs. Each has to work through personal angers before she can walk across the drumbeats. She slices off each of their heads so that she can enter them. She rises, like a serpent, over their backs, and rests as a crown over their heads.

Look into the eyes of the Rada Manbo and see that her power, mastery, and place in the world give her pleasure and satisfaction. She is radiant with life. Her intelligence is based on what the primordial waters of the body know. The serpent is her ally. The deep waters of her psyche contain deep knowledge, which is uncontaminated by intellectual deceit. She cuts off the lie with her sword.

She is to be invoked, not feared.

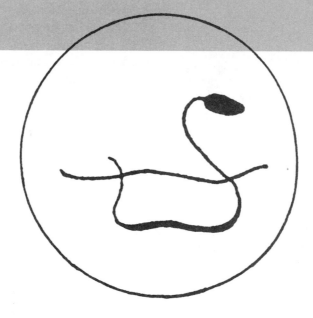

C ALL ON SANTERÍA SANTERA to raise and embrace the sacred, feminine force. Call on her when you are searching for a Mother of the Saints to be your teacher.

Santería Santera

OFFERINGS

Favorite foods of your Santera or of her Orisha, herbs, swamp water, Santería Santera image.

LITANY

"Pour la Santería Santera, qui marche sur les points de terre de l'eau. Santería Santera, Mère de l'Esprit, Mère spirituelle. Enseignez-nous les magies des marais. Acceptez nos offrandes. Entrez dans nos cœurs, dans nos bras, dans nos jambes. Entrez ici. Dansez avec nous."

SPANISH

"Para la Santera, quien anda en los puntos de la tierra de agua. Santera, Madre espiritual. Enseignanos las majias del pantano. Accepta nuestros ofrecimientos. Monta nuestros corazones, nuestros brazos, nuestras piernas. Monta y baile con nosotros."

TRANSLATION

"For the Santería Santera, who walks on the points of earth of water. Santería Santera, Mother of the Spirit, spiritual Mother. Teach us the magics of the swamp. Accept our offerings. Enter into our hearts, our arms, our legs. Enter and dance with us."

TRADITIONAL

The Santera is the female priestess of the Santería religion. Although she must go through the same levels of initiation as a Santero, she is traditionally somewhat more limited in her functions than a Santero. She cannot, for instance, confer the Initiation of the Warriors, or become a Babalawo, the high priest of Santería. She does maintain the characteristic strict adherence to the purity of tradition in her service to the Orishas and to her own Godchildren.

The path of Santería Santera represents earth of water, the material manifestation of the intuitive psyche.

VISION

Water of earth. Mistress of the Mysteries of the swamp, the Santería Santera is the all-accepting, all-receptive. All life grows from the swamp; all life is reabsorbed into the swamp. From viscous, dark water bubbles tellurian magic. Dark Mother and Shakti of the Tantrics, Santería Santera represents the ego. Not Freud's ego, but the ego that keeps us identified with life. Mesmerizing swamp Mother, pulsing with the rhythms of life and death and life, the Santería Santera is the beautiful, dark Mother of the Spirit. Full.

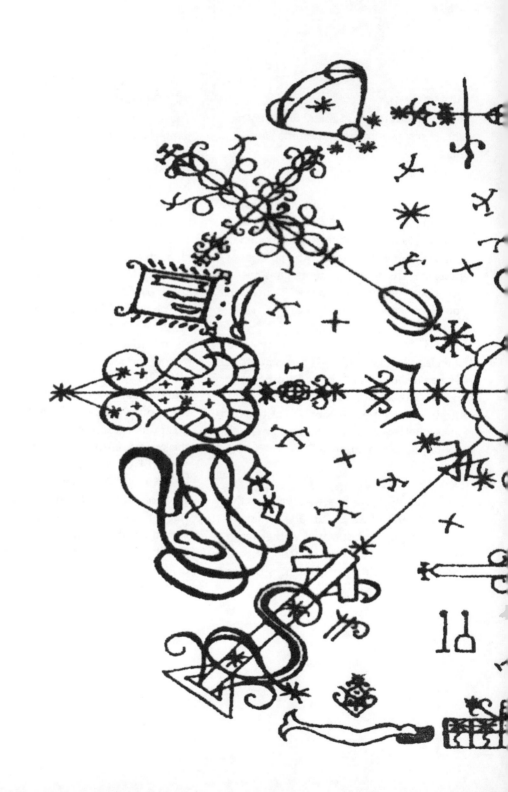

Laplas

THE LAPLAS is the master of ceremonies in the hierarchy of a Vodou Sosyete. The Laplas is usually an Oungan, is often the apprentice of the presiding Oungan, and is often in line to become the leader of the Ounfò after the presiding Oungan has passed.

The Laplas directs all the ceremonial details and the actions of all the participants in ceremonies. His ceremonial symbol is the machete, which he caries into the Peristil, flanked by two drapo carriers, and engages in mock battle with the Manbo or Oungan, moving around the centerpole, and honoring all the places, objects, and people of power within the Peristil. The Laplas cuts the air of the Peristil with his machete. He cuts crossroads into the atmosphere of the Peristil, through which Spirit enters.

In a traditional tarot deck, the Laplas would correspond with the knight. His machete would correspond with the sword, which, in turn, corresponds to the element air, the realm of intellect.

The Laplas corresponds to the Oriaté in Santería, who is the master of ceremonies in the rite of "making saint," or the Asiente.

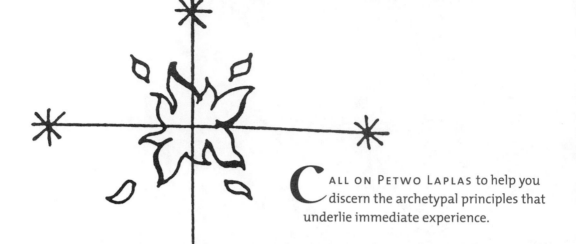

C ALL ON PETWO LAPLAS to help you discern the archetypal principles that underlie immediate experience.

Petwo Laplas

OFFERINGS

Olibanum incense, oranges, machetes, 151-proof rum. Petwo Laplas image.

LITANY

"Pour Petro la Place, qui marche sur les points de feu de l'air. La machette de la volonté revolutionnaire qui coupe l'air de l'intelligence. La pensée enflammée par la Volonté. Acceptez nos offrandes. Entrez dans nos cœurs, dans nos bras, dans nos jambes. Entrez ici. Dansez avec nous."

KREYÒL

"Pou Petwo Laplas, kap volé nan siel, kap maché sou difé. Manshèt revolision. Aksepté ofran'n nou. Antré nan kè nou, nan bra nou, nan jam'm nou. Antré vin'n dansé avek nou."

TRANSLATION

"For Petwo Laplas, who walks on the points of fire of air. The machete of revolutionary Will, which cuts the air of intelligence. Thought enflamed by magical Will. Accept our offerings. Enter into our hearts, our arms, our legs. Enter and dance with us."

TRADITIONAL

Petwo Laplas walks the points of fire of air. Intellect fired by Will. The Petwo Laplas's machete cuts the earth, creating change in accordance with his Will.

VISION

Petwo Laplas is the fiery master of ceremonies, a military figure who maintains decorum at rituals. He represents the fiery aspect of air. In alchemical metaphor, he is sublimatio, by which inherent Spirit is released from matter through the application of heat. In psychological terms, the application of rational thought allows one to rise above mundane circumstances to reach archetypal principle. The ego self rises to the archetypal through the application of the fire of religious aspiration. Petwo Laplas slices a crossroads into the earth with his machete, his magical weapon. The danger of this application is disassociation, if one avoids identification with experience by consistently rising above it to spiritual principle. The reward of this process is that through successive cycles of looking beyond mundane preferences, the eternal psyche is released from ego attachment. You begin to realize that you can add to the content of the archetypal. The Petwo Laplas disciplines the armies of the mind and fires them up to release the Eternal from the mundane mind.

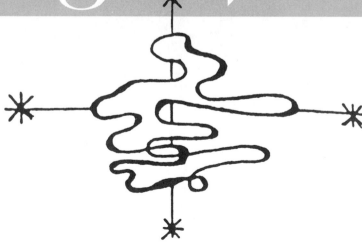

CALL ON THE KONGO LAPLAS to help you stay present with your emotions, to experience emotion fully.

Kongo Laplas

OFFERINGS

Myrrh incense, machete in water, Kongo Laplas image.

LITANY

"Pour Congo la Place, qui marche sur les points de l'eau de l'air. Congo la Place, maître de la fluidité et de la transmission de l'intelligence. Acceptez nos offrandes. Entrez dans nos cœurs, dans nos bras, dans nos jambes. Entrez ici. Dansez avec nous!"

KREYÒL

"Pou Kongo Laplas, kap volé nan siel, maché sou dlo. Mèt entélijans-nou. Aksepté ofran'n nou. Antré nan kè nou, nan bra nou, nan jam'm nou. Antré vin'n dansé avek nou!"

TRANSLATION

"For the Kongo Laplas, who walks on the points of water of air. Kongo Laplas, master of the fluidity and transmission of intelligence. Accept our offerings. Enter into our hearts, our arms, our legs. Enter and dance with us!"

TRADITIONAL

The Kongo Laplas represents water of air, the emotions in league with intellect, or the way in which emotions affect intellect, or the often tricky ways in which emotion and intellect reflect or distort one another. The waters of the world reflect images of identity and of the soul. The intellect can often reflect the distorted images of the fun house mirror. The social grace of the Kongo nation may indicate a posture that objectifies deep waters.

VISION

The Kongo Laplas cuts water with his machete. The separated flows of water collect in a pool, at the axis of the crossroads, forming a mirrored, reflective surface.

The Laplas and the element of air are concerned with processes by which the intellect rises above its conditions. Water of air, or the Kongo Laplas, deals with this objectifying or rising process in the arena of the psyche. Individual consciousness develops within time-bound reality. When something within one's own consciousness or psychology is objectified, it rises beyond time and space, becoming an archetypal fact that is no longer affected by temporal reality. This is much the process of a human transforming into a Lwa. The danger of such intellectual objectification within the element of water is that people can become disassociated from their emotions, and that the eventual descent from the heights can be disturbing or depressing. Often a Sèvitè feels let down on returning to daily consciousness after an initial possession experience. But successive possessions extend the experience of heightening, resolving, or harmonizing the conflicting elements within the person. A transpersonal, unifying, and archetypal factor can emerge. The Kongo Laplas cuts up the opposites in the personal psyche with his machete so that the eternal point in the center can emerge. The personal psyche can flood with the waters of the archetypal psyche.

The Kongo Laplas's ritual is elegant and dignified. Here we can see the disciplined elegance of the military master of ceremonies.

Rada Laplas

CALL ON RADA LAPLAS to direct the intellect, and to quiet destructive, distracting inner dialogues. Call on him to help sharpen the rational mind when you have to enter into debate or argument.

OFFERINGS

Popcorn, springs, tobacco smoke, Rada Laplas image.

LITANY

"Pour Rada la Place, qui marche sur les points de l'air de l'air. Rada la Place, l'intelligence de l'air. La machette qui coupe une idée d'une autre. Acceptez nos offrandes. Entrez dans nos cœurs, dans nos bras, dans nos jambes. Entrez ici. Dansez avec nous!"

KREYÒL

"Pou Rada Laplas, kap volé nan siel. Manshèt kap séparé youn lidé dé youn lòt. Aksepté ofran'n nou. Antré nan kè nou, nan bra nou, nan jam'm nou. Antré vin'n dansé avek nou!"

TRANSLATION

"For Rada Laplas, who walks on the points of air of air. Rada Laplas, the intelligence of air. The machete which cuts one idea from another. Accept our offerings. Enter into our hearts, our arms, our legs. Enter and dance with us!"

TRADITIONAL

Rada Laplas walks on the points of air of air, representing the intellect in its most intellectual mode. A mind that argues for the sake of argument, not for the sake of persuasion. Traditionally, this is a path of fleeting, ephemeral thought, and the intellect that leads one astray.

VISION

The Rada Laplas cuts whirlwinds in the air with his machete. Dusty spirals rise up out of the crossroads. The danger for Rada Laplas is the tendency of the intellect to brew up ideas, thoughts that have no real value or meaning, which blow away, like dust. But the power of Rada Laplas is to wield the air machete that cuts these thoughts off from the self. Rada Laplas lets each thought blow away in golden spirals. "Not this. Not this." His is the power to cut away each and every thought that is not the self. Rada Laplas stands in the center of the crossroads, holding his machete. The thoughts spiral out from him, first as yellow spirals of air. Then as golden, focused thoughts. Then four golden hawks take flight. Screeching, they leave. Rada Laplas is the center, the self, at the crossroads of no thought.

CALL ON ORIATÉ when you wish to tame the wiles of the intellect or when you wish to quiet the intellect so that you can receive internal guidance. Call on Oriaté before conducting a seashell divination.

Oriaté

OFFERINGS

Seashells, storax incense, rum, earth on a sword, Oriaté image.

LITANY

"Pour Oriaté, l'initié terrestre de l'Esprit qui marche sur les points de terre de l'air. L'Oriaté, qui tire l'epée de l'intellect hors des rochers du monde. Acceptez nos offrandes. Entrez dans nos cœurs, dans nos bras, dans nos jambes. Entrez ici. Dansez avec nous!"

SPANISH

"Para el Oriaté, discipulo del Espiritu quien anda en los puntos dela tierra del aire. Oriaté, quien arranca el espada de inteligencia de la piedra del mundo. Accepta nuestros ofrecimientos. Monta nuestros corazones, nuestros brazos, nuestras piernas. Monta y baile con nosotros!"

TRANSLATION

"For Oriaté, the initiate of Spirit who walks on the points of earth of air. Oriaté, who pulls the sword of intellect out of the rock of the world. Accept our offerings. Enter into our hearts, our arms, our legs. Enter and dance with us!"

TRADITIONAL

The Oriaté is a Santero who functions as master of ceremonies at the Asiente, or the making of a Santero. The Oriaté is also adept at seashell divination. Through the seashells, the Orishas "speak" to the Oriaté.

In the symbolism of the tarot, the Santería Oriaté walks the path of earth of air. The Oriaté pulls practical guidance and information from the spiritual airs.

VISION

Oriaté is the meditative aspect of prayer. The passion of his prayer is the perfume that draws the attention of the Gods. It is the power of this perfume to remind the Spirits where they came from, and who we are. Oriaté reveals the passion of prayer within the rock of reality.

In this tarot path, the machete transforms into a sword that—like Arthur pulling the sword from the stone—Oriaté pulls out of a cement Elegguá head. He claims his authority to rule his head through initiation. He also pulls the sword from the top of his head, opening his head to the influence of Spirit. Our intellects are like Elegguá, tricksters that can confuse and convolute the message of Spirit. The Hopis suggest opening a visionary hole in the top of the head to receive pure influence of Spirit. In certain Santería initiations, cuts may be made in the head into which herbs are placed so that the new Santero can receive his Orisha's Mysteries.

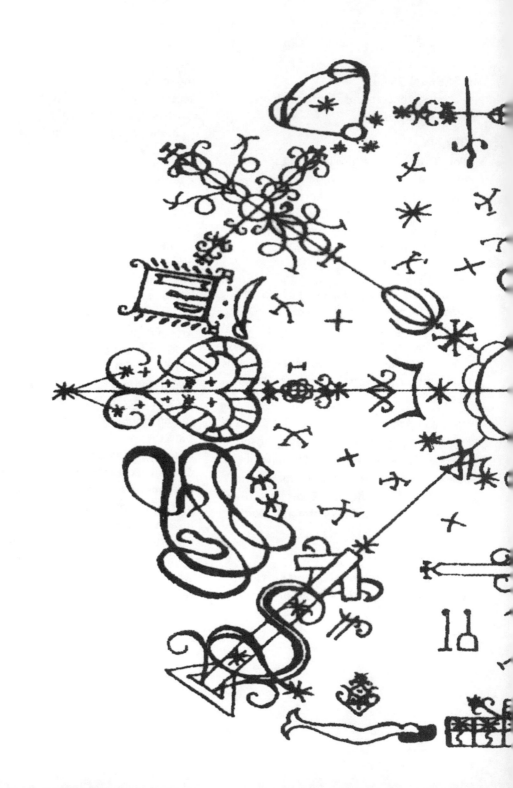

Ounsi

THE OUNSI are the initiated "spirit wives" of the Ounfò. They are the dancers, singers, and Sèvitè who have devoted themselves in service to the Spirit, to the community of the Ounfò. They carry on the myriad physical duties that keep the Ounfò working. The Ounsi are syncretized with the princesses or princes of a traditional tarot deck. They walk the points of earth, and their magical weapon, or ceremonial implement, is the calabash, rather than the cup. A calabash is a hollow gourd that is pressed into service in many ways in ceremony, from serving dishes to the assons that are strung with a bell and beaded with snake vertebrae.

The Ounsi represent the archetypal concept of initiated service and the ways that it can empower the work of a spiritual community.

The Yaguó corresponds to the Ounsi in Santería.

Petwo Ounsi

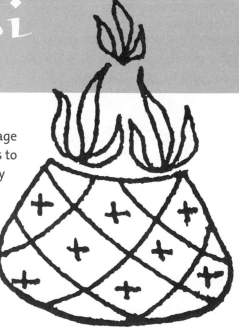

C ALL ON PETWO OUNSI for the courage
to face true vision. Petwo Ounsi helps to
maintain a steady gaze in the face of glory
or horror.

OFFERINGS

Cigars, charcoal drenched in lighter fluid and lit, benzoin, air of earth incense, Petwo Ounsi image.

LITANY

"Pour la Petro Hounsis, qui marche sur les points de feu de la terre. La Petro Hounsis, le combustible de feu, la prêtresse vierge et insatiable des Dieux Petros. Acceptez nos offrandes. Entrez dans nos cœurs, dans nos bras, dans nos jambes. Entrez ici. Dansez avec nous!"

KREYÒL

"Pou Ounsi Petwo, kap maché nan difé. Difé volonté kap boujé, kap transfòmé bagay sou la tè. Ounsi Petwo kap manyin chodiè sou difé—'Boulé zen'—Kanzo. Flam'difé pa ka boulé-l. Sé nan kalbas´ Ounsi nou jouen´ lespri Lwa La Flambo. Aksepté ofran'n nou. Antré nan kè nou, nan bra nou, nan jam'm nou. Antré vin'n dansé avek nou!"

TRANSLATION

"For the Petwo Ounsi, who walks on the points of fire of earth. Petwo Ounsi, the fuel for fire, the insatiable virgin priestess of the Petwo Gods. Accept our offerings. Enter into our hearts, our arms, our legs. Enter and dance with us!"

TRADITIONAL

Petwo Ounsi walks on the points of air of earth, and represents the spiritual fire of Will that moves and transforms earth. The Petwo Ounsi holds a flaming pot—the Boulé-zen—from the Kanzo trial by fire. Because her inner substance is fire, the flames from the pot do not burn her. The Petwo Ounsi's calabash holds the molten substance of the La Flambo Lwa.

VISION

The Petwo Ounsi's eyes are our eyes. They are on fire. Petwo Ounsi's vision is true. She sees the world as it wants to be seen, as it could be, but is not. Her eyes are on fire.

She is the Shakti, the initiated priestess of Tantric magic whose womb is on fire. She is a calabash that holds the flashing flames of Spirit.

The Petwo Ounsi indicates the initiatory process that leads to individuation. Individuation is the process of discovering and containing the True Will within the self. It is the process by which the ego and the self are fused. It is the process of fire by which the human and the Divine are fused. She steals fire from heaven. Like Prometheus's theft of fire, like Adam and Eve attaining consciousness, it is a punishable sin in the eyes of terrible Western Gods. But Petwo Ounsi is fire of earth. Prometheus's sin is forgiven; he is released from punishment when Charon replaces him in Hades. Earth magic submerges, goes underground, while the fire magic is permitted. Both the individual and the undifferentiated are sacred. Petwo Ounsi contains fire magic within the magic of earth. She maintains both in the steadiness of her gaze. Can you hold her calabash, her fiery grail? Can you hold her gaze in yours?

Kongo Ounsi

C ALL ON THE KONGO OUNSI when you want to see yourself as lovable and sweet.

OFFERINGS

Lotus blossom in water, dream drawn on paper and submerged in holy water in a calabash, gourds with water, water of earth incense, salt in water, Kongo Ounsi image.

LITANY

"Pour l'Hounsis Congo, qui marche sur les points de l'eau de la terre. L'Hounsis Congo—mignonne, belle, gentille, douce. La femme de l'esprit, l'enfant spirituelle, la manifestation terrestre des rêves d'Erzulie et de l'Hounfor. Acceptez nos offrandes. Entrez dans nos cœurs, dans nos bras, dans nos jambes. Entrez ici. Dansez avec nous."

KREYÒL

"Pou Ounsi Kongo, kap maché tout´ koté ki gen dlo. Ounsi Kongo—bel fanm, fanm dous. Fanm lespri, fanm Lwa-yo. Réprézantan Ezili sou tè-a. Aksepté ofran'n nou. Antré nan kè nou, nan bra nou, nan jam'm nou. Antré vin'n dansé avek nou."

TRANSLATION

"For the Kongo Ounsi, who walks on the points of water of earth. Kongo Ounsi—charming, beautiful, kind, sweet. The wife of Spirit, spiritual child, earthly manifestation of Ezili's dream and the dream of the Ounfò. Accept our offerings. Enter into our hearts, our arms, our legs. Enter and dance with us."

TRADITIONAL

Kongo Ounsi walk the points of water of earth. Libations are poured on to the earth in Vodou ceremonies to consecrate and purify, and to acknowledge that even the earth we walk upon comes from Water and will return to Water, as will the calabashes that are our bodies.

VISION

Through the Ounsi, we enter into Spirit. The Ounfò is a calabash that holds the waters of Spirit. The Ounsi serve the Ounfò. They serve the Spirit. Their strength and their gift is the steadiness of their nurturing. Water pours into earth. The earth receives it and is made fertile. Holding the Waters of the Abyss, the Ounsi are touched by Spirit. They float in the spiritual waters of love.

The Oungan or Manbo draws the Spirit out of the govi jar, but the Ounsi is the watery, intuitive field in which the Spirit is sustained.

The Ounsi is the ground into which Ezili's dream pours as a libation and manifests. Dreams made flesh. The flesh is the calabash that contains the blood, the water of life. The Ounsi's service is rewarded by the internal touch of the Spirit. To touch Spirit, enter through the Ounsi. Her calabash encloses the generative earth into which Spirit pours its Waters. Generation upon generation. Birth from dream into reality. The Ounsi is the spiritual child of the Manbo and the Oungan.

The Kongo Ounsi is a lotus that floats on the surface of the waters of return. Within her beautiful petals she cradles a jewel. Knowing how precious the jewel is, she treats it with devotion, with deference and greatest care. She is the calabash that holds the blood that is the water of life. Water within the earth. The intuitive knowing that resides within the body. Here and now, in the physical. Real dreams. The Kongo Ounsi carries a cosmology of Mystery in her calabash.

Rada Ounsi

CALL ON RADA OUNSI to lend you the humility needed to do service work. Call on Rada Ounsi to keep your ideas, aspirations, and ego down-to-earth.

OFFERINGS

Incense in calabashes, govi jars, flowers, Rada Ounsi image.

LITANY

"Pour Hounsis Rada, qui marche sur les points de l'air de la terre. Fixez ce qui est volatile. Initiez-nous. Nous nous donnons en service aux Loas. Acceptez nos offrandes. Entrez dans nos cœurs, dans nos bras, dans nos jambes. Entrez ici. Dansez avec nous."

KREYÒL

"Pou Ounsi Rada, kap volé nan siel. Inityé nou. Nou vlé sèvi Lwa-yo. Aksepté ofran'n nou. Antré nan kè nou, nan bra nou, nan jam'm nou. Antré nan dansé avek nou."

TRANSLATION

"For the Rada Ounsi, who walks on the points of air of earth. Fix the volatile. Initiate us. We give ourselves in service to the Lwa. Accept our offerings. Enter into our hearts, our arms, our legs. Enter and dance with us."

TRADITIONAL

The Rada Ounsi walks the path of air of earth, where the intellect is applied to practical, material ends. The Rada Ounsi must maintain personal integrity in the manifesting of hope, dreams, and aspirations, and must be able to put the needs of the Sosyete above their own ego desires.

VISION

The Ounsi are initiates who serve the Ounfò and the Lwa. They are powerful people who at the same time must contain themselves in humility in order to serve. Here an Ounsi cares for the Po tèt—containers of the Ti Bon Anj. Air of earth fixes the volatile intelligence in the earthenware pots or in the bodies of humans that are much like Po tèt. It takes tremendous trust to keep your Ti Bon Anj in a jar. It also takes tremendous trust for Spirit to entrust intelligence to the human containers of the body, given how we mistreat ourselves.

Here the intellect is contained in earth. The head is protected and nurtured in earth. By containing the intellect, it is empowered for service work. The Ti Bon Anj within its pot is an apt image for this path.

CALL ON YAGUÓ to help find Spirit in the most mundane, and to transform hard reality into the stuff of spirituality. Yaguó helps to transform hardship into opportunities for growth and understanding.

Yaguó

OFFERINGS

Fruit, flowers, warrior's weapons, earth in a calabash. Yaguó image.

LITANY

"Pour la Yaguó, qui marche sur les points de terre de la terre. Yaguó, la calabash qui contient les Mystères secrets du monde. Enseignez-nous vos magies réelles. Acceptez nos offrandes. Entrez dans nos cœurs, dans nos bras, dans nos jambes. Entrez ici. Dansez avec nous."

SPANISH

"Para el Yaguo, quien anda en los puntos de la tierra. Yaguo, la calabaza que tiene los Misterios secretos del mundo. Enseñanos tus majias verdaderos. Accepta nuestros ofrecimientos. Monta nuestros corazones, nuestros brazos, nuestras piernas. Monta y baile con nosotros."

TRANSLATION

"For the Yaguó, who walks on the points of earth of earth. Yaguó, the calabash that contains the secret Mysteries of the world. Teach us your real magic. Accept our offerings. Enter into our hearts, our arms, our legs. Enter and dance with us."

TRADITIONAL

The Santería initiate or novice must observe many taboos that are determined through divination by a Santero. It is said that as a person moves further into Santería initiation, an African worldview unfolds within the person's way of perception. The Yaguó develops knowledge and ability in the practices of the religion, and develops Ashé through devotion to Yoruba traditions.

The Yaguó represents the path of earth of earth, and is syncretized with the princess of pentacles in a traditional deck.

VISION

Earth of earth, Yaguó is the spiritual principle manifested within the most material reality. She is the flesh and blood manifestation of all the other vessels and powers. Her magic deals with the Mysteries of material existence. Hers is the magic of karma. The warriors guard and empower her.

As the most material issuance, she reflects back the initial spiritual impulse. Spirit hidden in matter. Matter, the dark container of Spirit. As the force that identifies us with ego, with the material, with cause and effect, she is also the force that inclines us to look within material identification to formless Spirit. That is the power of this path. The danger of this path is that in seeing Spirit within matter, in seeing the material as Divine substance, we can forget that the material world is not true. It needs repairing and transforming, which is the work of the initiate.

Glossary

Aksyon degras: Catholic litanies that are said at the beginning of a Vodou ceremony.

An ba dlo: "Beneath the water," where the Lwa live in Vodou cosmology.

Ashé: The creative life force.

Asiento: The initiation by which a Santero or Santera "makes saint."

Asson: Ritual rattle formed of a gourd, wrapped in beads and snake vertebrae, with a bell attached.

Ayibobo: "Amen" in Kreyòl.

Babalawo: High priest of Santería.

Banda: Dance and rhythm appropriate to the Gede.

Barbancourt: A Haitian rum.

Bilolo: Exclamation in Petwo ceremonies.

Bizango: A magical secret society in Haiti.

Bòkò: Vodou priest who "works with both hands" for benevolence and malevolence. To be distinguished from an initiated Vodou priest.

Bosal: Or "wild," characteristic of uninitiated possessions that can be turbulent.

Boulé-zen: Burning pot, or trial by fire during which the initiates are to put their hands into a boiling pot of oil without getting burned.

Ceremonial Magick: A highly intellectual form of ritual practice in which the conscious mind is overwhelmed by the symbolism utilized within the rites in order to attain heightened states of consciousness. The ultimate goal of this form of High Magick is the attainment of union with the higher self, and identification with the Divine.

Chakras: Points of physical and spiritual energy in the human body.

Chwal: "Horse." Person possessed by a Lwa.

Collares: Beaded necklaces given to Santería initiates.

Coucher: To put to sleep. The week-long ceremony by which an Oungan or Manbo is initiated.

Derecho: A ritual fee paid to the Orishas of Santería.

Dlo: Water.

Drapo: Ritual Vodou flags, sewn with sequins and beads, generally representing the presiding Lwa of a Sosyete.

Ebbós: Offerings for an Orisha.

Elekes: Necklaces. See Collares.

Ginen: The underwater world of the Dead, and the homeland of Africans where the Lwa live.

Govi: An earthenware pot that holds a Spirit. The govi are only used as sacred repositories, while kanari can be any earthenware jar.

Gwo Bon Anj: Big Good Angel. A part of the soul that remains by the grave for nine days after the death of the body. The Gwo Bon Anj then goes beneath the Waters of the Abyss, where it can become a Lwa. The Gwo Bon Anj can be stolen or trapped, and can be placed for safekeeping in a jar.

Hermetics: A mystical wisdom tradition that was based on the writings of Hermes Trismegistus, or thrice-great Hermes, who was a composite of the Greek God Hermes and the Egyptian God Thoth, Gods of wisdom, magic, and language.

Ibeji: The Sacred Twins in Santería.

Ile-Ife: Mythical city created by Obatalá.

Invisib/Invisibles: The Lwa, and the souls of all the Dead.

Kalfou: Or "carrefour." Crossroads or intersection.

Kanari: Any earthenware pot that can be used to house a Spirit.

Kanzo: Initiation involving a trial by fire. See Boulé-zen.

Kleren: Raw liquor. Moonshine.

Konesans: Ritual knowledge. Can refer to members of a Vodou community.

Kreyòl: Creole language, as spoken in Haiti.

Laplas: Master of ceremonies, and sword-bearer in Vodou ceremonies.

Lavé tèt: Head washing. A form of Vodou baptism that purifies a person's head, where the Lwa reside.

Lucumi: Yoruba-based religion.

Lwa: Vodou Spirit or demigod.

Macumba: Brazilian spiritism.

Madrina: Godmother in Santería.

Makout: Straw sack carried by Haitian peasants and associated with Azaka.

Manbo: Or Mambo. Vodou priestess.

Manman: "Mother." Name of largest of the three Rada drums.

Marron/Marronage: Escaped slaves during colonial times who lived in the hills of Haiti.

Mèt tèt: Master of the Head, a person's presiding Lwa.

Mistè: The Mysteries. The Lwa.

Mò: The Dead, Spirits of the Waters of the Abyss.

Nanchon: Vodou nation, such as Rada, Petwo, Ibo.

Oriaté: Santería priest who does seashell divination.

Orisha: The Gods of Santería.

Ounfò: Vodou temple. Can also refer to the community of serviteurs.

Oungan: Vodou priest.

Ounjenikon: Vodou choir leader.

Ounsi: Vodou initiate.

Padrino: Godfather in Santería.

Pakèt: Packet or wrapped, tied, and decorated bundle that holds the essential force of a Spirit.

Peristil: Usually a courtyard, covered with a roof, in which most Vodou ceremonies take place.

Petwo: Lwa nation and rites marked by the violent energy and practicality of the Petwo Lwa.

Po tèt: "Head pot." Earthenware jar that houses a person's Spirit.

Poto Mitan: Centerpole through which the Lwa enter into the Peristil.

Prèt Savann: Bush priest who says the aksyon degras at the beginning of a Vodou ceremony.

Pwen: "Point." Concentrations of power or magic, the point at which magic or energy is touched.

Qabalah: Jewish mystical system upon which tarot cards are based.

Quimbanda: A Brazilian black magic sect of Macumba.

Rada: Lwa nation and rites marked by benevolence and using particular styles of drumming and dancing.

Santera: Santería priestess.

Santero: Santería priest.

Scrying: A form of divination done by gazing into smooth, mirrored surfaces, such as crystals, crystal balls, polished stones, mirrors, or bowls of water, until trance states are achieved that reveal clairvoyant visions.

Segon: Middle of three drums used in a Rada ceremony.

Sèvitè: A Vodou serviteur, one who serves the Lwa.

Sosyete: "Society." The extended family of a Vodou community.

Tambour: Drum.

Tarot: A divination system based on playing cards.

Ti Bon Anj: Little Good Angel. Part of the soul that includes the personal identity and the conscience, which is incapable of lying.

Umbanda: A Brazilian white magic sect of Macumba.

Vèvè: Symbolic design, usually drawn in cornmeal on the ground, which represents a Lwa and serves as a focal point for invocation.

Wanga: Magic charm, usually malevolent.

Warriors: Santería initiation that confers the protection of Elegguá, Oggún, and Ochosi.

Yanvalou: Ritual dance or rhythm that marks the beginning of a Rada ceremony and is associated with Danbala and Ayida Wèdo.

Yoga: An experiential practice that leads to union of body, mind, and spirit. Through the practice of Yoga, an individual ultimately is liberated from matter and finds union with the Divine.

Zanj: "Angel." A Lwa.

Zonbi: Zombie. A soulless body. Someone whose soul has been stolen, generally for the purpose of slavery.

Bibliography ✳

VODOU AND SANTERÍA

Andoh, Anthony. *The Science and Romance of Selected Herbs Used in Medicine and Religious Ceremony*. San Francisco: North Scale Institute, 1987.

Bambara, Toni Cade. *The Salt Eaters*. New York: Vintage Books, 1981.

Bertiaux, Michael. *Vodoun Gnostic Workbook*. New York: Magickal Childe, 1988.

Bramly, Serge. *Macumba*. New York: St. Martin's Press, 1977.

Brown, Karen McCarthy. *Mama Lola: A Vodou Priestess in Brooklyn*. Berkeley: University of California Press, 1991.

Canizares, Raul. *Walking with the Night: the Afro-Cuban World of Santería*. Rochester, VT: Destiny Books, 1993.

Chesi, Gert. *Voodoo: Africa's Secret Power*. Vienna, Austria: Perlinger Verlag, 1974.

Clark, Veve A., Millicent Hodson, and Catrina Neiman. *The Legend of Maya Deren*, vol. 1. New York: Anthology Film Archives, 1984.

Cosentino, Donald J., ed. *Sacred Arts of Haitian Vodou*. Los Angeles: UCLA Fowler Museum of Cultural History, 1995.

Courlander, Harold. *The Drum and the Hoe: Life and Lore of the Haitian People*. Berkeley: University of California Press, 1960.

———. *Haiti Singing*. Chapel Hill: University of North Carolina Press, 1939.

———. *Tales of Yoruba Gods and Heroes*. New York: Original Publications, 1973.

Danticat, Edwidge. *Breath, Eyes, Memory*. New York: Vintage Press, 1994.

———. *Krik? Krak!* New York: Soho Press, 1995.

Davis, W. *Passage of Darkness: The Ethnobiology of the Haitian Zombie*. Chapel Hill: University of North Carolina Press, 1988.

Denning, Melita, and Osborne Phillips. *Vodoun Fire: The Living Reality of Mystical Religion*. St. Paul, MN: Llewellyn Publications, 1979.

Deren, Maya. *Divine Horsemen: The Living Gods of Haiti*. London: Thames and Hudson, 1953; New York: McPherson and Co., 1983.

Desmangles, Leslie G. *The Faces of the Gods, Vodou and Roman Catholicism in Haiti*. Chapel Hill and London: University of North Carolina Press, 1992.

Dow, Carol L. *Pomba-Gira: Enchantments to Invoke the Formidable Powers of the Female Messenger of the Gods*. Burbank, CA: Technicians of the Sacred, 1990.

———. *Saravá: Afro-Brazilian Magick*. St. Paul, MN: Llewellyn Publications, 1997.

Dunham, Katherine. *Island Possessed*. Garden City, NY: Doubleday, 1969.

Ecun, Oba. *Ita Mythology of the Yoruba Religion*. Miami, FL: Obaecun Books, 1969.

Fantunmbi, Awo Fa'Lokun. *Awo: Ifa and the Theology of Orisha Divination.* New York: Original Publications, 1992.

⸺. *Esu-Elegba: Ifá and the Divine Messenger.* New York: Original Publications, 1993.

⸺. *Obatalá: Ifá and the Spirit of the White Cloth.* New York: Original Publications, 1993.

⸺. *Ochosi: Ifá and the Spirit of the Tracker.* New York: Original Publications, 1992.

⸺. *Ogún: Ifá and the Spirit of Iron.* New York: Original Publications, 1992.

⸺. *Oshún: Ifá and the Spirit of the River.* New York: Original Publications, 1993.

⸺. *Oyá: Ifá and the Spirit of the Wind.* New York: Original Publications, 1993.

⸺. *Shangó: Ifá and the Spirit of Lightning.* New York: Original Publications, 1993.

⸺. *Yemojá/Olokun: Ifá and the Spirit of the Ocean.* New York: Original Publications, 1993.

Flores-Pena, Ysamur, and Roberta J. Evanchuk. *Speaking Without a Voice: Santería Garments and Altars.* Jackson: University Press of Mississippi, 1994.

Freeman, Bryant. *Le Creole Rapide.* Lawrence: University of Kansas, 1998.

Galembo, Phyllis. *Vodou: Visions and Voices of Haiti.* Berkeley, CA: Ten Speed Press, 1998.

Girouard, Tina. *Sequin Artists of Haiti.* New Orleans, LA: Contemporary Arts Center, 1994.

Gover, Robert. *Voodoo Contra.* York Beach, ME: Samuel Weiser, 1985.

Gray, John, ed. *Ashé, Traditional Religion and Healing in Sub-Saharan Africa and the Diaspora: A Classified International Bibliography.* Westport, CT: Greenwood Press, 1989.

"Haiti: Feeding the Spirit." *Aperture* 126, (Winter 1992).

Haskins, Jim. *Voodoo and Hoodoo.* New York: Stein and Day, 1978.

Herskovits, Melville J. *Life in a Haitian Valley.* New York: Alfred A. Knopf, 1938.

Hess, David J. *Samba in the Night: Spiritism in Brazil.* New York: Columbia University Press, 1994.

Hurston, Zora Neale. *Tell My Horse.* Philadelphia, PA: J. B. Lippincott, 1938.

Idowu, E. B. *Olodumare: God in Yoruba Belief.* New York: Original Publications, 1963.

Karade, Bab Ifa. *The Handbook of Yoruba Religious Concepts.* York Beach, ME: Samuel Weiser, 1994.

Kardec, Allen. *Collection of Selected Prayers.* Bronx, NY: De Pablo International, 1989.

Laguerre, M. *Voodoo Heritage.* Beverly Hills, CA: Sage Library of Social Research, 1980.

Marcelin, Milo. *Mythologie Vodou (Rite Arada).* Port-au-Prince, Haiti: Les Éditions Haitiennes, part 1, 1949; part 2, 1950.

Martinez, Raymond. *Mysterious Marie Laveau, Voodoo Queen.* New Orleans, LA: Hope Publications, 1956.

Métraux, Alfred. *Voodoo in Haiti.* Hugo Chateris, trans. New York: Oxford University Press (Schocken Books), 1972.

Montenegro, Carlos. *Magical Herbal Baths of Santería.* New York: Original Publications, 1996.

Murphy, Joseph M. *Santería.* Boston: Beacon Press, 1990.

Neimark, Philip John. *The Way of the Orisha.* New York: HarperCollins Publishers, 1993.

Olmos, Margarite Fernandez, and Lizabeth Paravisini-Gebert. *Sacred Possessions.* New Brunswick, NJ: Rutgers University Press, 1997.

Pelton, Robert W. *The Complete Book of Voodoo.* New York: Berkley Medallion Books, 1972.

Reed, Ishmael. *Mumbo Jumbo.* New York: Bantam Books, 1972.

Rhodes, Jewell Parker. *Voodoo Dreams.* New York: St. Martin's Press, 1993.

Rigaud, Milo. *Secrets of Voodoo.* San Francisco: City Lights Books, 1953.

⸺. *Vè-Vè.* New York: French and European Publications, 1974.

Riggs-Bergesen, Catherine. *Candle Therapy.* New York: Other Worldly Publishers, 1993.

Riva, Anna. *Voodoo Handbook of Cult Secrets,* rev. ed. Toluca Lake, CA: International Imports, 1974.

———. *Golden Secrets of Mystic Oils*. Toluca Lake, CA: International Imports, 1978.

———. *The Modern Herbal Spellbook: The Magical Use of Herbs*. Toluca Lake, CA: International Imports, 1974.

Rodman, Selden. *Where Art Is Joy, Haitian Art: The First Forty Years*. Randolph, NH: Ruggles de Latour, 1988.

———, and Carol Cleaver. *Spirits of the Night, the Vaudun Gods of Haiti*. Dallas, TX: Spring Publications, 1992.

St. Claire, David. *Drum and Candle*. Garden City, NY: Doubleday, 1971.

Saxon, Lyle, Robert Talland, and Edward Dryer. *Gumbo Ya-Ya: A Collection of Louisiana Folk Tales*. New York: Bonanza Books, 1945.

Seabrook, William B. *The Magic Island*. New York: Literary Guild, 1929.

Tallant, Robert. *Voodoo in New Orleans*. Gretna, LA: Pelican Publishing Co., 1990.

———. *The Voodoo Queen*. Gretna, LA: Pelican Publishing Co., 1983.

Teish, Luisah. *Jambalaya: The Natural Woman's Book of Personal Charms and Practical Ritual*. San Francisco: Harper and Row, 1985.

Thompson, Robert Farris. *Face of the Gods: Art and Altars of Africa and the African Americans*. New York and Munich: Museum for African Art; Prestel, 1993.

———. *Flash of the Spirit: African and Afro-American Art and Philosophy*. New York: Random House, 1983.

Voodoo Secrets of Haiti. New York: LBT Publisher, 1982.

Weaver, Lloyd, and Olorunmi Egbelade. *Maternal Divinity: Yemonja: Tranquil Sea Turbulent Tides*. Brooklyn, NY: Athelia Henrietts Press, 1998.

Weniger, Bernard. *La Médecine Populaire dans le Plateau Central D'Haiti* (Thèse, Docteur de 30 Cycles en Toxicologie de l'Environnement.) Metz, France: Centre des Sciences de l'Environnement de Metz.

Wilcken, Lois. *The Drums of Vodou*. Temple, AZ: White Cliffs Media Co., 1992.

Wippler, Migene Gonzalez. *Introduction to Seashell Divination*. New York: Original Publications, 1989.

———. *Powers of the Orishas: Santería and the Worship of Saints*. Plainview, NY: Original Publications, 1992.

———. *Rituals and Spells of Santería*. New York: Original Publications, 1984.

———. *Santería: African Religion in America*. Boston: Beacon Press, 1988.

———. *The Santería Experience*. Englewood Cliffs, NJ: Prentice-Hall, 1982.

———. *Santería, the Religion*. St. Paul, MN: Llewellyn Publications, 1998.

JOURNALS AND UNPUBLISHED DOCUMENTS

Breeze, William, and Cherel Ito, eds. *Conversations on Vodoun*, 1996.

Lerner, Michael, ed. *Tikkun: A Bimonthly Critique of Politics, Culture and Society*. New York, NY, 1995–present.

Willis, Courtney, ed. *Société Journal*. Burbank, CA: Technicians of the Sacred, 1986–present.

QABALAH

Dimont, Max I. *Jews, God and History*. New York: Signet, 1962.

Fortune, Dion. *The Mystical Qabalah*. New York: Ibis Books, 1979.

Halevi, Z'ev ben Shimon. *Kabbalah, the Divine Plan*. San Francisco: Harper, 1996.

———. *Psychology and Kabbalah.* New York: Samuel Weiser, 1991.

———. *Way of the Kabbalah.* New York: Samuel Weiser, 1991.

Kaplan, Aryeh. *Sefer Yetzirah: The Book of Creation.* York Beach, ME: Samuel Weiser, 1993.

Levertoff, Paul P., and Maurice Simon, trans. *The Zohar,* vol. 4. New York: Bennet, 1959.

Mathers, S. L. MacGregor, trans. *The Kabbalah Unveiled.* New York: Samuel Weiser, 1968.

Ponce, Charles. *Kabbalah.* San Francisco: Straight Arrow Books, 1973.

Regardie, Israel. *A Garden of Pomegranates.* St. Paul, MN: Llewellyn Publications, 1978.

———. *The Tree of Life.* New York: Samuel Weiser, 1969.

Telushkin, Rabbi Joseph. *Jewish Literacy.* New York: William Morrow and Co., 1991.

YOGA

Crowley, Aleister. "Eight Lectures on Yoga." *The Equinox,* vol. 3, no. 4. Dallas, TX: Sangrael Foundation, 1969.

Harish, Johari. *Tools for Tantra.* Rochester, VT: Inner Traditions, 1986.

Janakananda, Swami Saraswati. *Yoga, Tantra and Meditation in Daily Life,* revised with new English translation. York Beach, ME: Samuel Weiser, 1991.

Kundalini Research Institute. *Sadhana Guidelines for Kundalini Yoga Daily Practice.* Berkeley, CA: Arcline Publications, 1976.

Mookerjee, Ajit. *Kundalini, The Arousal of the Inner Energy.* New York: Destiny Books, 1983.

Satchidananda, Yogiraj Sri Swami. *Integral Yoga Hatha.* New York: Holt, Rinehart and Winston, 1970.

Svoboda, Robert E. *Aghora, at the Left Hand of God.* Albuquerque, NM: Brotherhood of Life, 1986.

———. *Aghora II: Kundalini.* Albuquerque, NM: Brotherhood of Life, 1993.

Vishnudevananda, Swami. *The Complete Illustrated Book of Yoga.* New York: Bell Publishing, 1959.

———. *The Sivananda Companion to Yoga.* New York: Simon and Schuster, 1983.

Walker, Benjamin. *Tantrism: Its Secret Principles and Practices.* Wellingborough, Northamptonshire (England): Aquarian Press, 1982.

TAROT AND CEREMONIAL MAGICK

Case, Paul Foster. *The Book of Tokens: Tarot Meditations.* Los Angeles: Builders of the Adytum, 1934.

———. *The Tarot: A Key to the Ages.* Richmond, VA: Macoy Publishing Co., 1947.

Crowley, Aleister. *777 and Other Qabalistic Writings.* York Beach, ME: Samuel Weiser, 1977.

———. *The Book of Thoth.* Ordo Templi Orientis, 1944. Reprint. York Beach, ME: Samuel Weiser, 1990.

———. *Magick: Book Four Parts I–IV.* York Beach, ME: Samuel Weiser, 1994.

Gray, Eden. *Mastering the Tarot.* New York: Signet, 1971.

———. *The Tarot Revealed.* New York: Signet, 1960.

Kaplan, Stuart. *Tarot Classic.* New York: Grosset and Dunlap, 1972.

Martinie, Louis, and Sallie Ann Glassman. *The New Orleans Voodoo Tarot.* Rochester, VT: Destiny Books, 1992.

Regardie, Israel. *The Complete Golden Dawn System of Magic.* Las Vegas, NV: Falcon Press, 1984.

Stanley, Thomas (English trans.), Patrizzi Francesco (Latin trans.). *Chaldean Oracles.* Gillette, NJ: Heptangle Books, 1989.

Waite, Arthur Edward. *The Pictoral Key to the Tarot.* New York: Samuel Weiser, 1973.

Wang, Robert. *The Qabalistic Tarot*. York Beach, ME: Samuel Weiser, 1983.

MISCELLANEOUS TITLES

Baring, Anne, and Jules Cashford. *The Myth of the Goddess*. London, New York: Penguin Books, 1991.

Brown, Norman O. *Love's Body*. New York: Random House, 1966.

Campbell, Joseph. *The Hero with a Thousand Faces*. Princeton, NJ: Princeton University Press, 1972.

———. *The Masks of God*. New York: Penguin Books, 1976.

Edinger, Edward F. *Anatomy of the Psyche*. La Salle, IL: Open Court Publishing Co., 1985.

Estes, Clarissa Pinkola. *Women Who Run with the Wolves: Myths and Stories of the Wild Woman Archetype*. New York: Ballantine Books, 1992.

Frazer, J. G. *The Golden Bough*. New York: Avenel Books, 1981.

James, William. *The Varieties of Religious Experience*. London: Longmans, 1910.

Raine, Kathleen. *Defending Ancient Springs*. New York: Inner Traditions, 1985.

Sardello, Robert. *Facing the World with Soul: The Reimagination of Modern Life*. Hudson, NY: Lindisfarne Press, 1992.

Thompson, William Irwin. *The Time Falling Bodies Take to Light*. New York: St. Martin's Press, 1981.

Index

INDEX

232

ABOUT THE AUTHOR

SALLIE ANN GLASSMAN has studied Ceremonial Magick, Vodou, and Yoga most of her life. She has been practicing Vodou in New Orleans since 1977, and was ordained as a Manbo, a Vodou priestess, in November 1995 in Port-au-Prince, Haiti. She is the co-owner of the Island of Salvation Botanica, and co-founder of Simbi–Sen Jak Ounfò where she presides over weekly Vodou ceremonies with her partner, Oungan J. Shane Norris. She has led her community in numerous public ceremonies. Ms. Glassman is an artist who exhibits her paintings and assemblage art pieces in several New Orleans galleries. She illustrated *The Enochian Tarot*, and was co-creator and illustrator of *The New Orleans Voodoo Tarot*.